THE QUEEN MOTHER

Fifty Years A Queen

THE QUEEN MOTHER

Fifty Years A Queen

Helen Cathcart

W.H. ALLEN · LONDON

Contents

Part Five:
QUEEN ELIZABETH THE QUEEN MOTHER

Part One

ELIZABETH LYON

1. *A Londoner Born*

In the autumnal fog-burdened London of 1899, everyone spoke hopefully of the dawning new twentieth century. It could not but bring change and progress, a new heart and fresh resolution to help lighten the depressing defeats inflicted on British troops by the Boers in South Africa. A new breeze was blowing, and it was in keeping with the times that the elderly 13th Earl of Strathmore just then gave up his substantial family mansion in South Kensington and moved into one of the new purpose-built 'flats' at Belgrave Mansions in Grosvenor Gardens around the corner from Buckingham Palace, 'close to Victoria Station, so convenient for the Continent', as he jovially explained to his many grandchildren. Whereupon, his eldest son and heir, Lord Glamis, followed the parental example and rented a similar new-century apartment at St Ermin's Mansions, within sound of the chimes of Big Ben.

The 500 suites, each with a sitting-room, bedroom and bathroom, offered a 'delightfully fresh idea, a residential mansion hotel of the highest class with all the comforts and privacy of home', as the prospectus claimed, and *Boyle's Court Guide* discreetly listed among the irreproachable residents a dozen peers and peeresses, a muster of Members of Parliament and their wives, and at least a bishop or two. Prince Louis Battenberg could often be seen in the breakfast-room before walking round to his naval intelligence job at the Admiralty. 'A staff of porters in best livery are always on duty,' the management mentioned, and above the wrought-iron gates a plaster set of heraldic beasts formed an impressive defence of respectability.

For their visits to town from their country home, St Paul's Walden Bury – only twenty miles by train from London though deep in the wooded recesses of Hertfordshire – Lord and Lady Glamis found St Ermin's a refreshing addition to their life-style. The sociable Lady Glamis loved going to tea with friends in London, perhaps taking in a concert or eagerly viewing the latest property in a ceaseless procession of prospective town houses. Her affable husband enjoyed directors' meetings for the insurance of Scottish widows and his companionable encounters at the Carlton Club by way of light relief to his farming interests. 'Claudie' and 'Celia' to their intimates, the couple had been married for eighteen years, together raising a good-looking family of five sons and three daughters, while remaining still deeply in love.

The girls all three resembled their slim brunette mother, the boys equally were 'their father again, true Lyons', Lyon the surname, Glamis a courtesy title, the perquisite of the heir. At thirty-seven and six years since the birth of their youngest child, Michael, Celia was aware of a phase of placid contentment; and then in the New Year and new century of 1900 she confided to Claudie her joyous surprise that she was anticipating another baby, perhaps in August or early September.

It hardly matters whether the newcomer could have been conceived at St Ermin's or upon a winter night in the quietness of the Waldens. But in the history of our times it matters significantly that the ninth of the Lyon children was to become Queen of England, and more besides: 'Queen of Great Britain, Ireland and of the British Dominions Beyond the Seas', last Empress of India and, for fifteen years, First Lady of the British Commonwealth. Moreover, when these dignities passed from Elizabeth Lyon upon the death of husband, King George VI, she personally chose her own style and title thenceforth and elected to become known as Queen Elizabeth the Queen Mother, while to her own Household and Court circle she remains simply 'Queen Elizabeth', an endearing Queen of Hearts in the imagined affection of millions.

With this writing we commemorate the Golden Jubilee of her Queenhood, fifty years on 11 December 1986, since the abdication of Edward VIII, when her husband succeeded to the British Throne as King George VI and she became his Queen Consort. 'My wife and helpmeet at my side,' he complimented her amid the gravity of his Accession Council.

Like the Diana of our own day she had been a girl of nineteen or twenty when first welcomed into the Royal Family and in fact was no more than twenty-two when she married the then Duke of York in Westminster Abbey. Thirteen years of happy wedded domesticity ensued in the comparatively gentle light that shines upon a royal duchess, followed by the challenging fifteen years of her husband's reign and her thirty-five years and more of valiant widowhood, the ever-changing turbulent decades that have constantly acclaimed her as one of the most popular women in our world.

In the beginning, newspapers continually reminded their readers
that 'the little Duchess' had been born a commoner, a chilling emphasis
quickly diminished when she proved herself an uncommonly royal
lady. Researchers who consulted the Register of Births, that vast listing
of the population, found her indeed in the volume for June-September
1900, indexed on page 325 merely as Lyon, Elizabeth A.M. although
the details of birthplace are now known to be incorrect.

For more than half a century, relying upon the birth certificate attes-
ted by her father, every relevant reference book gave her place of birth
as St Paul's Walden Bury, Hertfordshire. In the ancient parish church
of St Paul's Walden moreover, soon after her Coronation, the Queen
Mother with her husband had unveiled a creamy commemorative
plaque '. . . in this parish she was born and here she worshipped'. Not
born at Glamis, therefore, nor at the Earl of Strathmore's other home,
Streatlam Castle in County Durham, which had been ironically demol-
ished to its foundations in the year of her wedding. Two months before
her eightieth birthday, in response to an enquirer, the Queen Mother
astonished all save her closest friends and kinfolk by announcing
through her Clarence House staff that she had always known she was
born in London.

To this statement she has declined ever since to add details. An
explanation which does not take us very far has been provided by
Dorothy Laird, one of her best-trusted biographers: 'Some things
remain very private and secret. She dislikes all things being known
about her at all times, and will keep little inconsequential matters to
herself, even from her own Household.' To the British with their
overweight of tradition, and to their American cousins, a monarch –
and his wife also – needs a birthplace like a baker needs flour. Where,
then, in the teeming metropolis? 'No one, including Her Majesty, will
ever know,' asserts a press attaché, and the world confronts a wry
riddle.

The younger school of royal biography has had a hard time of it
lately, what with disowned birthplaces, erasures in baptismal registers,
vanished medical records and missing letters. It has been authorita-
tively denied to the present author that the child was born at St
Ermin's: some residual knowledge, then? One could be warmer with an
opening scene in the Strathmores' fresh-painted new apartment in
Grosvenor Gardens, the night of 3 August. In the Waldens, around
Queen Elizabeth's childhood home, there remains an abiding folk
memory that she was born in a carriage, a closed four-wheeler, a cab,

perhaps even a growler from the rank at Victoria Station; all but a gaslight steeplechase past streets and landmarks the passengers could not have noticed, a jolting transit in a nativity unique among the grand-daughters of earls. How could Her Majesty ever know precisely where she was born?

The one certainty is that Claudie Lyon had gone up to Glamis Castle earlier than usual that year to help his ageing father, the 13th Earl, with preparations for the grouse-shooting season, the so-called Glorious Twelfth. The Strathmores went on to Glamis having enjoyed their usual July sojourn at Streatlam, and in her husband's absence Celia needed no second invitation to join her youngest sister-in-law, Claudie's spinster sister, Maud Bowes-Lyon, at the new flat for a day or two's shopping before the August Bank Holiday.

There was no doubt the convenience of Lady Strathmore's resident housekeeper or possibly the alternative hospitality of Claudie's widowed sister, Isobel, at her house in Chelsea. Telephones were still a novelty, and it seemed of no consequence that neither house nor flat were in the slim newly-organised London telephone directory. But London was sweltering, the shopping tiring, and on the Friday evening of 3 August Lady Glamis experienced an entirely unforeseen inti-mation of approaching labour.

On the eve of the holiday weekend her accustomed London doctors had already left town, and as the evening wore on other neighbourhood doctors were not readily found. One can well imagine the flurry of mess-engers and clatter of door-knockers. Normally the nearby Smith stables in Cadogan Mews would have had twenty or thirty horses and carriages plying for hire but most had been bedded down in their stalls early that night ready for the holiday demands early next morning. There even remains an unsubstantiated and romantic possibility that Celia's good friend and Cavendish-Bentinck cousin, Mrs Arthur James, exercised a privileged understanding for one of the Prince of Wales' fleet of carriages and coachmen from Marlborough House. In growing dis-tress, at all events, the expectant mother was driven to hospital, where in the small hours of 4 August night nurses hastened to attend the mother and new-born child.

But which hospital? St George's at Hyde Park Corner, not a mile from either flat or house, was long held in regard by Londoners as a good samaritan of emergencies. It is tempting to consider the very site of the familiar old stuccoed building, all but overlooking the garden walls of Buckingham Palace at the summit of Constitution Hill, doubly felicitous if the future Queen Mother was delivered under the banner of St George.*

Yet the evidence is purely circumstantial. The essential documentation – the admissions register, maternity day-books and ward records of 1900 – were destroyed some sixty years ago. If they survive, the appropriate record of St Thomas's, the Westminster and other local hospitals rest in the Greater London Record Office, at present denied to researchers under the Public Records Act. One potential clue nevertheless remains in the conundrum. Not half a mile across the park, St Mary's, Paddington, was one of the first hospitals to gain the patronage of the Queen Mother as Duchess of York. 'I include St Mary's in my prayers every night,' she once assured a puzzled Matron, and it must encourage conjecture to learn that in 1980 a trustees' fund presented two much-needed benches for a waiting-hall suitably carved in commemoration of their patron's eightieth birthday.

Lord Glamis would have learned from his young sister by telegram that he had a new daughter and that mother and child were fine, and he remained with the house-party in a carefree frame of mind. Nothing could have appealed more to his wife's advanced liberal inclinations than her unexpected involvement in the changing trend of social reform in the new century, while her letters from hospital would have stressed the blessing of being in good care. But the Glamis agent-archivist, Mr Philip Ord, knows of no correspondence of that time. It may yet lie secure in private papers elsewhere.

Other than the gratified, triumphant new aunt, Maud Bowes-Lyon, probably the first to see the baby were Celia's twin sisters, Anne and Hyacinth, 'good sensible girls' in their middle thirties, ready to accompany her safely home when the doctor permitted. Celia's two daughters Mary and Rose, young innocents of sixteen and twelve, could ask no questions and accepted unquestioningly that Mama had gone to London to visit Aunt Maud and mysteriously returned with a new little sister for them.

It was not until 21 September when his infant daughter was nearly seven weeks old, that Lord Glamis appeared before the Registrar of Births in the Hertfordshire market town of Hitchin and was mildly

---

* On the expiry of the Grosvenor lease, St George's was transferred in 1980 to new hospital premises in southwest London.

cautioned on being liable to a fine of forty shillings for failing to report the birth within the statutory period of forty-two days.

Claudie took the rebuke lightly. He knew the form. Over the years he had registered his children in districts as varied as Kensington (for his first-born daughter Hyacinth), Kingston, Hitchin and Glamis itself, where his eldest son, Patrick, had uttered his first cry at the height of the shooting season and the Registrar, a meticulous Scot, had brought his book to the Castle. Besides, a widely accepted convention had gained currency that the place of birth could be regarded as the place where the parents were normally resident. Upper-class babies were seldom known to be born in hospital, at a nursing home or in a mid-wife's cottage. To this day there are few maternity homes in the annals of the peerage. And so to the question, 'When and where born?' Claudie responded, '4 August, 1900, St Paul's Walden Bury'. On the birth certificate he approved the entry of his name and surname as Claude George Bowes-Lyon, and signed himself 'Glamis', with his occupation as 'peer's eldest son'. The name, surname and maiden name of the mother were formerly entered as 'Cecilia Nina Bowes-Lyon, formerly Cavendish-Bentinck', and the baby's name was given as 'Elizabeth Angela Marguerite'.

All was as it should be and unquestionably Lord Glamis returned home to lunch without a twinge of conscience. He could never have dreamed, during the British difficulties in the Boer War, that his little Elizabeth would one day be Queen of South Africa nor ever imagined that his one misstatement would prove of interest to posterity.

Plain Elizabeth Lyon . . . or Bowes-Lyon? Into her twenties she usually introduced herself as 'Elizabeth Lyon'. Her younger brother, David (born in 1902), ultimately preferred Bowes Lyon, without the hyphen. And following the rules observed in the Register for the double indexing of compound names, Elizabeth Lyon appears earlier on page 60 as Bowes-Lyon, Elizabeth A. Marguerite, thus gaining a trick of gamesmanship from the cradle.

Her father remembered something of the fireside discussions of his boyhood when *his* father, having succeeded as 13th Earl of Strathmore and Kinghorne, had also assumed 'by habit and repute' the surname of Bowes-Lyon from the century-old name of Lyon-Bowes. In 1865 the classic *Debrett* remained firm for Lyon-Bowes, while by 1869 the early editions of *Who's Who* unequivocally supported the plainer Lyon. Ingeniously skilled in inventing distinguishing names for his new crossbreeds of sheep and cattle, the 13th Earl also took a romantic Victorian pride in his proven noble descent from Sir John Lyon, Keeper of the Privy Seal in 1371 to the Scottish King Robert II. But in 1767 the Bowes heiress, Mary Eleanor, married the 9th Earl of Strathmore on her nineteenth birthday, and in uniting her considerable fortune with his estate he had agreed 'to take and use the surname Bowes next, before and in addition to his titles of honour', a bargain equally binding by Act of Parliament upon his children.

Lyons they nevertheless all remained, between themselves and among friends and neighbours. As Lyons the sons had their names put down for Eton or occasionally Harrow, while one of Elizabeth's Lyon uncles was acclaimed lawn tennis champion of Scotland and another won his Lyon's share of the doubles championship of England. 'There are lions everywhere' wrote the essayist-traveller, Augustus Hare, after paying a visit to the 13th Earl at Glamis Castle; 'gilt lions on either side of the drawingroom fireplace, lions as nutcrackers, on the letterbox, the very doorscraper, while at dinner is produced the gold Lion of Lyon for holding a whole bottle of claret.'

The Hare among the Lyons found the sons of the house charming, cordial boys, the eldest 'Claudie Glamis very handsome, strikingly so, especially in Scottish dress'. A good-looking romantic bridegroom in his red Life Guards uniform, he married the eighteen-year-old Cecilia Nina Cavendish Bentinck at Petersham parish church a year or two later, with the name of bride and groom alike unhyphened. It remains perhaps of richer interest that the ceremony was conducted by Robert Liddell, a kinsman of none other than the Alice Liddell who inspired Lewis Carroll in writing *Alice in Wonderland*. Official documentation rarely leads so readily through the Looking Glass.

Lyons and Liddells were entwined on the family tree by ties of both marriage and cousinhood. An old family album enshrines photographs not only of the 12th Earl – the 13th Earl's elder brother and thus Elizabeth's great-uncle – but also a charming photograph of Alice and her two sisters strikingly reminiscent of the Orchardson portrait of the three Cavendish Bentinck sisters (Cecilia and the younger twins) on the walls of the Queen Mother's drawing-room at Clarence House.

A more sombre link lay through the pleasantly named Reverend Tristram Valentine, vicar of St Paul's Walden, who was to christen Elizabeth. In his earlier days, as a chaplain of the London Hospital, Whitechapel, he laboured in the nearby courts and alleys at the height of the grisly Jack the Ripper murders and may have officiated at the funerals of some of the victims. From this horror, he was transferred in the following year to the tranquil village church, where glass from the time of Crècy glowed in one of the windows, and the history of England seemed written in every stone. Happily, he assumed his rural duties in time to baptise each of the three youngest Bowes Lyon children in turn, Fergus in 1889, Rose Constance in 1890, and Michael in 1893, their surnames all inscribed in his hand in the parish register. Careful as he was, Mr Valentine nevertheless made a hash of his baptismal entry for the infant Elizabeth, 'somewhat tatty', as a county archivist describes it, 'with some corrections made at the time'.

Elizabeth was baptised at the fourteenth-century font of All Saints after morning service on Sunday 23 September. Many of the congregation remained for the ceremony with family guests from the Bury, and the junior element was substantial. Patrick, the eldest son of the house, had celebrated his sixteenth birthday the previous day and was due back at Eton that evening, and probably all his four brothers were present: Pat, Jock, Alex and Fergus, down to seven-year-old Michael, with their two sisters, Mary and Rose, and a batch of Bentinck-Cavendish cousins, young and old. There were Harrison neighbours from King's Walden and no doubt an indulgent friend or two from Hatfield. There are hints that Claudie's youngest brother, Malcolm, while serving with the Life Guards in South Africa, was a godfather by proxy, an apt figure, aged twenty-six and born on St George's Day, 23 April. Regrettably, however, the godparents failed to sign the register and the Queen Mother can name only two of her godmothers with certainty.

Both without children of their own, the two were happily to gain a secure hold on her youthful affections. Her Aunt Maud was of course a sponsor, shielding the secret of Elizabeth's first appearance, her very initials, for Maud Agnes, bestowed in reverse upon the baby. The other well-remembered Cavendish-Bentinck godmother might have escaped attention if she had not some years earlier married a rich American named Arthur James and tumbled forthwith into a world of discreet affairs, horse-racing, fast pioneer motoring and close royal friendship.

Not a year after the christening, in fact, King Edward VII's secretary, Frederick Ponsonby, took careful note of two of the King's guests at Homburg, 'Arthur and Venetia James, he charming but not having much in common with the King except racing; she full of humour and high spirits, walking with the King and keeping him amused'. At Marienbad, Sandringham and elsewhere on the royal round, Mrs James helped to amuse this earlier 'Bertie' for the rest of his life and, indeed, Ponsonby chronicles her at Buckingham Palace, playing bridge with the King and Mrs Keppel only three days before the King's death. A surprising figure at the font, her public image as a celebrated Society hostess preceded her, and perhaps with so many onlookers, flustered the vicar.

Although Lady Glamis had intended that her new baby daughter should be christened Elizabeth Angela Marguerite, partly to satisfy a penchant for floral girls' names, Violet, Hyacinth, Rose and Marguerite among them, Mr Valentine misheard the latter name as Margaret or Margerite, and the name Elizabeth recalled a favourite cousin on the distaff side, a Baroness Bolsover. The baptismal entry describes Elizabeth Angela Marguerite as 'the daughter of Claude George Bowes Lyon, commonly called Glamis, a peer's eldest son, and of his wife, Cecilia Nina'. But erasures defying decipherment were scratched with a sharp knife after Elizabeth: the U was clearly inserted into 'Marguerite' in the same ink and the same hand, and the title of 'Lord' added as an afterthought with a different pen before 'Glamis'. The figure of Tristram Valentine bending over the parish register with his sharp erasing knife might have stepped from Victorian melodrama, a reminder that Elizabeth Lyon was born in the fading twilight of Victorian times. On the afternoon of the christening, the old Queen at Balmoral took one of her last carriage rides through the Scottish hills, and in four months and a day her long reign had closed.

2. Home and Family

St Paul's Walden Bury, the childhood home of Queen Elizabeth the Queen Mother, has stood for 200 years in its rolling acres, a Georgian country house in a setting of garden glades that rise and fall through woods of oak, beech and hornbeam. The intersecting green avenues where Elizabeth Lyon once raced on her pony, her cloak flowing in the wind, are still to be seen with their guardian hedges.

Thirty miles north of London, the Waldens seem sheltered from change, an oasis of chalk uplands within a circlet of five towns: eastward the new environment of Stevenage, westward industrial Luton, northward Hitchin and to the south Harpenden and Welwyn Garden City. This is commuter country, edging the suburban belt of Cobbett's despised 'Wen'. On the southern fringe lies Hatfield, where another Queen Elizabeth began her Tudor reign, and where, in modern times, the world's first passenger jet airliner was built and the Queen Mother once flew with the test pilot to the Mediterranean and back between lunch and tea. Hereabouts is much of the tourist Britain that flaunts its traditions between the mists of ancient times and the nuclear present. Yet the Waldens are much as they were, sequestered and drowsing, the essence of rural England.

At King's Walden, the Saxon King Ethelred had hunted his red deer. At Abbot's Walden, granted by one Wulfgar to St Alban's Abbey, the monks had reserved all the cheese and 1,000 Easter eggs for the abbot's kitchen; and at the dissolution of the monasteries Henry VIII had exchanged the manor of Waldenbury for other lands with the Dean and Chapter of St Paul's Cathedral. Hereabouts a manor house is styled a Bury, that is a hide or retreat, hence Aston Bury, Ayot Bury, Bayford Bury, King's Walden Bury and more besides.

Originally, the Queen Mother's so-called birthplace was a Bowes acquisition. The Bowes tend to be neglected in her ancestral history, although a fourteenth century lawyer, Adam Bowes, amassed a fortune

sufficiently substantial to be useful two centuries later to Sir John
Bowes, Queen Elizabeth I's ambassador to Russia. Adam, moreover,
married the heiress of Streatlam which, within another two centuries,
was found to stand on a black immensity of coal. Hence the impressive
wealth of George Bowes, coal-owner and sportsman of the early
eighteenth century, who married a girl of fourteen whom, upon her
death the following year, he longingly described as 'the most accom-
plished of her sex'. It was indeed twenty years before he found anyone
to rival her attractions. Then he wedded Mary Gilbert, whose father
owned St Paul's Walden Bury, and in 1767 their only daughter and
heiress, Mary Eleanor, espoused the 9th Earl of Strathmore, thus uniting the Bowes and Lyon estates.

Through the next sixty years the Strathmores and their heirs added
some piquant strains to the Queen Mother's ancestry. In 1782, for
instance, a certain George Carpenter 'of an ancient and respectable
family' took to wife at sixty a roguish plumber's daughter aged eighteen;
and the only child of this unequal match, a girl, married Mary Eleanor's
youngest son, the 11th Earl. Their eldest son in turn hastily married at
nineteen the daughter of another Hertfordshire landowning family,
Charlotte Grimstead, whose tragic fate it was ten months later to give
birth to a malformed son, the so-called 'monster' of Victorian legend.

Charlotte's portrait, in the lace cap and shawl of old age, shows a
woman of anxious disposition, but she coupled an eager sociability with
a mordant sense of humour. The sorrow of her first baby was known to
few and there is strong evidence that it was born and died on the same
day. In any event, Charlotte outlived her husband and lived to see her
young son, Claude – the Queen Mother's grandfather – succeed as 13th
Earl.

Paying a visit to friends at Blendon Hall (near Bexley, Kent) in the
1850s, Claude wooed and won one of the daughters of the house,
Frances Dora Smith, and so introduced the most common of English
surnames into the Royal Family. (As an incidental augury, Fanny
Smith's father also owned the Blendon village inn which chanced to be
named the Golden Lion.) Destined to be the Queen Mother's paternal
grandmother, Fanny in due course presented Claude with a large Victorian family of seven sons and three daughters, 'all born musicians', as
Lord Frederick Hamilton fondly recollected. 'I have never heard such
finished part-singing. At Glamis, in the middle of dinner, even, the
irrepressible family could not help bursting into harmony, and such
exquisite harmony too. Until their sisters grew up, the young boys sang

the treble and alto parts, but finally they were able to manage a male-voice quartet, a trio of ladies' voices, and a combined family octette'.

The ensemble consisted, of course, of Elizabeth Lyon's future uncles and aunts, who were ultimately to marry and surround her with innumerable cousins. Augustus Hare, too, was equally impressed by the 'charming, cordial boys, so very nice. Claudie (Glamis) is very handsome, strikingly so in Scottish dress'. Now we are meeting the good-looker who was in fact, Claude's son, Claude George, and the Queen Mother's father.

Simple-hearted, kindly, courteous yet unsophisticated, Claudie was Charlotte Grimstead's favourite grandson. His strict sense of family duty had led him to enter his father's old regiment, the 2nd Life Guards, but Army life was not without disillusionment. At twenty-five he found himself, apparently immured at Windsor Barracks, despondent at military gaming and drunkenness and above all shocked at the outspoken gossip in the officers' mess of the easy morals of the heir to the throne.

Neither the Windsor draghounds nor other local diversions could compensate for the lost sport and broad acres of Glamis Castle. In 1880, however, his hours of reprieve from barracks found him frequently at the home of a Mr and Mrs Harry Warren Scott, to whom he had been introduced by his commanding officer, Major Burnaby. The Scotts had married as widow and widower and their house at Ham, near Richmond, was enlivened by the presence of Mrs Scott's three daughters by her former marriage, Cecilia Cavendish Bentinck, who was just eighteen, and her younger twin sisters, Violet and Hyacinth.

Claudie fell in love with the slim, dark-eyed 'Celia'. Warm-hearted sincerity, kindness and hospitality unfailingly greeted him at the Scotts' threshold, a house fragrant with flowers and colourful with old Italian furniture, and in Celia he found a love of music and the simple domestic pleasures together with an underlying seriousness and religious faith that matched his own. Her father, who had taken Holy Orders, had died when she was only three and the twins still babes in arms, but her family was well connected: the Rev. Charles Cavendish's grandfather was none other than the celebrated 3rd Duke of Portland, twice Prime Minister, and his young widow encountered no financial stress during the five years before she married Harry Scott. Claudie in his younger generation nevertheless worried over the financial responsibilities of taking a wife and the necessity of dutifully managing, as his father had done, upon his army pay plus a paternal allowance. Pondering these problems during the January gloom of 1881, Lord Glamis was saddened by the death of his Grandmother Grimstead, but the next month, when he was summoned to the reading of her will, a broad and sunlit highway suddenly opened in his affairs.

Charlotte had not made her last testament without exercising her sardonic sense of fun. The will was long and complex, and Lord Glamis heard with astonishment that she had left him a couple of pubs: 'and to my grandson Claude George my public-house known as the Strathmore Arms at St Paul's Walden, the beerhouse known as the Woodman at Whitewell with the paddock adjoining and all my other real estate in the parish of St Paul's Walden or any adjoining parish referred to as my Walden property'. Disappointment must have warred with despair until, the next instant, Claudie realized that the real estate comprised the Georgian mansion and park of St Paul's Walden Bury with hundreds of acres of the finest farming land in Hertfordshire, and he must have experienced a rosy vision of release in which he blithely resigned from the army, married his lass of Richmond and was happy master of all he surveyed. At this point his grandmother's posthumous jest turned decisively sour, for she had added a codicil. After fifteen months of anxious thought, Charlotte had changed her mind and in a few brief sentences the estates devolved upon his father, the 13th Earl of Strathmore, for life, while Claudie's interest was reduced to an annuity of £400.

Fortunately, Lord Strathmore was a sensible parent, and with his pride in already owning 24,700 acres – a claim to celebrity which he entered in Who's Who – he prudently perceived that, far from gilding the gingerbread, another large estate and an impecunious son would only add to his burdens, and he happily saw a way through the difficulty. The will could be observed in the letter, if not in the deed. Claudie could receive not merely his annuity but also the tenancy and income of St Paul's Walden Bury, both having his cake and improving it.

Within the month Lord Glamis successfully proposed to Celia – with Mrs Scott's permission since she was still a minor – and on 16 July 1881 they were married by special licence at Petersham. The charm of the bride was enhanced by her twin bridesmaids; her cousin, the 6th Duke of Portland, gave her away; her uncle Major Burnaby signed the register as best man and the congregation was enlivened by the presence of the bridegroom's six brothers, ranging from their twenties down to seven-year-old Malcolm, who remembered something of the wedding in his old age when Elizabeth II was Queen.

For more than 100 years the Strathmore heirs had invariably married for love rather than for wealth or other worldly considerations. The fond mama, the Countess of Strathmore, who followed Claudie and Celia into the vestry to sign the wedding register, was of course the Fanny Smith whom the 13th Earl had carried off from Kent. The happy accidents of love thus brought the ducal strains of Devonshire and Portland and the acumen of the Bentincks into Elizabeth Lyon's heritage, and the Queen Mother has never failed to put visiting Dutch diplomats at ease by reminding them that she has some Netherlands' blood in her veins.

The Lyons have been somewhat less Scottish than they seem since the late seventeenth century when the 4th Earl of Strathmore married the English rose Elizabeth Stanhope and raised seven sons, four of whom, with their partly English blood, succeeded one another as Earls of Strathmore. The romantic gloss of the Scots dates from the documented reality of Sir John Lyon, nicknamed the White Lion from his platinum beard, who in the fourteenth century married a daughter of King Robert II of Scotland, gained the estates of Glamis as her dowry and begat heirs able to boast of their Scottish blood royal. Successive Lords of Glamis fought at Sauchieburn and Flodden. Yet with a single Irish exception the Earls of Strathmore have married Englishwomen for the past seven generations.

For the benefit of his wedding banns, Claudie, Lord Glamis, gave his address as the Hyde Park Barracks, but his four-week honeymoon was timed to conclude on the eve of the grouse-shooting season, and his bride found Glamis Castle en fête to welcome her. Family correspondence of the time tells of the 'immense party in the house', much as when the Prince of Wales had been expected a year or so previously and they had sturdily failed to invite Lillie Langtry. 'To the great inconvenience of everyone' the Prince pleaded toothache and did not come. The 13th Earl and his Kentish Countess, née Fanny Smith, spared no effort of hospitality, and Celia found that her father-in-law lived for Glamis and his guests, his tenantry and his northern estates. Her stepfather, one of the Scotts of Ancrum, had often swept his young family north for holidays to imbue them with Scottish tradition, but at Glamis everything was always 'better than best'.

A guest of the old days has told of the family pipers circling the table and retreating until the last echoes of the music died away in the corridors and the vast vaulted room was left in candlelight. 'Then out came a tuning fork, third beat, and off they went, singing exquisitely, glees, part-songs, anything and everything from madrigals to Gilbert and Sullivan'. There was even a stage on which the old Earl's seven sons and three daughters performed *The Pirates of Penzance* and *HMS Pinafore*. All this, of course, was years before Elizabeth Lyon was born, but the atmosphere of her parents' first summer of married life was little changed twenty and even thirty years later, and when Claudie took his young wife home to St Paul's Walden Bury they had the happy knowledge that their marriage would be blessed by a child.

The couple had already inspected the house that summer. The first glimpse from the road was not impressive. Ivy half-blanketed the roof and darkened the windows, and the place bore the marks of Grandmama Charlotte's long occupancy. But now the new bride arrived as chatelaine, and the servants were assembled under the watchful eyes of the steward and housekeeper – housemaids, scullerymaids, footmen. The presentation of the keys to Her Ladyship would have been followed by the introduction of the outdoor staff, coachmen and gardeners, shed boys and woodsmen lined up in the stableyard. The faithful head gardener had been left a small annuity under the Grimshaw will, subject to withdrawal without notice, and a coachman was similarly privileged provided he remained sober. Such was the friendly, but infinitely graduated 'upstairs-downstairs' domestic world into which a new generation of Lyons was born.

Lord and Lady Glamis's first child, a daughter born in April 1882, was named Violet Hyacinth, after Celia's twin sisters, and a second daughter, Mary Frances, arrived sixteen months later. Great was the rejoicing in September 1884 when, within a week of her twenty-second birthday, Lady Glamis presented her husband with a son and heir, Patrick. A second son, John, was born in April 1886, and a third boy, Alexander, in the following April. For ten years the fond parents demonstrated a fecundity as dependable as the espalier pears and peaches on the red-brick walls of their fruit garden. A fourth son, Fergus, appeared two years to the week after Alexander, and the Bury had to be enlarged under the pressure of this ever-growing family, with a new frontage in neo-Elizabethan red brick to flank the roadside. A third daughter, Rose Constance, arrived in May 1890, three weeks after Fergus had celebrated his first birthday anniversary.

With this remarkable regularity, the children fell into convenient social age-groups: first the trio of Violet, Mary and Patrick; next three boys, John, Alexander and Fergus; and then Rose, matched some three years later by her brother Michael. Behind the baize-padded doors of the new wing, the passages echoed to junior comings and goings, for the children were never long in the nursery. Claudie and Celia were agreeably determined that their home should be a family home in every sense. The boys presently found that the former Georgian entrance hall on the garden front formed an excellent skittle alley. Outside the sash window, Lord Glamis preferred to trim but not strip the ivy rather than deprive the nesting wrens of shelter. The drawing-room then lacked, I think, its later sumptuous chimney-piece and the beautiful windowbays were heavily curtained against draughts. In the music room, only the children paid much regard to the plaster fiddles and lutes of the smoke-darkened ceiling. Becoming plump with the years, Lady Glamis loved nursing her ever-present babies, reading to them as they perched on her knee, teaching them to read and write, and taking one or two of the elder ones to call on neighbours, thereby inaugurating decades of friendship. All this, as time passed, came to be mixed with an endearing casual vagueness. A friend once could not resist pointing out that a leaking gutter was spreading damp on a wall. 'Oh, dear,' came the answer, 'I really must move that sofa.'

Lord and Lady Glamis were in the thirteenth year of their marriage when they faced their first great sorrow. In the late summer of 1893, while Celia prepared for her eighth baby, the eleven-year-old eldest child, Violet Hyacinth, was sent to stay with her Scott grandmother and young unmarried aunts. A son, Michael, was born to Celia on 1 October but within the week Celia had received alarming news from Richmond that Violet had fallen ill with diphtheria, that dreaded scourge of Victorian childhood. The baby boy was only seventeen days old when the little girl died, and her funeral had to precede Michael's christening.

From this moment the grieving parents regarded their family as complete. Their garden, dappled for so long with babies and nurse-maids, was approaching a new phase of schoolboys and tutors, and the company of a young tutor was considered advisable for nine-year-old Patrick, who was missing his elder sister. Lady Glamis drew what solace she could from designing a tablet for the church showing two small figures holding a wreath, and gradually the parents emerged from their sorrow and entered upon six settled and tranquil years.

Boys and girls alike, it was generally agreed that the Lyons added good looks and exceptional qualities of charm to the junior social life of the neighbourhood. Benevolent uncles were forever appearing in wide variety: a diplomat, a barrister, a soldier, and especially an Uncle Frank who assumed a halo of romance when his nephews and nieces discovered that he was a member of the Queen's Bodyguard for Scot-land and satisfyingly skilled in archery. Household cricket matches of the Bury versus the village were a delight of the summer, with the eldest girl, Mary – often 'May' to the family – knowledgeably keeping score. Neighbourhood tea-parties were enlivened by a trio of young boys who suddenly appeared, sang part-songs and encores – as their father had at Glamis – and then mixed amiably with the company. Lady Glamis, people agreed, had a genius for family life. 'At six or seven,' wrote one of the brothers, 'we could each have written a fairly detailed account of all the Bible stories, knowledge entirely due to our mother's teaching.'

In her mid-thirties, Celia took up gardening, one of the ever fresh enthusiasms ranging from embroidery to London house-hunting that sustained her from time to time. The children were encouraged to till and plant, and to care for special shrubs. Claudie had embarked on a long-term programme of clearing decaying trees and planting afresh in the woodlands, and retrieving weedy lawns and moss-grown walks. The ground of the Bury had been laid out in the eighteenth century with a cultivated observance of the precepts of Le Notre; the sculptures that enhance the glades were reputedly by John Nost, but the children improvized names of their own for the welldraped ladies and men of marble muscle – the athletic discobolus became the 'Running Foot-man', a decorous fountain was the 'Frying Pan'. A lead female figure of Charity, preoccupied with her babies, alone escaped ridicule and, in token of sentiment, a replica adorns one of the glades of Royal Lodge, the Queen Mother's Windsor home.

As the nineteenth century drew to its close, the parents noticed that life at the Bury was undeniably quieter. Their four elder boys were at school, Patrick at Eton, John mapped for Sandhurst; while Mary (the future Lady Elphinstone) had coiled up her hair and was leaving the schoolroom. Only Rose, aged nine, and Michael, aged six, still inha-bited the nursery rooms, with their worn rocking-horses and scrap-book screens and sentimental prints by Marcus Stone. In their secure existence, the Lyons were nevertheless not immune from far-off events. In October 1899, the outbreak of the Boer War produced an emotional shock through every grade of society, particularly felt in the overnight leap from flag-waving to the dire lists of casualties and then the incred-ible news that British troops were hemmed in under siege in Ladysmith, Kimberley and Mafeking. Lord Glamis's youngest brother, Malcolm, had sailed in one of the troopships with the Black Watch, and from Magers-fontein a Glamis neighbour, David Airlie, wrote of disastrous leadership and of seeing men 'tired and desperately thirsty and completely disorganized', mown down from the Boer trenches. What worse news had the new century in store?

In the climate of gloom as the year 1900 dawned, *The Times* carried an antidote of correspondence. Was a new century indeed beginning, or should one wait until 1901? On 1 January 1900 Queen Victoria firmly settled the argument for herself. 'I begin today a new year and a new century.' Then, in February, Kimberley was relieved, the first turn of the tide, and after her long quiescence Lady Glamis could confide to her husband the equal surprise that she was expecting another baby.

Although a precipitate arrival, Elizabeth Lyon was a decided late-comer to the large and pleasant family at the Bury. Celia's twin sisters must have been among the first to see her, 'sensible girls', then in their mid-thirties: Hyacinth, who was being ardently courted by an American, and 'the quieter one', Violet, who never married. They would have travelled up from Richmond with their mother, Mrs Scott, to gaze rapturously at the blue-eyed newcomer, cradled in Celia's arms in hospital. From a Waldens farmhouse near the Bury a tall gangling girl presently helped to welcome Lady Glamis home and to assist the household as nursemaid. This was Clare Knight, herself the sixth of a family of twelve children, the redoubtable 'Alah', as infant lips framed her name, who was to remain with the family for fortyfive years: first as nanny of Elizabeth Lyon, and then the Elphinstone children, and later the two Princesses, Elizabeth and Margaret. 'In all these rooms children certainly *were* heard,' a visitor once described Alah's unchanging scene. 'After admiring all the scrap-book screens, you pass through the precautionary high gate of nursery tradition. The clamour of young voices seems still to linger, a nursery suggestive of precious, shabby, hugged-out-of-shape toys . . . the high fender recalls comfortable dryings by the fire and the delicious smell of toasting bread.'

We also have Clare Knight's testimony that her charge was 'an exceptionally happy, easy baby; crawling early, running at thirteen months and speaking very young'. And little Elizabeth was no sooner running than Lady Glamis, in her fortieth year, had another surprise for her husband with the intimation of another baby. Her tenth child, a younger brother for Elizabeth, was born on 2 May 1902, and named David, by way of blessing and sanction among the giant Goliaths of his five elder brothers.

His christening had perhaps to be arranged with regard to the Coronation of King Edward VII in June 1902. It was doubtful whether Claudie's father, the old 13th Earl of Strathmore, now nearly eighty, could endure the fatigue of attending the long Abbey ceremony of the crowning, and while Claudie debated whether he could or should take his father's place, the unexpected appendicitis of the King caused the Coronation to be postponed until 9 August, clashing irredeemably with family arrangements to go to Scotland.

In a social context, the new reign had brought the Lyons a step closer to the court. Their friends along the ridge at King's Walden, the Harrisons, were on terms of personal friendship with the Tecks, particularly Prince Frank, the youngest brother of the new Princess of Wales (later Queen Mary), while the Princess had invited their own close Glamis friend, young Mabell Airlie, to be one of her ladies-in-waiting. Mabell was still wearing the deep black of widowhood; her husband, David, the 9th Earl of Airlie, had survived the Magersfontein rout only to be killed in the decisive Boer War battle at Diamond Hill; and with her unfailing sympathy and thoughtfulness Lady Glamis preferred to keep her friend company on learning that she had been excused from Coronation Day duties in London. 'The Lyons and Ogilvys had been friends and allies for centuries,' Lady Airlie affectionately wrote later. 'The two children at the extreme end of the big family had been brought over to Cortachy before they could walk.' At about this time Aunt Hyacinth also appeared briefly to take her farewell of the babies, for she had married her American, Augustus Jessup, and would be going to live in Philadelphia.

The fuller future of the twentieth century was gradually emerging. In 1903, Katharine, Duchess of Atholl, chanced to call on Lady Glamis at a family flat in London and was 'very impressed by the charm and dignity of a little daughter, two or three years old, who came into the room . . . as if a little princess had stepped out of an eighteenth-century picture'. This is the first we hear reliably of the regal attributes of the blue-eyed, brunette, chubby and endearing child who was to become, as Harold Nicholson said, 'in truth one of the most amazing Queens since Cleopatra'.

Part Two

LADY ELIZABETH BOWES-LYON

3. *All That Children Could Desire*

In February 1904 the old 13th Earl of Strathmore died in his eightieth year. Born in the reign of George IV, he had seemed to the last a central figure of the family and his portraits at Clarence House and Glamis Castle afford a remarkable link between the Georgian era and the Queen Mother. His widow, Fanny, survived him until February 1922, and lived to take delight in the possibility that her grand-daughter Elizabeth might marry into the Royal Family.

The 13th Earl had been a patrician by inclination rather than upbringing. He had been only nine when his father died, and thirty-one years elapsed before he succeeded his elder brother to the earldom. As a boy, he could remember his father's hard-drinking dinner-parties at Glamis when a page lurked under the table to loosen the men's collars as they rolled from their chairs, and roisterers were often carried insensible to their carriages. Yet the 13th Earl, with his sad, wan looks, sat as a Scottish peer in the House of Lords and was a staunch pillar of the Scottish Presbyterian Church. 'Silent and moody with an anxious look', Lord Halifax described him, aware of his supposed secret knowledge of the so-called Glamis monster. But his innumerable grandchildren and great-grandchildren remembered the happiness of his old London home in Queen's Gate Gardens, and then his surprising modernity in leasing a new flat in Grosvenor Gardens. He and Lady Strathmore had taken to wintering in Italy, and he breathed his last in the warm clime of Bordighera.

Taking fuller charge of affairs as his father aged, Lord Glamis had been aware of untouched reserves of family wealth, much of it accumulating from the Bowes chemical and industrial interests of Tees and Tyne. This did not lessen the shock on learning that his father had left a personal fortune not far short of £250,000, perhaps akin to £10,000,000 today, not including the assessed £716,000 value of his various estates in Forfar, Hertfordshire and Sussex.

As the 14th Earl of Strathmore, Claudie's new family titles were impressive: Viscount Lyon and Baron Glamis, Tannadyce, Sidlaw, and Strathdichtle in Scotland, they ran under a charter of Charles II, with the added 'Baron Bowes, of Streatlam Castle, County Durham, and Lunedale, County York, and Earl of Strathmore and Kinghorne in the United Kingdom'. Sadness for his father and astonishment at the new-found financial reserves did not diminish the new Earl's satisfaction that his own son and heir, Patrick, would now be serving in the Guards as Lord Glamis. His old dislike of Army restraints was forgotten, and the repetition of old family ways and traditions had an increasing appeal. Among his younger sons, the old arguments of the family name came up afresh. Bowes-Lyon was a mouthful but the prefix for an Earl's son – the Honourable Fergus, the Honourable Alexander – provoked mirth, and it was droll to see letters to Mother addressed as 'The Right Hon The Countess of Strathmore'. The daughters of lords were not always ladies, with or without a capital L, but despite the teasing May and Rose were now Lady Mary and Lady Rose . . . and their little sister was Lady Elizabeth, too.

If the sallies went over Elizabeth's head, a more immediate concern was with Curly-Love, the ring-dove, and the Shetland pony, Bobs, who could walk up steps and was suffered to follow her into the house. At the age of four, she amused the Glamis factor with her demure politeness. 'How do you do, Mr Ralston? I haven't seen you look so well for years and years.' And another friend long remembered her as a small girl of five, with dark beribboned hair, confidently detaching him from the main group in the drawing-room. 'Shall us sit and talk?' she invited, and maintained her full share of the conversation.

She was naturally imitative, self-possessed, a shade precocious, in her world of indulgent elders. With not two years between them, her younger brother, David, came on the scene in time to soften the risk of her being spoiled. 'They were almost like twins,' Mary Lyon (Lady Elphinstone) remembered, and in the haze of affectionate recollection the two children run down the slope of the lawn in their smocked pinafores and floppy sunhats and there was rarely an hour without young David's cries of 'Elizabuff! Elizabuff!' Laughing together, searching for wild strawberries, the girl's dark tresses against the boy's golden curls, the two belong to a Rivière print. Through an eternity of June afternoons the white cloth was spread for tea on the lawn, with Mother and Alah and perhaps Rose, in the shadow of the statue of the goddess Diana.

When in her twenties, as Duchess of York, the Queen Mother was persuaded to set down some notes on her childhood while her impressions were still immediate. The hot sunshine could be felt: 'At the bottom of the garden is THE WOOD – the haunt of fairies, with its anemones and ponds and moss-grown statues, and the big oak under which she reads and where the two ring-doves contentedly coo in their wicker-work "Ideal Home". There are carpets of primroses to sit on and her small brother David is always with her. . . . Now it is time to go haymaking, which means getting very hot in a delicious smell. Very often she gets up wonderfully early – about six o'clock – to feed her chickens and make sure they are safe after the dangers of the night. The hens stubbornly insist on laying their eggs in a place called the FLEA HOUSE, and this is where she and her brother go and hide from Nurse. Nothing is quite so good as the FLEA HOUSE, but the place called the HARNESS ROOM is very attractive too. Besides hens there are bantams, whose eggs-for-tea are so good.'

Ten years later, one suspects, she glanced at these impressions in preparing material for a Coronation supplement of *The Times*, for the same author's hand is evident: 'Here were all the things that children could desire – dogs and tortoises, Persian kittens and "Bobs" the Shetland pony, hay to make, chickens to feed, a garden, a friendly stillroom, the attic of a tumbledown brew house to play truant in, bullfinches to tame, fields to roam, flowers to love, ripe apples to drop, providentially, about the head, and on wet days the books that are best read on the floor in front of the fire. . . .'

The childhood picture was unexaggerated, neither warmed nor softened. The Bowes-Lyon family always insisted that Elizabeth's happiness had mirrored their own, drawn essentially from their mother's serene outward-going personality. Lady Strathmore had brought up her large family to her own high principles, managing them all 'in much the way she handled her outdoor and indoor staff, with a peculiarly individual tactful persuasion that rarely tightened in sternness, and in which a sense of gaiety was never long absent'. 'I never heard her say a harsh word,' Lady Elphinstone once said, 'but we had to obey her.' If her elder children felt that she was often less strict with the younger, experience had shown that it caused no harm to be lenient. With her recent change of name and title, Lady Strathmore claimed vivaciously that her new family gave her a sense of being young again. Seldom at a loss for a Biblical simile, she often introduced her two youngest children as her 'two Benjamins'. No one better knew the Biblical reference to the two youngest children born to Jacob and Leah and she protested comically that her last two were often mistaken for her grandchildren.

Early in 1905 a new governess joined the household in the petite person of Mlle Lang, who retained a life-long recollection of Elizabeth, meeting her in the hall, 'an enchanting child with tiny hands and feet and rose-petal colouring, murmuring with perfect politeness, "I do hope you will be happy here".' Elizabeth invariably spoke with careful precision, but with the difficult 'Mademoiselle' abbreviated to 'Madé', Mlle Lang remained a focus of youthful affection for the next six years or more.

Lady Strathmore's choice of a French governess, rather than English, was characteristic. As a girl, she had been taught French, Latin and a little German and Italian; the Scotts ensured that she was widely read, and lessons from both a Richmond drawing-master and a music teacher developed her artistic and musical talents. In middle age, after attending a concert, she could return home to play much of the music perfectly by ear. She admired the Froebel precepts of teaching by play, an advanced view in those days. Mlle Lang found that Elizabeth knew psalms by heart as well as poetry; her mind was stocked with Bible stories; she could already read the simpler stories of *Little Folks* magazine by herself, and her mother had given her elementary music, dancing and drawing lessons. Family charades brought some familiarity with the kindlier stories of English and Scottish history aided by, in the Queen Mother's phrase, 'a wonderful chest full of period costumes and the wigs that went with their gorgeousness'.

Forty years later, when Elizabeth was Queen Consort, just such a chest was brought out for charades at Windsor, to the King's delight and Winston Churchill's disgruntlement. Over teatime at Royal Lodge there hangs Mlle Lang's wisp of anecdote concerning her pupil at the age of six, playing hostess with composure when visitors called one afternoon and Lady Strathmore, busy in some distant recess of the garden, could not be found. Elizabeth rang for tea and her mother returned to find her successfully handling the teapot in the drawing-room and 'making conversation'. Lady Strathmore invariably included her children at the lunch or tea table the moment she thought them 'old enough to behave'. Lord Gorell remembered David being imperiously enjoined by his six-year-old sister not to bother him, 'the unconcealed object being to bother me by herself', and two years later she was to confide self-reproachfully that at six, she was sure, she 'must have bothered him most awfully'.

As a budding author and publisher, part of Ronald Gorell's own sympathetic attraction for the child was his ability to make up stories on demand, among them his saga of the Michelin man in the motor-tyre suit who fell off the castle roof 'and bounced and bounced until they strewed the courtyard with tintacks to puncture him'. Twenty years later, he found that his young disciple could still retell the story. Another thirty years on, indeed, I expressed the hope that I 'had not bounced about the courtyard too much' and the Queen Mother immediately smiled at the reference.

The stories linger, as they might around any child after gaining world celebrity. From Madé the story of the death of a tame bullfinch at the claws of a cat, and his interment in the finest coffin the schoolroom could provide, namely, a pencil-box, while Elizabeth intoned an improvized burial service. From David Bowes Lyon the drama of the highly intelligent pigs, Lucifer and Emma, who grew so stout that it was decided they should furnish a prize in a village raffle. The two horrified children broke open their money-boxes, cajoled their relatives for sixpences and are credited with buying half the raffle tickets themselves. Unhappily, the pigs were won by strangers and vanished from the Bury farm, their ultimate fate cloaked in desirable mystery. Earlier, Bruce Lockhart recalled the little girl at Glamis who clapped her hands and jumped around with partisan glee every time a wicket fell to the Castle fast bowler. 'That's James,' she explained. 'I'm going to marry him when I grow older.' The much-admired James was one of the footmen.

Perhaps conveniently forgotten, few stories survive of naughtiness. Given her first pair of sewing scissors, Elizabeth practised by injudiciously snipping a new pair of nursery sheets. 'What will Mother say?' was the question. 'She will say "Oh, Elizabeth!"' replied the culprit, with an instant thumbnail impersonation, and so it was. Repression was little known among the Bowes Lyons. With mock severity, David was once punished for some boyish misdemeanour by being flipped with a hunting-crop. The victim screamed with laughter, though his tender-hearted sister, thinking the worst of the distant commotion, sat up in bed and sobbed.

Years later, Lady Strathmore pleaded inability to recall many childhood stories, perhaps as an excuse to prevent distortion if the tale were retold by others, as it unfailingly would be, yet she considered one instance as characteristic. The affairs of a young man who, though wealthy, was unfortunately unpersonable, were being discussed by the grown-ups one day unaware that the little daughter of the house was still in the room. 'How sad', said one, 'to think that the poor man will be married only for his position and money.'

A faintly reproachful small voice chimed in from behind the sofa. 'Perhaps someone will marry him 'cos she loves him.'

'One must face the world,' Lord Strathmore would say when, as occasionally happened, his children sought his views on their own small personal problems. His youngest pair accepted the phrase more literally than he intended and in the loft of the fleahouse they kept, according to David, 'a regular store of forbidden delicacies, acquired by devious devices . . . apples, oranges, sugar, sweets, slabs of chocolate, matches and packets of Woodbines', iron rations for facing the world. The cigarettes were reserved for a future attempt at smoking which in the event was forever postponed.

At fifty Lord Strathmore was a modest, country-loving man who enjoyed the solitudes of nature and yet revelled in genial sociability, his ambivalent nature as marked and matching as the carefully-parted sides of his moustache, which he permitted to luxuriate as he grew older. His sons came to believe their invention that at Glamis, in the autumn, he spent every Saturday afternoon watching the Forfar football team. He was a man of regular habits, from his hour of useful exercise spent cutting wood to his time-table for visiting the farms or his days devoted to the Scottish Widows insurance or other business meetings in London. A sense of duty ordained his daily routine, as it would one day for his youngest daughter. On inheriting his father's title, as he carefully put it, he had been touched by the tributes to the late Earl as a civic figure and the invitations that he should continue in the same course. He gave much thought to his public responsibilities. He had long been a Justice of the Peace, and as a magistrate he rarely omitted his duties on the bench, sympathetic and unhurried yet shrewd. The earldom, one of the ten oldest of Scotland, was soon enhanced by his appointment as Lord Lieutenant of Forfarshire; he treated the sudden assumption of seniority, rank and wealth, with a gravity at odds with his nonchalant, still youthful outlook.

In the Edwardian era of opulent and fashionable display, a favourite phrase, 'We've room enough', might have summed up his private opinion of his castle in Scotland and his country mansion in Hertfordshire. Plans for the sale of Gibside, a Bowes property in Durham, were not concluded without considering the sentimental worth of a fine

chimney-piece, rich in heraldic devices, which was subsequently transferred to the Glamis billiard-room. His other northern property,
Streatlam Castle, was allowed to remain in hand for summer holidays
for a few more years. But the Grosvenor Gardens apartment no longer
appealed to Lord Strathmore's sense of family dignity. His children's
matrimonial needs and prospects were to be borne in mind, and his wife
returned from a house-hunting expedition one afternoon glowing with
the adventure of discovering a house to rent in St James's Square.
Number 20 was in fact an Adam mansion which had been in the posses-
sion of the Williams Wynn family from the time they built it in 1771.
There were delicately painted Adam ceilings, two drawing-rooms with
decorations by Angelica Kauffmann or her husband, Antonio Zucchi,
and an impressive staircase recommended as ranking with any in
London.

Lord Strathmore could not but agree with his wife's rhapsodies when
his inspection also disclosed a secluded garden courtyard and sensible
stabling. In the heart of London, No 20 was only around the corner
from the Carlton Club, of which he was a member, and was both peace-
ful and arrogantly spacious: a battalion could have fed in the so-called
Eating Room. The interior was also graced by characteristic Adam
alcoves and desirable chimney-pieces, and at the head of the staircase on
the first floor, a mural copy of Raphael's painting of the 'Transfigur-
ation', had impressed Celia with persuasive force.

With its palatial stone façade, handsome pilasters and pedimented
windows, the mansion still outshines its neighbours today, and it
doubtless annoyed Lord Strathmore that his splendid residence was not
ready for occupation when he rode to Buckingham Palace to receive his
credentials as Lord Lieutenant. Yet Celia set about the task of refur-
bishment with all her 'immense zest', in David Bowes Lyon's phrase,
'for something fresh, something new, not necessarily something
prudent'. The house was the central setting of Lady Elizabeth Bowes-
Lyon's London activities from 1907 to 1920. A key to the gardens of St
James's Square accompanied the lease, an amenity for the nursemaids
and children of families in town, and today I can never pass through the
Square on my way to the London Library without thinking of the
Queen Mother as a child, playing with David around the equestrian
statue of William III.

Every August the annual move to Glamis Castle was undertaken with a
junior maelstrom. Alah's firmest management was needed throughout

Elizabeth's fever of indecision in choosing which toys, books and pets should be taken or which livestock could be confided to friendly domestic care and left behind at the Bury. Governess, nursemaids, footmen, lady's maid, valet – all were transported in the great migration. The journey of 400 miles north by the Flying Scotsman was an adventure of steamy roaring speed and swirling fields that always delighted the children until, heavy with sleep, they reached the Castle in time to see its turrets and towers shining in the sunset.

Madé's schoolroom curriculum, never strict, would be forgotten. Beaming and companionable uncles, aunts, cousins and friends converged on the annual gathering, eager for 'the best of company, fun and games that the war-free world had to offer' and the fond recollections glowed untarnished decades later. 'It was an enormous family party and the nicest way of life in the world,' David Bowes Lyon recalled. 'And as we were stuck with one another every day, a lot of head-knocking went on which was very good for us. We learnt that family life is a wonderful thing, and tremendous fun, too.' Ostensibly, for the tender-hearted Elizabeth, the hospitable festival was for 'the cricket season', not the shooting, and ghillies and house servants alike exercised a stream of devious wiles to keep the pathetic carcases out of her sight.

'I always loved that cricket up there,' wrote Michael Bowes-Lyon. 'I shall always remember Jock opening the bowling, later on relieved by Plowright and my father, very round arm. The special umpire, Mr Arthur Fossett, short, round, red-faced and fat, was perfectly trained never to no-ball Father and always to give his appeals out.' Clearly the cricket was not too serious, and when Lord Strathmore, bowling his leg-breaks, once achieved the hat-trick of three wickets in three balls against the redoubtable Dundee Drapers, his triumphant team subscribed to buy him a much-needed new Panama hat.

The alternative days on the moors after grouse or woodcock were similarly disguised with finesse as picnics, on which Elizabeth was long remembered 'exercising an aged donkey, reputedly housed in the Castle stables for a quiet retirement'. Determined that he should still enjoy life, his rider however gave him free rein, while her escorts were running breathlessly at her stirrups, ever faster, until a final frenzied struggle ensued to prevent both donkey and joyously shrieking rider from plunging down a steep bank into a stream.

At seven or eight years old, Elizabeth revelled in playing miniature hostess, conducting guests to their rooms, explaining 'I must make sure you are quite comfortable' and then inveigling newcomers, 'May I take

you around?' The date 1621 on the ceiling of the drawing-room, formerly the Great Hall, sets a period to all the old rooms leading off the
spiral stone staircase which she would 'show' with enthusiasm. Overnight guests would be pleasantly cautioned, 'If you should hear shuf-
fling sounds and clanking chains at midnight, don't be afraid. It is only
the cords and chains of the Great Clock being rather a nuisance.' Lady
Scott, wife of the explorer, came to tea and reported to her husband in
the Antarctic, 'What a glorious place! Little Lady Elizabeth Lyon
showed me over.'

Such encounters so deeply appealed to the child that when asked to
set down her favourite pastime in an autograph album she reflected and
then carefully inscribed, 'Making friends'. She had the gift even then of
not merely insinuating herself into good graces but almost commanding
captivation by instinctively knowing the right thing to say. A family
group were once discussing the entertainment of an anticipated guest
who was known to be difficult. 'Let's ask Elizabeth,' Rose proposed.
'She can talk to *anyone*.'

It was a rare morning, moreover, that did not bring mail for Elizabeth, so wide already was her correspondence. As a grown-up
acquaintance, twelve years her senior, Arthur Penn happened to send
her a birthday card, and her response the following day began a close
lifelong friendship. She was allowed to stay up late for birthday parties,
but on other evenings family and guests frequently conspired to mis-
count thirteen at table so that she might remain up to make a
fourteenth.

Much has been heard of a children's party at Montagu House when
Elizabeth, aged five, had prised the cherries off her cake to give to the
thin little boy next to her, her supposed first meeting with her future
husband, King George VI. Neither, in fact, ever remembered the incident. Two or three years later, however, at Lansdowne House, another
small boy found himself urged to 'Come and talk to this little girl – she is
called Elizabeth Lyon'.

'For the next two summers,' Lord David Cecil confessed years later,
'she figured largely in my life. I remember her playing in the Park, racing beside her yellow-haired brother, or sitting demurely at the tea-
table, or best of all at a fancy-dress party . . . When I was ten years old,
too ill to go to school, she came to tea with her governess. I lay upon a
sofa, watching the gale and feeling very small and lonely. She was taller,
paler and darker, but her charm was the same, her soft eyes glowing
with sympathy. I felt it worth being ill a thousand times over . . .'

Not that everyone was enslaved by 'the drowsy caressing voice, the slow sweet smile, the delicious laughter'. When a domestic crisis recalled Madé to France for a time, a temporary governess chanced to set her pupil an essay on an unwelcome subject. Years later, the result came to light in an old exercise book. 'Some governesses are nice,' it began, 'and some are *not*.' And there ended this rare literary fragment.

The chronology of childhood is measured less by time than in the exposition of developing character. The moppet who begged cook, 'Please may I have a cream?' was followed within a year by the more dignified child who enquired, 'May I come in and eat more – *much more* – of that nice chocolate cake than I could eat upstairs?' The two fierce junior Redskins who burst into the dairy at Glamis demanding biscuits and milk were followed in due course by two deft confidence tricksters. David would roll beseeching eyes at susceptible guests and pointedly remark, 'We haven't had no presents lately, Elizabuff!' Whereupon his sister would conjecture 'No, but I expect we shall have soon . . .' and the atmosphere was roseate with hope until the victim obliged. Lord Strathmore's views on pocket-money were stringent; Elizabeth was limited to ninepence a week and Mrs Thompson, the housekeeper, devised small services, such as shelling peas or hulling gooseberries, to help broaden the budget. 'May we perhaps have silver pennies this time?' Elizabeth begged, during a financial difficulty. And ultimately, when nearing her teens, she invested a week's pocket-money in a desperate telegram to her father which read 'SOS LSD RSVP ELIZABETH', and the economic system was amended.

The trivial memories gain emphasis after fifty years of queenhood. When Patrick, Lord Glamis, became engaged to Lady Dorothy Osborne, daughter of the 10th Duke of Leeds, after an energetic courtship, his young sister wrote with excitement, 'Me and Dorothy's little brother are going to be bridesmaids'. Elizabeth in fact made her first appearance in public ceremonial on 21 November 1908, at the Guards Chapel at Wellington Barracks, wearing a frock of white muslin and satin, the youngest of six bridesmaids, and gravely concerned with the good behaviour of David and the bride's own younger brother as fidgety trainbearers in suits of pale blue silk. At the Chapel doors the spectacle was enhanced by the Strathmore pipers in full Highland dress, and later in the glittering swords of a Scots Guards arch of honour.

None could have guessed that a future Queen of England was among the bridesmaids nor that Buckingham Palace and Clarence House just across the park would both be her future homes. Or might the prospect have been discerned even then? When the present Queen Elizabeth II was christened in 1926 as Princess Elizabeth, elder Bowes-Lyon kith and kin noticed the stray coincidence that within the family circle her mother had been fondly dubbed with the nickname 'Princess Elizabeth' and played at being a princess almost from infancy. 'I always addressed her as Princess Elizabeth, kissed her hand and invariably made her a low bow, which she acknowledged haughtily yet courteously,' one amused friend wrote to Lady Cynthia Asquith. And we have the firm documented evidence that in 1908 when Leonora Lang, wife of the historical writer Andrew Lang, published her children's book *Princes and Princesses* it carried into thousands of homes the printed, if slightly inaccurate, homage:

Dedicated To
Elizabeth Angela Margaret
Bowes Lyon

The young dedicatee must have read every one of the 361 gilt-edged pages, which hindsight enriches with curious interest. 'This book about princes and princesses is not one which a child is *obliged* to read,' said the author's preface. 'It cannot be said that the princes and princesses in this book were too happy. . . . They were obliged to marry first and fall in love afterwards if they could, which is quite the wrong arrangement. . . . However, certainly the lives of princes and princesses are rather more interesting to read about than the sons and daughters of the Presidents of Republics.' And the final chapter, entitled 'The Troubles of the Princess Elizabeth', opens boldly with question and answer: 'What reign in English history do you like best to read about?' 'Oh, Queen Elizabeth, of course!'

With such encouragement, the game gathered strength and Lady Strathmore obligingly made her daughter a party frock of rose brocade, high-waisted and full-skirted, trimmed with silver ribbon and satin-buttoned from neck-line to hem in the early seventeenth century mode, satisfyingly based on the Van Dyck portrait of Princess Elizabeth, daughter of James VI and I.

The following summer, the Minister of Glamis, the Rev James Stirton, was invited to attend a tea-party of local ladies at Glamis Castle and, as he noted, was rewarded by a bright and fascinating scene. 'After some conversation the Countess of Strathmore sat down at the piano and suddenly, as if by a magician's touch, two small figures seemed to rise from the floor and dance a quaint old minuet. The mingled fragrance of beeswax and sweet peas never afterwards failed to evoke the scene.' Through Mr Stirton's eyes we are watching Elizabeth in her long rose gown and David in the motley of a jester, with cap and bells and sagging stockings . . . with the finishing touch that when the Minister asked 'the dark-haired graceful girl whom she was supposed to be, she replied with great *empressement*, "I call myself the Princess Elizabeth"'.

Mr Stirton considered it a 'crystal ball experience'. On the other hand, the sustained masquerade may have been set off by the child's question. 'Mother, where was I born?' and the inconsequential reply, 'Next door to Buckingham Palace', playful but possibly truthful. In that pre-war world crowded with royals, more children enjoyed games of royal make-believe than today, and Elizabeth knew more of royalty, especially Scottish royalty, than most. Mr Stirton noticed the keen interest 'she took at a very early age' in his portrait of Bonnie Prince Charlie and the sympathetic and unusual background knowledge she displayed in his own family collection of curios. 'She wanted very much to go down into the burial vault of her ancestors, but I drew the line at that.' No doubt the friendly minister told her that the artist who painted the sixteen Biblical pictures in the Glamis family chapel had also painted the alleged portraits of the Kings of Scotland in the Palace of Holyrood. At all events, the princess's gown remained in use longer than most fancy costumes and was either copied or else inspired the style of a dress Elizabeth wore in her late teens. Indeed the original or its close semblance reappeared first for Lilibet at children's parties, and then Princess Margaret. Besides, it was soon the accession summer of King George V and Queen Mary, when kings and queens were in every mind. There is the story of the garden fête at which the young Lady Elizabeth patronized the amateur lady palmist in her tent, and Madé enquired, 'What did she say?'

'She was silly. She said I'm going to be a Queen when I grow up.'

'That isn't possible unless they change the laws of England for you,' said Madé, incautiously.

'Who wants to be a Queen anyway?' retorted Elizabeth, and danced gaily around the room singing one of her governess's French nursery rhymes, '*S'il fleurisse je serai reine*.' ('If it blossoms, I shall be Queen.') To Elizabeth a more impressive event was the wedding in July of her eldest sister, Mary, to the 16th Baron Elphinstone, a match destined to provide happy enmeshments of cousinhood through three generations. The family of Elphinstone is as old and historic as that of the Lyons, and for the ceremony in St Margaret's, Westminster, David wore ceremonial Highland dress with the Lyon tartan while, with Elizabeth in attendance, the bridesmaids were dressed in blue-sashed white Romney gowns with large picture hats, prettily carrying fans instead of posies, a tribute to the bride's second name, Frances.

Romance was in the air in the new reign and, not long afterwards, to the complete astonishment of her two young pupils, Madé disclosed an entirely unsuspected side of her private life and informed Lady Strathmore that she hoped shortly to be leaving to marry a young man named Edmund Guerin, with whom she would settle in France. After the first dismay, the children went into days of earnest discussion on their choice of a wedding gift. They had hitherto contributed pennies to 'share with Mother' in any family wedding presents but now Elizabeth felt that a more personal keepsake was imperative. David was permitted to join in this offering with a contribution of tenpence and, since Madé had once confessed the difficulty of making good tea in France, a silver spoon for infusing tea was purchased 'because you like tea'. The presentation card, however, carried an anxious postscript, 'We hope Edmund will be kind to you.'

4. *The Widening World*

Between the fleeting high summers at Glamis, the placid weeks and companionable weekends of St Paul's Walden Bury and the tasks and treats of the Strathmore London home, there was no lack of sociable options in the pervading happiness of Elizabeth Lyon's childhood. It may be that Glamis guests have filled the canvas of reminiscence more thoroughly; the hospitality, like the turrets and pinnacles, all more impressive; the ghosts highly-coloured rather than spectral grey. Old Mr Neal, the Scottish dance teacher from Forfar, with his black frock-coat and gleaming shirtcuffs, his white beard almost entangling with his fiddle, was remembered years after the prosaic local dancing classes in Hitchin. Travelling at twenty miles an hour in a motorcar to the Ogilvys at Cortachy Castle was infinitely more exciting than jaunting in the pony-cart to Hatfield. But with all their country occupations neither Glamis nor the Waldens could rival the annual London thrill of being taken to the Drury Lane pantomime where, as David Lyon testified, 'we sat enthralled, usually with violent headaches from the unaccustomed glare'.

Elizabeth, indeed, was nearly ten before she heard very much of the Glamis ghosts, or a mention of the hapless monster concealed in a secret room. The story of Earl Beardie dicing with the Devil in a top-most tower or Michael's horrific yarns of the days when the Lyons maintained a private hangman were not for younger ears. Perhaps the spooks scared only believers: on a moonlit night any scurry of wind in the drive, any whirlwind of leaves, might be the spectral rush of Jock the Runner, though perhaps the local poacher had more solid cause to take to his heels. The unpleasant atmosphere of a haunted bedroom disappeared after the joists were treated for dry-rot; and when Lady Strathmore had a rutted old floor smoothly boarded over it was more to remove a hazard to unwary visitors than to conceal alleged bloodstains. Rose and Michael however could truthfully tell of sleeping guests disturbed when bedclothes were twitched away by unseen hands. The elder brothers had enjoyed many such larks before Elizabeth was born, and at Christmas there occurred a terrifying manifestation of scampering, giggling phantoms looking remarkably like David and Elizabeth draped in sheets and towels.

Yet these pranks had a scaring quality. Lady Rose was fond of recollecting a stormy night when the two children came to bid their mother goodnight and, with a timid look, David asked if he could ring for a footman to fetch a story-book he had left in the crypt. 'Certainly not,' said his mother, 'you must fetch it yourself. There's nothing to be afraid of. A big boy of eight, you don't need anyone to take care of you!' Nervously the boy set out, but Elizabeth skipped after him. 'Mother said you weren't to ring for someone, but she didn't say you couldn't have me.' It was an eerie journey, past the shadowed eyes of the portraits, down the stone staircase to Duncan's Room, where a huge stuffed bear stood sentinel, and on to the silent suits of armour in the crypt. With its endless rooms and passages Glamis was a wonderful place for hide-and-seek, but only in daylight. The incident was remembered as characteristic of Elizabeth's tender protective tact. 'She was an ideal sister,' Rose testified, 'original and amusing – and always full of fun or sympathy whichever you happened to need.'

Later on, nearing his teens, David occasionally claimed to see shadowy 'grey people' at Glamis, although his elders discounted his 'second sight' as juvenile showing-off, much as they did his successful water-divining with a hazel twig. The sudden appearance or disappearance of the grey people never caused him alarm, and Elizabeth readily supported her brother with a chilling account of the strange lady whom she met on the stairs and who smiled and passed without speaking. They were imaginative youngsters and Elizabeth, especially, read everything she could lay hands on. When sociable adults or her brother's willing company failed her, she would be found propped over a book full-length on the floor, a habit which, Alah complained, made her elbows red and raw.

The migration to 20 St James's Square in early summer and autumn was less to follow the fashion of the London season than for family convenience. The junior world in the attics enjoyed no more than the views of treetops and chimneys, but constant forays were made to the park and to friends, to music and dancing lessons. It was from No 20, during Madé's earlier absence in the autumn of 1908, that the two children first went to school. A young Froebel-trained teacher named Constance Goff had opened a kindergarten at 25 Marylebone High Street, a youthful, venture-some educational experiment which appealed to Lady Strathmore, and for two terms little Elizabeth arrived by carriage, electric brougham or limousine with six-year-old David in tow.

Garbed in matching tussore smocks, they read, painted, sketched, and 'took to languages happily', as a fellow-pupil remembered, even to acting playlets in French and German. The boys of Miss Goff's learned boxing and the girls practised fencing. Years later, Elizabeth ruefully remembered being rebuked for showing off when she began an essay on *The Sea* with a Greek quotation, *'Thalassa! Thalassa!'* ('The sea, the sea!'), which seems a feat for a child of eight, but Madé had simply done her work too well.

At Madame d'Egville's dancing classes in Knightsbridge, Elizabeth was already a practised and accustomed dancer, gliding over the polished floor to the one-two-three of an elderly French ballet-master, self-assured in the waltz, the polka and the Highland shottische, 'a graceful and intelligent pupil . . . very pretty and vivacious', according to Madame. These attainments qualified her for the junior dances in the pale-plastered drawing-room of Lansdowne House and, at ten, she began taking piano lessons at the Mathilde Verne school in the Cromwell Road. 'I used to lift her on and off the piano stool oftener than was necessary just because she was so nice to take hold of,' Miss Verne's younger sister remembered. Though Elizabeth's hand was too small to span an octave, the difficulty was outweighed by her talent. Lady Strathmore wrote that she considered her children (David and Elizabeth) had 'made extraordinary progress in two terms. Knowing nothing of music when they started, they can now play quite nicely.' Indeed, at the school's first children's concert, Elizabeth and her brother represented the star turn, a feat not achieved without extra practice. One afternoon Miss Verne felt that a difficult and detested exercise had gone on long enough, and thought it best to enter the torture chamber. 'We have only just begun,' declared the assistant teacher, but her pupil slid from the piano stool. 'Thank you so much,' she said firmly. 'That was wonderful.' The resourceful Vernes subsequently gave her the stool as a wedding gift, but in fact Elizabeth had only 'rather sad recollections' of her concert performance. 'I "got out" in the piece,' she noted, 'and felt terribly ashamed of myself.'

Lady Strathmore considered that her daughter's musical gifts stemmed from her own mother, Mrs Scott. A plump little figure in her seventies, the twice-widowed Mrs Scott now lived near Florence with her unmarried daughter, Anne Violet, and as a sequel to Mary's wedding Aunt Violet escorted Elizabeth and David on the first of several visits to Italy between 1911 and the untroubled spring of 1914. The Queen Mother vividly remembered the magic of night travel, the restaurant-car meals on the Rome Express, and then the enchantment of the Villa Capponi, her grandmother's old Medici villa high up at Arcetri, outside the town. 'Tier upon tier of terraces with walls covered with roses and sweet-scented flowers . . . magnificent cypresses standing against the blue distant mountains . . . the ding-dong clamour as the Angelus floated up every evening,' was how Mrs Scott's niece, Lady Ottoline Morrell, has described her impressions. The house moreover possessed an organ, inset against the dark panelled walls of the living-room, and some years later Mrs Scott's lessons to her grand-daughter led to Elizabeth playing the organ at St Paul's Walden church, with unexpected effects after Sunday service when young fingers strayed into a pianissimo Yip-i-Addy-i-Ay!

As so often, the villa also had its chapel, where small dark icons hung upon red damask walls and Elizabeth accompanied her grandmother to morning prayers. The afternoon saw expeditions in the ramshackle pony carriage into Florence, where Aunt Violet expertly guided the young girl through the marvels of the Pitti and Uffizi palaces and yet was a sympathetic escort also through the narrow, strident and exciting streets.

Lady Ottoline found the devotions of the Villa Capponi 'rather too High Church' but their fervour illustrates the deep inward religious faith with which Lady Strathmore invested her youngest daughter. With the boys away, the custom of early morning prayers at the Bury faltered, yet there was rarely a morning when Elizabeth did not first go to her mother's room to read a chapter of the Bible together.

Regular church attendance was an acknowledging duty to God. Lady Strathmore was fond of recalling an occasion when a heavy cold prevented her from attending morning service at St Paul's Walden, and ten-year-old Elizabeth and young David went to church alone but reached the church door to hear the first hymn being sung. Rather than seem unpunctual, Elizabeth felt that they should stay outside, but the duties of the sabbath were still to be performed and so brother and sister sat down behind a hedge and steadfastly read through the service in their prayer-books, the prayers, the responses, the collect, and psalms, and only then returned home carefree and content.

The new King George V and Queen Mary were crowned on 22 June 1911, and for the first remembered coronation of her life Lady Elizabeth rose in the dawn to see her mother and father in their robes making their early departure from No 20 to gain their places in Westminster Abbey. With David and Rose, and probably Michael and Fergus, Elizabeth watched the spectacle of the carriage processions from the windows of a family friend on the route. The identity of their hostess now eludes memory, but younger friends and acquaintances were to be seen – and cheered – in the procession, among them fourteen-year-old Princess Mary in an open carriage with her brothers. Among these in turn was Prince Albert, Elizabeth's future husband. That make-believe of childhood, the imagined Princess Elizabeth, was not yet banished, but now the princes and princesses of real life rode by, ahead of the ultimate splendour of the crowned King and Queen in the golden Coronation coach drawn by eight cream Hanoverian horses.

Earlier that month, Lady Strathmore's 'Cousin Willy', the 6th Duke of Portland, had sparked a family rumour that his wife might soon be appointed Mistress of the Robes to the dowager Queen Alexandra, and Elizabeth presently gained junior honours of a different calibre. On 2 July a daughter was born to her sister Mary (Lady Elphinstone), a first niece and namesake for Elizabeth, and christened indeed as Elizabeth Mary.

Lady Elizabeth, however, had already been created an aunt in the previous year with the birth on New Year's Day, 1910, of a nephew, her eldest brother's son, John Patrick. Now change was everywhere, and even Alah was transferred to the young Lady Glamis's household, while the youthful aunt was encouraged her into a correspondence reporting Master Patrick's progress. In Alah's place a Scottish nursery-maid, Catherine (Catta) Mclean, remained at St Paul's Walden as children's maid and devoted slave. In that Coronation summer the illness of Alec, the third of the Bowes-Lyon brothers, also caused family anxiety. He was twenty-four – Lady Strathmore often referred to him as 'my middle son' – and on his convalescence, the Glamis Castle season went on as usual.

Elizabeth and David devoted hours to frenzies of tennis. 'You will always find them,' enquirers were told, 'either on the tennis courts or near the stables.' After the big shoots of September, Fergus, Michael and Lord Strathmore went on more casual forays for pheasant, hare and rabbit, while the ladies supervised the picnic baskets. Alec liked to sit about in the garden and on 19 October young Elizabeth heard almost casually that he felt unwell and had gone to bed. And then suddenly Glamis was silent in incredulous grief, for Alec was dead.

The effect of this early childhood bereavement as a factor of the Queen Mother's personality has rarely been discussed, but clearly her brother's tragic death evoked a radical flowering of compassion. She was 'old enough to understand' and her consideration for her mother revealed a sensitive perception beyond her years. Perhaps it was Rose who suggested that it would be better to keep Mother occupied, and Elizabeth beguiled her into Italian practice or suggested that David should not miss his lessons. Slowly such solicitous threads of persuasion drew both Lord and Lady Strathmore from their mourning and, not for the first time, family strength was drawn from the family motto carved in Latin on one of the great Glamis chimney-pieces. Elizabeth had been taught its meaning long before, and was one day to find personal solace within it herself, 'In thou, my God, I place my trust without change to the end'.

David was ten in May, 1912, and his sister faced the irrevocable fact that he would be going away to prep school in Broadstairs in September. The boy and girl were now nearly the same in height, still as near twins as ever, as Rose said, in their 'wonderful and very close relationship'.

Clearly one way of celebrating David's heightened status was to sweep off together on 'a holiday of their own', involving a magnificent train journey to stay with Elizabeth's godmother, their Aunt Maud, in the Cotswolds. Four or five years earlier, Aunt Maud had 'transformed', as she liked to say, an old farmhouse at Broadway, and Elizabeth loved the fairytale lattice windows, the timbered ceilings, while David drank in the architectural changes. The summer house had been a cart-shed until the red stone floor was put in. The sitting-room had unbelievably been a barn until a passage and stairway were built. There was also a schoolroom where Aunt Maud expected *all* her godchildren, nephews and nieces, to busy themselves with books on a wet day, but what other schoolroom could boast of once being part shop and part bake-house? None must interfere, similarly, when Aunt Maud practised her violin and, later on in her teens, Elizabeth accompanied her godmother on the piano, and could picture herself living in a similarly transformed old house and perhaps one day taking her own children or godchildren on excursions to Stratford-on-Avon.

Presently, at home at the Bury, Elizabeth probably supervised Catta Mclean in packing David's school trunk, hiding surprises among his shirts and socks, but little could alleviate the disconsolate courage of parting. 'David went to school for the first time on Friday,' she wrote to a friend. 'I miss him horribly.'

5.   *Girlhood and Peace*

With David's departure to prep school, Lady Strathmore felt sympathetically that Elizabeth would benefit from a wider company of girls of her own age. Elizabeth had grown 'taller and paler and darker', a friend noted, no longer the rosy, plump little pippin who had enthralled Gorell Barnes, although 'her charm was the same . . . the delicious gurgle of laughter'. Once again Lady Strathmore enquired among her acquaintances about the private schools in central London, and an irreproachable recommendation emerged for the 'select classes for girls' held by the sisters Dorothy and Irene Birtwhistle at 30 Sloane Street, near Knightsbridge.

Daughters of a Somerset parson, sometime Rector of Withycombe, who had died in their childhood, the Misses Birtwhistle were in the van of that timely spur of feminist education which took root in the receptive soil of the early twentieth century. Miss Dorothy had studied at the Bedford Training College for teachers, while her younger sister had taken an arts degree at St Andrews. As with Constance Goff, the Froebel influence persisted, and the sisters applied the credo of self-activity with such success that they soon surrendered their first small classes at Clifton and moved to London. A former pupil recollects that Miss Dorothy was 'so straight and honest that she never over-praised work. *Good* was indeed her highest and well-earned word of commendation.' Young Elizabeth, however, readily distinguished herself, and within eight months had the considerable satisfaction of winning a literature prize for an essay. It has been argued that her schoolgirl career may have had a traumatic side, the distress familiar to teachers of the lonely child, accustomed to the company of adults, when suddenly flung into a mêlée of contemporaries. But the Birtwhistle classes of those days numbered only thirty pupils, and within this number Elizabeth formed a lifelong friendship with a near namesake, Elizabeth Margaret Cator, daughter of a Unionist parliamentarian. Betty Cator's

41

parents indeed lived just around the corner in Pont Street, an enticing sanctuary for tea and cakes after school, and the friendship became so close and enduring that, some ten years later, Betty became Elizabeth's bridesmaid and, within fifteen years, her sister-in-law by her marriage to Elizabeth's elder brother, Michael – and presently 'Aunt Betty' to Queen Elizabeth II and Princess Margaret.

A release from school nevertheless came in April 1913, with the arrival of Kathie Kuebler as a temporary German governess at St Paul's Walden Bury during the Easter holiday. The daughter of a Nuremburg civil official, blonde, tall and buxom, Kathie found her new pupil 'charming to look at, a small delicate figure with a sensitive, somewhat pale little face, dark hair and very beautiful violet-blue eyes . . . a child far more mature and understanding than her age warranted'. Years later David Bowes Lyon wrote playfully of Kathie 'shaking the foundations of Glamis Castle with her Teutonic tread' and pretended to have rueful memories of the first time he went out with a gun, triumphantly returning with a hare for the schoolroom lunch only to find that Elizabeth and the governess had practically emptied the stewpot, leaving the hunter only the head. The Fräulein was, however, a welcome figure and Elizabeth stage-managed everything so admirably that Kathie – then scarcely twenty herself – agreed to stay as her permanent governess, taking over her entire teaching from piano lessons to modern science.

'The systematic German time-table was quite strange to her,' Kathie Kuebler acknowledged. But with relief at being 'always near Mother', her pupil swung happily into a routine of piano lessons before breakfast and a clocked curriculum of French and German, history, geography, mathematics, nature study, needlework and gymnastics. 'We were both ambitious,' wrote the governess, and Elizabeth's adolescent enthusiasm and application delighted her, 'in teaching such a gifted and willing pupil.' Nature study and drawing lessons were shifted to the garden and Elizabeth soon had a string of ready excuses to transfer less amenable studies out of doors. A photograph shows the two trudging the lanes with their walking sticks, the Fräulein in shapeless grey serge and her young pupil with a modish, flower-trimmed and beribboned sun-hat. This walk in itself was a language lesson, for the governess insisted upon her native tongue for ordinary conversation until Elizabeth soon spoke fluent German.

They must have looked an odd couple. On summer afternoons, a pony was harnessed to the wagonette, the butler handed up a basket with sandwiches and cakes and they drove off together into the woods, seeking out a spot for a picnic tea and botany precepts. Kathie Kuebler had never before been in an alien land, nor so far from her own home, and Elizabeth was quick to notice and alleviate the symptoms of homesickness. 'Tell me about Germany, and your own home,' she would say, and one recognizes the comforting technique of the Queen Mother.

The family group at the Bury was closer knit than of old, with Lord and Lady Strathmore, Rose and Elizabeth, and at weekends nineteen-year-old Michael occasionally appeared from Oxford or fair-haired Jock made jokes of breathing great draughts of fresh air after the city, and a jubilant reunion occurred when Fergus came home on leave dark and bronzed from India. Tennis tournaments, eccentric family golf and – inevitably – household cricket maintained their everchanging pageant on the lawns. But it was the walks and rides in mid-week serenity, the blue lakes in the woods that were swards of bluebells, the kettle boiling on the brushwood fire, that Kathie Kuebler cherished in her reminiscences years later, and not least the coming home and Elizabeth's instant search for her mother. . . . 'How often I heard her clear voice calling, "Mother darling, where are you?" in tones that rang through the house. . . .'

David came home for the holidays to demonstrate that he was now a full inch taller than Elizabeth, and an amusing snapshot supported his claim, 'I am catching up'. Elizabeth evinced a liability to snuffle and catch cold, so that the grown-ups flustered about her with coats and scarves, yet the two remained children at heart. Eluding the vigilance of Mr Keeling, the gardener, they crawled under the strawberry nets one afternoon and sampled the illicit early fruits so unwisely that David was sent to bed with the inevitable penalty of stomach-ache, as it seemed. Next morning the local physician diagnosed appendicitis, necessitating an urgent operation, but the sufferer was too ill to be moved and surgeons and nurses were summoned from London.

Suddenly the memories of Alec's death eighteen months before were revived with terrible apprehension. The operation on King Edward VII in 1902 had made the removal of the appendix a familiar and even fashionable procedure, but the doctors could not discount the natural hazard to a child of eleven, and in the privacy of her room Elizabeth desperately prayed that David would not die.

Kathie was able to offer very practical comfort. By coincidence she also had a brother of nearly the same age and he, too, had fallen ill with appendicitis only four weeks earlier; the surgeons had operated, and only that morning a letter from Germany announced that he was fully recovered. Not that this lessened the fervour of Elizabeth's supplications. At root, her youthful faith was simple and personal: to seek to do one's best, and to love one another, in the life that God had given; and with this her mother had taught an unwavering belief in the direct link of prayer, or petitions that might be answered if such was His will.

The operation was performed and, as Kathie Kuebler wrote, 'We lived through anxious hours before we knew that the outcome would be a happy one. How happy we all were then!' Prayer had been answered, and Elizabeth's happiness was complete when, a day or two later, she was allowed to see David and sit beside him.

With her brother's recovery, the delights of the summer were all the more exhilarating. Brother and sister revisited the White City at Earl's Court where, beyond the pleasure domes of the exhibition palaces, the cafés and orchestras, they persuaded Kathie to join them on the giddy ascents and headlong swoops of the scenic railway, which Elizabeth 'enjoyed greatly, screaming loudly'. At a magical show the conjuror produced roses out of the air to present to the two ladies – 'a man who knew how to behave', Lord Strathmore said, on hearing the story when they got home.

It was customary for governesses to chaperone their charges to the junior dances given by friends of the family, where one day Miss Kuebler noted pleasurably that Elizabeth 'met the children of the King' and indeed noticed the enjoyment which her pupil – just turning thirteen – and Prince Albert shared in dancing together. One cannot afford to disregard this romantic trimming, an overlooked link of continuity between the possible first acquaintance at the children's party at Montagu House in 1905 and their meeting at a dance given by Lord Farquhar in 1920.

The facts for once fit the evidence. In July, 1913, the future George VI was a naval cadet of seventeen, just back from his first transatlantic cruise aboard the *Cumberland* and spending a week's leave in London. Among the Canadian girls in Quebec none would tempt him onto the dance floor and 'conversation soon flagged', yet within four months he had lost his shyness and danced every dance at a naval ball in Alexandria. Among his interim partners, pretty Elizabeth Lyon may have contributed her own share of confidence.

Punctually every morning the house in St James's Square resounded to Elizabeth's piano practice, with an interlude when Kathie studied a

Wagnerian piano score, perhaps that of *Parsifal* which Rose Lyon had seen that year during the great German season at Covent Garden. In the fresh beauty of her early twenties, Lady Rose enjoyed the whirling excitements of the 1913 season to the full: it was nothing, she reassured Kathie, to attend three or four balls in a night and still be fresh to practise Schumann next morning. Thanks to Rose's entreaties, Lady Strathmore assumed responsibility for sponsoring the coming-out of the widowed Lord Curzon's daughter, Cimmie, though if she chanced to see the bills she may have been shaken at the £2,000 cost of decorating the Curzon House ballroom with orchids.

Elizabeth was introduced to the pleasures of London more gradually, chiefly in companionable explorations when David was home for the holidays. 'We used to go to theatres as often as we were allowed – usually in the cheaper seats. Our purses never bulged,' he recollected. 'I think Barrie's plays were Elizabeth's favourites.' Perhaps for convention's sake he added cautiously that 'Shakespeare was by no means slighted', but it was Cyril Maude in *The Headmaster* and *Grumpty, The Lights of London* at Drury Lane, *Eliza Comes To Stay* and the like that usually sent the two hurrying expectantly into the pit or the back of the circle to bask in the world of illusion. The opening by Sir George Alexander of the New Gallery Cinema on the site of a former art gallery was among the landmarks that made the moving picture industry socially acceptable, and Elizabeth would hardly have failed to persuade some friendly adult to take her to see Sarah Bernhardt in the title-role of the film, *Queen Elizabeth*, which had created a sensation. At Christmas Herbert Ponting's great travel documentary *With Captain Scott in the Antarctic* undoubtedly drew brother and sister to the Philharmonic Hall, while the mammoth production of *Quo Vadis?* offered the excuse of historical entertainment to which any governess could conscientiously conduct her pupil.

On entering her teens, Elizabeth was promoted from the comparative purdah of childhood to join her parents' luncheon-table at 20 St James's Square; and in the greater formality of the white-and-green Adam dining-room, still curiously called the Eating Room, this exacted a grown-up social responsibility more circumspect than her earlier début at Glamis or the Bury. Obviously Lord Strathmore realized the asset of her unselfconscious and peculiarly sympathetic charm in conversation, and his wife and younger daughter, usually with Miss Kuebler, balanced the affable pleasure he took in such occasions. He specialized in hospitably collecting elderly widowers and other lonely statesmen of the House of Lords; and No 20 made a change from the Carlton Club. When Elizabeth was very young, it was noted that his table once seated four ex-Viceroys of India: the Marquess of Lansdowne, Lord Elgin, Lord Curzon and Lord Minto. Now in addition Elizabeth turned her serene smile upon Viscount Goschen, a Viceroy of the future, and in her early teens met at her father's table senior statesmen who now seem the full-dress personalities of another age, peopling a vanished Imperial past.

Thus it is strange to discover that Queen Elizabeth the Queen Mother, so essentially a central figure of the twentieth century, should have met Lord George Hamilton, who had served under Disraeli, and Lord Rosebery, who had accepted the British premiership in succession to Gladstone; and that she knew them when both were still in the vigour of their power. Lord Rosebery and Lord Lansdowne, for example, were guests at luncheon at No 20 at the time when they were summoned as elder statesmen to advise King George V on the thorny Irish problem of Home Rule. The King's dilemma had subjected the Royal Prerogative to controversy at the table of every great house in the land; the more's the pity that sound tapes had not been invented.

Lord Rosebery was apt to observe that it was a symptom of the modern British monarchy that every word of the King's was as treasured in England 'as if it were God's . . . he cannot speak without the chance of his words being noted, and carried', and the Queen Mother always conducted herself as if his precept had been deeply impressed on her mind. In his own handwriting, in fact, Rosebery had submitted to the King a list of desirable royal qualities which is still preserved in the Royal Archives at Windsor. 'The King,' he urged, 'should show that he is willing to deny himself any pleasure to do his duty. Besides devotion to duty and reticence, there is something else . . . and that is the instinct of striking the imagination.' Nor is it improbable that he repeated the tenor of this to Lady Elizabeth when he sensed her interest in royalty, and that she vividly remembered his words years later.

There were times, too, when Lord Strathmore's guests drew Elizabeth's German governess into the conversation by talking pleasantly of their own studies and friendships in her native land. 'When I beamed at such revelations,' Miss Kuebler wrote, 'Lady Elizabeth was glad for my sake and secretly pressed my hand under the table.' It is a characteristic sidelight.

By the chance skeins of family acquaintance, Elizabeth had also struck up a youthful friendship with Diamond Hardinge, whose father was then Viceroy in Delhi. One might extend these varied interlocking spheres of her budding social ambiance almost indefinitely: through Hardinges and Cecils, Hamiltons and Ogilvys, Egertons and Leveson-Gowers. If it became a secret vexation to be considered too young to attend the reception at No 20 with which the Strathmores embellished the 1913 season, the strains of the hired orchestra drifted enjoyably up the staircase, and from a vantage point on the third floor Elizabeth leaned over the banisters to admire the scene, precisely as her two young daughters were to do twenty-five years later at Buckingham Palace.

It was a byword that everything she undertook was followed through with great thoroughness. 'If you give of your maximum, you then do it as well as possible,' Lady Strathmore used to say. 'Give your maximum and you receive more in return,' precepts that Elizabeth applied to her sociabilities and studies alike. The topics of conversation at a reception reached her so swiftly that she mystified the family by recounting amusing titbits at breakfast. Probably she discovered from Cimmie that Lord Curzon was an inveterate ghost-hunter who slept in every well-attested haunted room his friends could provide, and so Elizabeth ensured that when he visited Glamis that September he spent each night for eight nights in a different haunted room. The fruitless investigation would surely have tried any but Strathmore patience. This was the last great pre-war season at the Castle and each of the twenty-eight guest-rooms were occupied, with lady's maids besides in a service wing, and innumerable valets who were lodged elsewhere.

Kathie Kuebler recounts with astonishment that six women coped with the baskets of linen which a platoon of domestics carried down the service stairs every morning. In the kitchen a French chef presided over a staff prepared to provide family luncheon for fifty, while never omitting the personal plum pudding served to Lord Strathmore, so his sons alleged, every day of his life. The unexpected arrival of ten officers of the Black Watch to lunch caused no disarray. With a rent-roll of around £20,000 a year from sixty tenanted farmsteads, the entertaining at Glamis was not an undue extravagance.

Early in her teens Lady Elizabeth was increasingly initiated by her mother into the hostess's responsibilities for such a household, from the morning orders for the chef to an occasional inspection of the snowy table-cloths and napkins stacked in the linen-room. With Lady Rose to counteract any vagueness, Lady Strathmore shared in the conferences in the greenhouses on the promise of the melons, figs and grapes expected to be in perfection by the time of stipulated crosses on the calendar.

In that last pre-war Scottish summer, the new formal gardens which Celia had been developing for five or six years were in their first full maturing flower: the sunken Dutch garden, the Italian garden, with its memories of the Villa Capponi, and a rose garden, each within its beech or yew hedges. Gesturing towards the trimmed yews, she loved to explain that one day they would each house a statue of one of her children, one for Pat and one for Jock, one for May, one for Rose and so on, perhaps 'one for you, too, Elizabeth'. Fortunately, the plan was never carried out, and the fond mother contented herself with the names of the garden craftsmen carved on the seats of a summer-house.

As a token of growing up, Elizabeth now occasionally 'followed the guns', her sociability outweighing distaste of the slaughter. David, in any case, was improving his marksmanship, and sisterhood demanded that she should share his target practice. All the same, it was more to her taste to watch the expertise of fly-fishing for trout in the Glamis burn or to take part in a tennis tournament. One day it was suggested that the best player should be partnered by the worst, which led to certain asperities until Miss Kuebler, blandly innocent, was chosen to partner the family champion.

The separate life of the schoolroom continued meanwhile, though often out of doors, and when the moors fell silent the Glamis stay was prolonged, as if ebbing time were suddenly precious, until at last only Rose and Elizabeth and her parents, with the governess, sat at table in the panelled dining-room. There was talk of war, but the opening of the Palace of Peace at The Hague had seemed auspicious; there was talk of friendship, too, and a few language students in Forfar, having formed a German conversational club, enquired whether Fräulein Kuebler and Lady Elizabeth would care to join. Elizabeth was enthusiastic. Practice in speaking German was the principal object: 'I was very proud of my pupil, who chatted so uninhibitedly in German,' Miss Kuebler recalled – an odd glimpse of the future Queen conversing in German with her loyal Scottish subjects.

Although Elizabeth and the family returned to St Paul's Walden Bury for Christmas, they immediately hurried to Glamis for the New Year of 1914. The hills were covered with snow and tobogganing was the order of the day, Scottish ski-ing then being unknown. A New Year resolution was obviously directed to passing the 'Oxford Local' examination, a project in which Elizabeth drove herself so assiduously that Lady Strathmore grew alarmed at her thinness and pallor. 'Good health is more important than exams,' she reminded Miss Kuebler. The exam was nevertheless attempted in April and her daughter 'passed with distinction'. Delighted with this success, Lady Strathmore drew up elaborate further plans, and the German governess was invited to remain another four years, during which Elizabeth's gifts for languages, music and art could be cultivated. The vista embraced an annual visit abroad, to Germany for the Bayreuth Festival, to Vienna and Rome. But this was never to be.

One morning at the end of June, the Fräulein came down to breakfast to find stricken faces, and Lord Strathmore thrust a copy of the *Morning Post* towards her. 'Here, read it,' he said. 'This means war!' and she saw the news of the assassinations at Sarajevo. For all that, the prospect of war seemed so incredible that when the governess went on holiday two weeks later to visit Germany for her parents' silver wedding, Lady Strathmore embraced her fervently, begging her to promise to return. Strolling in Hyde Park, glancing critically at the riders in the Row, Rose and Elizabeth discussed their summer plans for Glamis, heedless of the wild rumours.

On 4 August 1914, Lady Elizabeth awoke to the greetings and gifts of her fourteenth birthday and the newspaper headlines of Army mobilization. As a birthday treat that evening, her mother had booked a box at the Coliseum, and the car had to crawl to the theatre through London crowds gone mad with excitement, 'feckless masses waving Union Jacks,' so one witness described them. In the theatre Elizabeth and her brothers looked down on a packed and excited audience. The vaudeville programme featured sketches with Charles Hawtrey and G P Huntley, and an alto tenor of curious ability, 'The Man with the Tetrazzini Voice'. Every chance topical allusion was cheered, and the ballerina Fedorovna received the ovation of her life . . . for were not the Russians potential allies? When the British ultimatum to Germany expired at midnight, Elizabeth Lyon was already at home in bed at No 20, and the distant cheering of the crowds outside Buckingham Palace sounded like the soft wash of surf on a distant shore.

6. *Girlhood and War*

'It will all be over by Christmas. . . .' Widely shared as it was, the fourteen-year-old Lady Elizabeth's first view of the war was naturally a romantic optimism. Her two eldest bachelor brothers, Jock and Fergus, lost no time in proposing to the ladies of their choice and the family was flung into a ferment of mobilization and marriage. At the gate of his thirtieth birthday, Pat was called up with the officers reserve of the Black Watch, and Jock and Fergus were soon serving in the same regiment, though in different battalions. Rose instantly entered herself for nursing training, and young Michael enlisted in the Royal Scots.

Elizabeth found herself caught up in running errands for them all and vividly remembered, as she put it, 'the bustle of hurried visits to chemists for outfits of every sort of medicine, and to gunsmiths to buy all the things that people thought they wanted for a war, and found they didn't'. Fergus, who was twenty-five, was married on 17 September to Lady Christian Dawson-Damer, a daughter of the Earl of Portarlington. In the 13th-century parish church at Buxted, Sussex, the bride, to Elizabeth's admiration, compromised with wartime exigency by wearing just 'a white travelling dress'. Michael was best man, and the Bury was lent for the brief honeymoon, while the rest of the family rushed to Scotland for Jock's marriage to Fenella Hepburn-Stuart-Forbes-Trefusis, whose mystifying chain of hyphens requires the explanation that, as a daughter of Baron Clinton, her family stemmed from the year 1299 and the marital links of twenty generations. There had been preparations for Michael to celebrate his coming-of-age at Glamis in October. Instead, he dispatched a telegram that his leave had been cancelled, the beacon fires were never lit and the Forfar locals felt that events in Flanders must be catastrophic.

Then, suddenly, bentwood chairs and iron bedsteads were unloaded at the Castle door. Red Cross helpers prepared the huge dining-room, the crypt and other rooms for hospital use, and abruptly Glamis seemed empty of family and full of village folk sorting out a muddle of voluntary duties. Lady Strathmore wished to move as little family furniture as possible rather than spoil the homely welcoming aspect for the expected wounded soldiers, and young Elizabeth supervized the responsibility of stacking household treasures in the upper rooms out of harm's way.

In the dining-room family portraits soon looked down at rows of white hospital beds. As if resuming its old guise as a banqueting hall, the crypt was arranged as a mess-hall full of trestle tables grouped beneath the hunting trophies and medieval shields. In the billiards-room Nebuchadnezzar gazed from his tapestries at tables piled with 'comforts' and bookshelves stored with thick shirts and socks, mufflers and vests, while mounds of sheepskin coats awaited waterproofing with varnish. 'Lessons were quite neglected,' Lady Elizabeth told her early biographer, Cynthia Asquith. 'During these first few months we were so busy knitting, knitting, knitting and making shirts for the local battalion, the 5th Black Watch. My chief occupation was crumpling up tissue paper until it was so soft that it no longer crackled, to put into the linings of sleeping bags.'

When no more tissue remained to be tenderized, endless knitting awaited the volunteer, varied with the task of sewing khaki shirts. Lessons were neglected through the early autumn months, and only two letters got through from Kathie Kuebler, reporting that she was serving as a nurse in a reserve hospital in Erlangen, near her parents' home. In December the first 'boys in blue' – as the wounded became known from their blue flannel hospital suits – arrived at Glamis Castle Hospital from Dundee Royal Infirmary. They were, in fact, convalescents, doomed to be returned to the trenches. But Elizabeth made herself useful in popping down to the village, to buy unfamiliar brands of cigarettes and tobacco, Gold Flake and Navy Cut, as she recalled. Wartime Christmas at Glamis saw a glistening tree brushing its topmost spurs against the vaulted ceiling of the crypt. The 'comforts' were disguised as Christmas parcels, and the boys in blue, some in slippers, some in heavy black boots, made the best of opening the 'gifts'.

Noticing how few parcels arrived for the men, Elizabeth indeed decided that each should have a personal gift package from herself, a last-minute gesture that emptied the village shop of fountain-pens, pencils, books and playing-cards. David, on holiday from school, joined in the lark of being dressed up as a lady visitor, complete with skirt, cloak, buttoned boots, furs, veil and feather hat, whom Elizabeth escorted around the ward and introduced as her cousin. Through his veil David softly asked the questions ladies were supposed to put to wounded soldiers and, whether deceived or not, the men played up nobly, feigning utter astonishment next day when twelve-year-old David was produced and the joke made known.

Ignoring the gaps at her family table, Lady Strathmore was determined that the first – and surely the last? – wartime Christmas should be as happy for her two Benjamins as possible, and so the two went to the pantomime in Dundee and rode into Forfar to giggle at Charlie Chaplin. The men themselves gave a concert and blacked their faces with burned cork for a minstrel show. Whist-drives were arranged, with nurses, family and domestics as extra players. Though 'only just learning to play whist' and 'often in need of advice', Lady Elizabeth was a popular partner – even a cause of occasional jealousy and complaints against Tommies who seemed 'unfairly too pushing to get to her table'.

Illusions comforted these men so far from home. A corporal in his late twenties constantly assured her that she was just like his fiancée, and she made friends so readily, with such genuine warmth, that it seemed a continual sadness for her to hear of 'discharges' leaving to make way for fresh 'admissions'. It became a custom of the house to give each departing group a farewell supper, with Christmas-style crackers, caps and mottoes, speeches and photographs and little packages of 'gifts from Glamis Castle', which invariably meant presents from Elizabeth, purchased with her own money.

Early in 1915, however, the arrival of the badly maimed and disfigured men who had been exchanged as prisoners of war, deeply affected her. To echo Dorothy Laird: 'She teased and charmed them into good spirits, played and sang for them, wrote letters for those unfit to write and helped to restore them to normality. . . . Some of the men were shattered in body and spirit. It was then that she had her early lessons in complete, selfless control, in the iron discipline and sense of duty that lay beneath the smile.'

Rose returned newly-qualified from her London training to assume a strange authority as the Glamis hospital sister, and Elizabeth was immediately eager to train as a nurse and emulate her, but had to agree with good grace that she was obviously too young. Lessons were resumed under an English governess, Miss Boynard, who admirably combined athletic tennis with her teaching, but there remained the never-neglected duty of sorting the hospital mail. Many Glamis patients were to remember 'little Lady Elizabeth' waiting for the postman or hurrying down the drive to meet him with her black cocker spaniel, then rushing up the staircase, calling her mother whenever 'British Expeditionary' envelopes arrived from her brothers.

Whenever the ambulances or buses brought new arrivals, Lady Strathmore would visit the ward with her young daughter to be introduced but, quick to greet every shy stranger with a smile, Elizabeth had usually already met the newcomers. She had her stock of questions in readiness to break the ice. 'Where do you come from? Does your wound – your shoulder – your leg – hurt you? I do hope you like Glamis. . . .'

'I can see her now,' one of the Glamis patients, Corporal Ernest Pearn, has written of those days. 'She was very fond of cycling about the grounds, often with both her eyes tight shut. I've seen her roll off, spring up, grab her sun-bonnet and jump on again laughing and enjoying my fright immensely. . . . She was quick to see a joke, and didn't she laugh when I and another lad, who had one arm in a sling, tried to carry a large tray of dishes, and the whole lot of crockery got smashed to pieces.' With the Spring, it was thought that she would be confirmed by the Bishop of Brechin in the Castle chapel, but she elected instead to take her place with the village lasses in St John's Church, Forfar, a quest for anonymity not altogether successful. Word got around and the church was well-filled with Sister Rose's 'walking cases'.

Striving to look older, Elizabeth 'put her hair up' early, with a 'bun' and a fringe on her forehead in the style that became her hallmark for years. A minor anxiety was to be a better cyclist than David, lest he assume a status appropriate to commencing his first term at Eton. In September her brother Fergus also came home on leave to spend his first wedding anniversary with his wife at Glamis and to see his two-month-old baby daughter, for what was so soon to be mourned as the first and only time. He left as darkness fell on the Monday and on the Friday a telegram arrived that sent Rose hurrying to her mother's side. Captain Fergus Bowes Lyon had been killed the day after returning to France.

All the hospital patients signed a letter of sympathy to Lady Strathmore. It was not until a day or two later that, emerging from their first terrible shock, Elizabeth and her mother noticed the curious silence. None of the men were to be seen in the grounds. As a mark of respect, they had agreed among themselves not to play the gramophone or the piano, not to use the billiards-room – which was nearer the family quarters – nor the lawns for games, and to use only a side door of the Castle to avoid intrusion. Touched by the gesture, the Strathmores sent a message bidding them to continue recreations in the usual way 'for you are our guests'. But for many weeks it was Elizabeth alone who punctiliously said goodbye to each departing soldier.

Old wartime photographs show a little figure in black, skirts flapping near her ankles, though still with that open smile which made every man regard her as a special friend. And indeed she knew them all by Christian names, knew about their parents and civilian lives . . . and remembered them years later on seeing them again, among those who survived. It was one of the elements of friendship that she took a snapshot photograph of each man to send to his family. Posing one youngster to avoid showing his arm in a sling, this produced an unfortunate illusion that the arm was missing. Learning of this, she at once wrote to his parents to reassure them, enclosing a second picture clearly showing both arms.

'We needed no photographs to help remember her,' one patient gallantly acknowledged years later. 'She had the loveliest eyes, expressive and eloquent eyes, and a very taking way of knitting her forehead when speaking . . . that sweet, quiet voice, that hesitating yet open way of talking. For all her fifteen years she was very womanly, kind-hearted and sympathetic.'

Elizabeth was a wartime bridesmaid at St James's, Piccadilly, when her sister Rose was married to Commander William Spencer Leveson-Gower on 24 May 1916. A lull had occurred in the London air-raids and no warning police-whistles or wailing maroons disturbed the congregation. It was a wedding flecked with naval pageantry. The three bridesmaids wore frocks of white chiffon with little Dutch bonnets, a bridal picture much to the taste of the wedding guests, so predominantly feminine in that second year of the war. At the wedding reception at No 20 people no doubt gaily reminded the bride's young unmarried sister that she would be next. Auspicious naval emblems decorated the wedding-cake. If some nautical fragment of icing were in Elizabeth's slice, it would have been apt, for her future husband had just rejoined his ship *Collingwood* as a young lieutenant and within the week would face his baptism of fire in the Battle of Jutland, that 'battle of the mists and rout of the German fleet'.

In the complex embroidery of events, Elizabeth passed through Windsor only the following week on her way to enjoy the Fourth of June celebrations with David at Eton. Prince Henry (later Duke of Gloucester and father of the present Duke) had also attended Wellesley House school at Broadstairs and was now David's Eton contemporary in Mr Lubbock's house. Though he was by no means an intimate, other links imperceptibly furthered Elizabeth's path to the altar, including her friendship with Diamond Hardinge, with Lady Mary Thynne (youngest daughter of the then Marquess of Bath), and Lady Mary Cambridge (a niece of Queen Mary), all of whom were to be bridesmaids with her at Princess Mary's wedding not six years later.

At Glamis Castle, in her sister's absence, the responsibility of the enormous place now rested more heavily on Elizabeth's slim shoulders. Her mother had far from overcome the shock of Fergus's death and was often unwell and listless, depressed by the fear of another tragic telegram. Mary Elphinstone came to stay, bringing her own two-year-old toddler 'to help cheer up Mama'; and Dorothy Glamis, Elizabeth's eldest sister-in-law, brought her own son, the five-year-old Master of Glamis, who was forever commanding his 'Aunt Elizabuff' to be 'funny'. Thus something of the old family life was revived in the upper rooms of the Castle, while from the hospital quarters the gramophone strains of *If You Were the Only Girl in the World* or the mouth-organ plaint of *There's a Long Long Trail* came drifting as usual up the stairwell.

Fortunately, Lady Strathmore found solace in resuming a domestic pattern, which Elizabeth was quick to encourage. Every morning, their heads mantled with little crochet lace caps, the two went to the Castle chapel for private prayers. On discovering this custom, some of the soldiers expressed a wish to attend, and so a bell was briefly rung. Afterwards, Elizabeth and her governess, Miss Boynard, shut themselves away for lessons in a room high above the courtyard or else in a summer eyrie on the highest roof-leads where stout old railings formed a balcony among the turrets. The flap of the Union Jack on its flagstaff provided cheerful punctuation; one could not miss seeing an aeroplane if one of these still novel machines should come buzzing over the Grampians, and sometimes governess and pupil were disturbed when a chimney-stack caught fire and the more mobile soldiers came hurrying up with plates of salt to pour down the chimney and help quench the flames.

In September 1916, a more serious blaze occurred. One Saturday evening, Elizabeth noticed unaccustomed smoke from high in the central keep, and had the presence of mind to telephone the local fire brigade while two soldiers raised the alarm. Most of the patients had been taken to a cinema and there were no bed cases in the ward; David appeared with his mother, and Elizabeth telephoned for the extra help from the Forfar and Dundee brigades before organizing a panicky squad of domestics into a chain with buckets and dressing-room jugs of water. Over ninety feet high, the keep was now emitting smoke and sparks like a factory chimney. The Glamis firemen had no sufficient length of hose to pump water from the river Dean and the Forfar brigade were little better equipped. Before long a lead water tank in the roof burst under the pressure of the heat, its precious water cascading down the stone stairway where Elizabeth and David redeployed their force with brooms and mops to sweep the deluge away from the doors of the drawing-room. By now the whole village had been attracted by the sound of the fire-engines and the glow of the flames, and again it was the young châtelaine who sufficiently organized some thirty people in line to pass pictures and furniture hand to hand to safety. 'It was her little Ladyship told us how, and kept us at it.'

Unaccustomed to Glamis faces, a young Dundee reporter plied Elizabeth with questions. How had the fire started? What damage had been done? 'I've no time to make conversation,' she cut short his flow.

'Who's yon prood lassie?' the discomfited youth enquired. The next issue of the local paper however devoted a page to the fire, and sister and brother read with roars of laughter of the 'defiance of discomfort' and 'indefatigable energy' with which they had fought the flames, their first accolade in print.

In the fertile soil of Glamis folklore, a belief persisted that the Lyons had the gift of second sight. Under the dire food shortages in the third year of the war, Lord Strathmore sought to improve his young daughter's proficiency with rod and line, and some old people attributed her angling success in the Dean Water to the 'giftie'. Even Mr Fairweather, the gamekeeper, was certain that the little Lady's early summoning of the Dundee firemen owed more to intuition than the seriousness of the blaze at the time, akin to Mr Michael so often knowing 'where the birds were'. And hardly had the plaster ceilings dried out than a more impressive instance of 'the family gift' was to occur, though involving David rather than Elizabeth. As her parents' amanuensis, she wrote constantly to all three of her fighting brothers, Patrick, Jock and Michael – 'Elizabeth will always know what they want from her'. That autumn her letter to Captain Michael Bowes-Lyon was one of the last before he was reported killed and Lady Strathmore's own dreadful foreboding seemed to be fulfilled.

The official notification from the War Office was a further terrible blow to the Strathmores, not two years after the loss of Fergus. In the hope that David's company would help their parents, the sisters arranged for him to come home from Eton, but his boyish consolation took an unexpected line. Michael was not dead, he urged, with a conviction so positive that he refused to wear either a black tie or black armband. On his return to school, an elderly friend chided him for not wearing even a dark suit. 'But Michael is not dead,' David persisted. 'I have seen him twice. He is in a big house surrounded by fir trees. I think he's very ill, his head is tied up in a cloth. I don't care what the War Office says. I *know* he's alive.' A sceptic may claim that his circumstantial picture was coincidental, yet within three months Elizabeth's last letter was acknowledged with the news that Michael was a prisoner in Germany and too ill to communicate. He had been shot through the head and the family learned later that when he could have been repatriated in an exchange through Holland he had yielded his place to another severely wounded officer.

In 1917, Lord Strathmore began to entertain groups of Australian and New Zealand officers during their spells of leave, and matchmakers were not slow to suppose that Elizabeth might ultimately find a husband among them. If she had been an only child, unaccustomed to older brothers, she might indeed have lost her heart to any one of the good-looking lively young men and the course of history would have been different. Not only was this forecast unfulfilled: Lord Strathmore is said to have given an irrefutable demonstration of his own inability to foretell the future. A young New Zealander on the General Staff, Delhi, a boy from Tamaki named Robert Sencourt, asked him one night about the opportunities and careers that his sons – and the topic included Lady Elizabeth – might follow when the war ended. 'Well,' Lord Strathmore replied, with great emphasis, 'if there is one thing I have determined for my children, it is that they shall never have any sort of post about the Court.'*

Between 1914 and 1919 some 1500 men passed through the Glamis Castle Hospital, and Elizabeth gave each guest an individual tonic of companionship while still maintaining an extraordinarily wide and skilful correspondence. Each group, in invalid blue or regulation issue dressing-gowns, must have looked very like another, yet she seldom faltered in memorizing the wounded men as individuals. With youthful hilarity she was quite capable of imitating herself on a tour of the ward. 'Are you sleeping well? Have you really plenty of tobacco?'

* Background circumstances unknown to Sencourt make this story highly suspect.

Behind the mimicry of bedside visits lay her girlish satisfaction in a worthwhile job. Former patients talked of 'dear old Glamis' and 'little Lady Elizabeth', unaware how steadily, unknown even to herself, she had gained working practice in the techniques of royal memory. At St Paul's Walden Bury the coming and going of overseas house guests created a running correspondence with comparative strangers. Letters, meetings, reunions, all were unwitting rehearsals in 'the ties of Empire . . . the connecting links of a Commonwealth'.

Hardly aware at seventeen of her latent powers of persuasion, she threw herself energetically into the fund-raising endeavours of the Angus (Forfar) Red Cross. When Princess Mary came to inspect the Forfarshire Girl Guides, the King's daughter found herself being publicly introduced to the twinkling Lady Elizabeth in her local role as deputy District Commissioner of Glamis. Off-stage meetings had, in fact, already occurred through the widowed Lady Airlie, who had known them both from babyhood. Herself a lady-in-waiting to Queen Mary, and indeed the Queen's firm friend from when they were children together, Mabell, Lady Airlie, eased the wheels of royal friendship and even romance more than she knew. In her memoirs Elizabeth especially goes on early record 'with her dark brown hair and vivid blue eyes . . . the only daughter at home, and the constant companion of her mother, who was one of my oldest friends'. Princess Mary she describes as 'the least inhibited' of the royal youngsters . . . 'and her father's favourite, although his jokes at her expense often made her cheeks crimson'.

Airlie Castle, the family dower house, was not ten miles from Glamis but throughout the 1914–18 War, Lady Airlie spent much of her time in London. There her flat in Ashley Gardens was accessible to her sons and their girl-friends when on leave, and on Elizabeth's occasional visits to town, two or three chance meetings with Princess Mary at the flat heightened their growing friendship. The Princess saw in the younger girl, who was more than three years her junior, a sense of family responsibility allied with an inner loneliness akin to her own. 'She never complains. She's far too unselfish and conscientious,' said the then Prince of Wales in discussing the Princess with Lady Airlie, and friends equally saw tougher fibres emerging in Elizabeth's character. The friendly but no longer unpractised charm masked considerable self-reliance, and the sweetness was edged by cool appraisal. 'She never tried to shift any weight from her young shoulders,' Cynthia Asquith shrewdly summed up her forming personality. 'The observant saw on her face a look of experience beyond her years.'

All her life before her —
Elizabeth Bowes-Lyon in her high chair, 1902.
A rare family photograph.
CATHCART ARCHIVES

Lady Elizabeth Bowes-Lyon, youngest daughter of the 14th Earl of Strathmore, 1904.
CATHCART ARCHIVES

In the wood at the bottom of the garden.
CATHCART ARCHIVES

With her parents, the Earl and Countess of Strathmore, Glamis, 1919.
CATHCART ARCHIVES

The Princess and the
Jester: with brother
David in fancy dress.
CATHCART ARCHIVES

In the 'Princess
gown' for the New
Year Ball, 1920.
CATHCART ARCHIVES

'Aunt Elizabeth' with Elphinstone nephews and nieces.
A rare family photograph. CATHCART ARCHIVES

Bride and groom: the Duke and Duchess of York on their wedding day, 26 April 1923. POPPERFOTO

Leaving Buckingham Palace for their honeymoon.

*The Duke and Duchess of York
with their 8-month-old daughter
Princess Elizabeth, Christmas, 1926.*

*Crossing the Line:
King Neptune
awards the Order of
the Golden Mermaid.*
CENTRAL PRESS

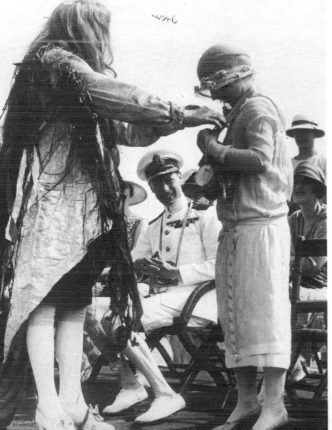

*New Zealand 1927: a
notable catch on the
Torgariro River.*
POPPERFOTO

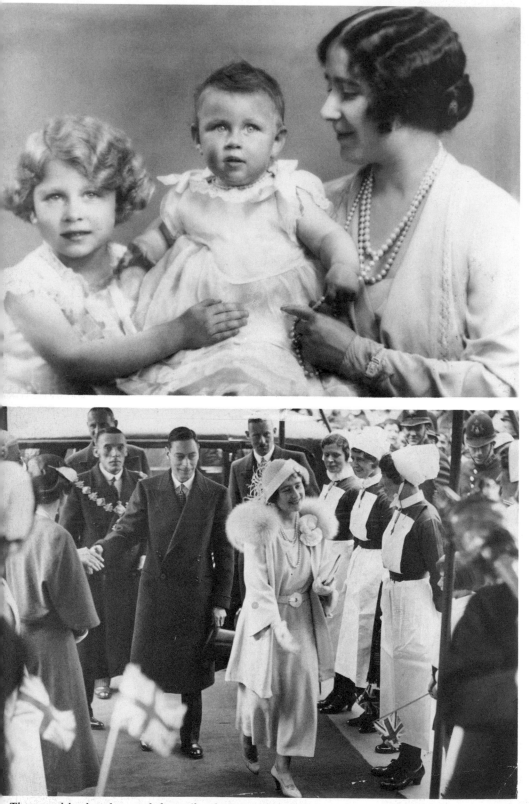

Princess Margaret at ten months old, with her mother and sister. POPPERFOTO

The proud husband — and the smile, the gesture, the total charm. . . the Duchess of York aged 34. POPPERFOTO

The moment
of Queen
Elizabeth's
crowning,
Westminster
Abbey,
12 May
1937.
POPPERFOTO

Their Majesties, King George VI
and Queen Elizabeth,
December 1936. BERTRAM PARK

On the
balcony of
Buckingham
Palace on
Coronation
Day, 1937.
POPPERFOTO

The Royal Family at home.
RADIO TIMES-HULTON

The crinoline and accessories created by Hartnell for the State Visit to Paris, 1938.
CECIL BEATON
POPPERFOTO

On the royal train in Canada, May 1939.
POPPERFOTO

Towards the end of the war Lady Strathmore fell seriously ill under the stress of anxiety for Michael, and the 'daughter at home' inevitably took on the tasks of assistant nurse, with the burden of running the domestic side of Glamis, her hospital correspondence and, in addition, the secretarial help her father sorely needed as Lord Lieutenant of the county. Her sisters' lives lay elsewhere: Rose faced the seaport uncertainties of any naval officer's wife, and the eldest sister, Lady Elphinstone, in her mid-thirties, was expecting her fourth baby – her son Andrew – who was born a few hours before the Armistice silenced the guns. Thus it was Elizabeth to whom Lady Strathmore turned for strength and comfort as she grappled with her ever-increasing dread that Michael might yet die in the prisoncamp.

'A day of emotion and thankfulness,' wrote Queen Mary on 11 November, and next morning the newspapers carried pictures of the excited crowds outside the Palace cheering the King and Queen, with glimpses – of more personal interest to Elizabeth – of Princess Mary and Princess Pat of Connaught among the royal group on the balcony.

At Glamis Castle, as under every roof in the land, rejoicing was commingled with sadness for the fallen, but photographs of the hospital group suggest that Lady Elizabeth produced some comic hats out of the old boxes, and the day ended with a singsong. Perhaps her forage through the fancy-dress chests brought to light her old Princess Elizabeth gown from the pre-war world of childhood. With her brothers Pat and Jock safely home, though both had been wounded, plans for a New Year fancy-dress ball helped to strengthen their mother's confidence, and Elizabeth needed little prompting to have the old dress copied in adult style and fit: the gathered sleeves, high waist, neckline, epaulettes, buttons and embroidery deliciously the same.

In February 1919, public attention focused on the Westminster Abbey wedding of Princess Pat, daughter of the Duke of Connaught, and Commander Alexander Ramsay, which was to prove first of a popular chain of post-war royal marriages. The press applauded the match as contributing to 'the democratization of the Throne' and agreed with public opinion that the era of foreign matrimonial alliances was over. History repeated itself and the bride left for the Abbey from Clarence House, then her parents' home which, in another post-war world forty years on, would be the London home of Queen Elizabeth the Queen Mother.

The marriage was close to Lady Elizabeth's heart: the bridegroom was a Forfarshire neighbour; his best man, John Bowlby, was a family friend of the Lyons and, but for the sustained anticipation of Michael's homecoming, it would have been curious if the Strathmores had not been wedding guests, among the Portlands, Buccleuchs, Ogilvys, Plunkets, Annalys and Spencers. Only two days before the wedding, word of Michael's return came at such short notice that there was only time to dash to the station to meet him, and his health and well-being sent the Bowes-Lyons into a prolonged domestic huddle of happiness. From this emotional gala Elizabeth also looked forward to her role as bridesmaid to her close friend Lady Lavinia Spencer, who was to marry Lord Annaly in April. Youngest sister of the 7th Earl Spencer, 'Lavvy' had been one of the bridesmaids with Elizabeth at Rose's wedding three years earlier. Now, supposedly to help the bride prepare her trousseau, Elizabeth went to stay with the Spencers at Althorp. Lavvy's brother had also married a Hamilton, whose family had always been welcome at 20 St James's Square, and so we see another link forged in the mesh of social consequence which would gradually evolve around Elizabeth and lead ultimately to the marriage of Lavvy's great-niece, Diana, to the Prince of Wales.

Lavvy's country wedding passed without mention in *The Times*. In 1919, as in 1945, everyone shared a sense of battling for the climate of peace against headstrong winds. The wounded were still being returned or were transferred from one hospital to another, and the Glamis ward did not close until the end of the year. As 'demobbed' staff returned, St Paul's Walden Bury was reopened and more overseas officers came there to spend their leave. As one visitor said, 'the vista of sheep peaceably grazing on the lawns was itself welcoming and reassuring'. Nor had Elizabeth's interest in the domestic affairs of her 'hospital boys' ceased with the Armistice. Not yet nineteen, she found herself still sympathetically concerned with the problems of 'work and homes for returned heroes', and jobs were found on the estate for a number of men who had first met the Bowes-Lyons as hospital patients.

Peace was signed in June. The searchlights of London swept through the night sky in broad sweeps of jubilation and as the great houses were reopened for their last echoes of past splendour Elizabeth entered with youthful enjoyment upon the revived London season. In July she witnessed the Victory March and long remembered the tremendous ovation given to Marshal Foch at the head of his procession. The brilliant sunshine of Royal Ascot saw her in a white lace frock and a hat charmingly akin to a poke bonnet. At Goodwood, too, we find the young racegoer with her lifelong friend, Lady Doris Gordon-Lennex (later Lady Doris Vyner) whose father in fact owned the racecourse.

Then once again the weekends lengthened at the Bury. 'It's so perfect here,' Elizabeth wrote, 'but it's so perfect at Glamis, also.' Nevertheless, when settled once more within the familiar castle, she appears to have shared the sense, so prevalent in the immediate post-war atmosphere, of being a little at a loss, of finding oneself at the end of a chapter. The old park merged with the woods, the new plantations with the heathlands and moors towards the mountains. And then? Lady Elizabeth could still renew the picnic camp-fires of her childhood with her local Girl Guides. She resumed her piano studies with Madame Verne. She could and did help to revive her mother's garden-parties for local good causes. And there were, of course, fish to be caught in the Dean, and perhaps fish of a different kind to be caught and thrown back, elsewhere.

7.   The Persistent Prince

Prince Albert, King George V's second son, was not among the figures on the Palace balcony on Armistice Day. Wishing to learn to fly, he had been transferred from the Navy and was then serving with the RAF in France, so little known that when he rode mounted at the right hand of the King of the Belgians for the joyous entry into newly liberated Brussels he was mistaken by many for his elder brother, the Prince of Wales. In July 1919, he was, however, present at the Victory Parade in London, and to his great pleasure he received his wings that same week, the first member of the British Royal Family to become a fully qualified air pilot.

Apart from the brief acquaintance of pre-war children's parties and junior dances, it is often said that Lady Elizabeth Bowes-Lyon first met Prince Albert in May 1920, at a dance at Lord and Lady Farquhar's house in Grosvenor Square, yet circumstantial evidence points to a friendship founded at least a year earlier. The Prince of Wales' liaison with the attractive Mrs Freda Dudley Ward was progressing at the time, alerting his next younger brother to the prospects of new friendships. In the spring of 1919, however, when Prince Albert was assigned to the Air Ministry in Whitehall, Princess Mary often enlivened Buckingham Palace with gramophone dance sessions in her private apartments, impromptu dansants at which it would have been strange if Elizabeth and the Prince were not occasional partners. At this juncture, Bertie, as he was known in the family, had just passed his twenty-fourth birthday, nearer in age to Mary – with only sixteen months between them – than to all his brothers. Elizabeth was now discreetly within the junior circle, and destined within three years to become one of the Princess's bridesmaids. At the Farquhars' she and Bertie waltzed together with enjoyment and accustomed expertise, and gossipy souls dubbed Elizabeth 'the best dancer in London'.

Far from being shy and reserved, the Prince danced with the panache expected of any young bachelor of twenty-three with a pretty girl. 'He told me long afterwards that he had fallen in love that evening,' wrote Lady Airlie, 'although he did not realize it until later.' If one catches a hint of love at first sight, the Annalys, who had chaperoned Elizabeth to Grosvenor Square, never stirred this ingredient into the record. Elizabeth's godmother, Venetia James, was also soon back in town, with the same 'menservants of untouchable dignity' and 'the same kind heart', as another protégée, Mrs Keppel's blonde daughter Sonia, observed. With her friendship with Queen Alexandra and another 'Bertie', Mrs James hastened to add the younger Bertie to her guest list. Probably only Elizabeth knew her personal secret that, in contrast to her lavish parties, she charitably ran a working girl's club which she visited every week of her life.

Horace Farquhar nursed less reputable secrets. In his seventies, with bristling military moustache and fierce expression, he was considered equally rich and irreproachable. Master of the Household to Edward VII and later Lord Steward to George V, he had acted as foremost royal financial adviser since his 'services rendered' at the Duke of Fife's marriage to King George's closest sister, Princess Louise. Some murky mining transactions of Edwardian times had been forgotten, and his finances were clearly beyond questioning. 'He is so gaga that one does not know what to make of him,' wrote Bonar Law, when enquiring into £80,000 missing from the funds of the Tory party, of which Lord Farquhar was treasurer. He in fact left a grandiose will in which handsome legacies were left to nearly every member of the Royal Family, though without any money to meet them. Certain trust funds which he managed for Princess Pat's mother, Princess Arthur of Connaught, had also disappeared with other credits, leaving the Princess in stringent financial straits. It seems poetic justice to deprive him of introducing the future King George VI and Queen Elizabeth.

Yet certainly nothing but the pleasantries of friendship passed between the Prince and Lady Elizabeth Lyon during the leisurely summer before Bertie went up to Cambridge. His troublesome stammer, his 'fear of talking', as he once put it, diminished to the merest hesitation in congenial company; and Elizabeth, who liked to tease friends with mild argument, knew when to give way amusingly at the first sign of constriction. In 1920 the lease of 20 St James's Square had to be relinquished, and she could make the Prince chuckle at the absurdities in which her mother was involved in searching for a successor. In the end a remarkably similar Adam mansion was found a few doors east of Berkeley Square at 17 Bruton Street. But all the reputed second sight in the family could not have given Elizabeth a clue that within three years she would leave its threshold as Bertie's bride.

On the eve of the Farquhar dance, King George V was considering whether he should confer the traditional title of Duke of York on Prince Albert, 'the fine old title which I bore for more than nine years, the oldest Dukedom in the country'. The advancement was announced in his Birthday Honours, and his son's manifest pleasure and appreciation made the King respond in his most affectionate vein: 'Dearest Bertie. . . . I feel that this splendid old title will be safe in your hands and that you will never do anything to tarnish it. I hope you will always look upon me as your best friend and always tell me everything . . . Yr. very devoted Papa.'

Elizabeth no doubt sent Bertie a note with a thought for the occasion. Within her light-hearted social scan there were now young Guards officers, young men from *The Times* and the publishing world, tyro diplomats and junior stock brokers, banking and accountancy types, one or two indirectly linked with her father's presidency of the Scottish Widows Fund, his fellow directors on North British Assurance or even his role as a deputy Governor of the Royal Bank of Scotland. A rich young American, 'Chips' Channon, was one day to write regretfully of being more than a little in love with her. 'I called her Elizabeth' he said and in later days, when she was Queen, he noted pleasurably that 'she saw me and smiled, with a touch of the twinkle which she reserves for old friends.' As wise old Lady Airlie made a point of noting, 'her radiant vitality and a blending of gaiety, kindness and sincerity made her irresistible to men,' but her admirers, though numerous, were kept comfortably at bay.

One hapless young bachelor attempted to discover the cause of his 'intense desire to please her', but did not get very far. Among her virtues he listed her 'unruffled serenity', this despite her ability to 'express opinions very trenchantly' and 'a great love of argument'. 'Those she is with feel themselves all they would wish to be. If to be witty, they become scintillating. In companies of the shy and silent, she will launch one of those inexhaustible topics on which everyone wishes to talk. . . . When discussions become exasperating she can interject a remark to distract immediately.'

Not that her apparent spontaneity was at times without forethought. At Bruton Street, before a luncheon party with some predictably stuffy guests, she conspired with a friend across the table to laugh whenever she raised an eyebrow. At a dullish remark, Elizabeth flashed her signal and laughed with her charming naturalness, her friend took the cue and the solemn atmosphere was dispersed.

Nearing her twentieth birthday, she was of no age to take anyone or anything very seriously. A friend recalled being given a lift to St Paul's Walden Bury on a hot summer afternoon in a high old-fashioned family touring car comically resembling the limousines used by Queen Mary. Elizabeth could not resist sitting bolt upright, raising her umbrella like a parasol and bowing and waving right and left to the startled passers-by in the Edgware Road. 'The smile and gracious bow were full of charm and grace during our pantomime,' recollected her companion.

There remains the oddity that the future Queen of England was never presented at Court. The befeathered parades of debutantes and mamas were revived in 1920, but without her name on the presentation lists. In 1921 no Courts were held and, when the ceremonial was resumed in 1922, she yielded family precedence to her senior sister-in-law, Mrs John Bowes-Lyon, who was presented that year. When the Courts were next held in 1923 Elizabeth was already a member of the Royal Family, but it may be that in fact she attended one of the crowded royal garden-parties of 1919 which 'constituted a presentation'.
In September 1920, Princess Mary was staying with Lady Airlie in Scotland when, by way of neighbourly counterpart, the Strathmores invited the Duke of York to visit Glamis. Events had raced on in the few months since the conferment of the dukedom. The Duke had nervously taken his seat in the House of Lords, had won the RAF doubles with his friend, Louis Grieg, at Wimbledon and had held an investiture for the first time as his father's deputy at Buckingham Palace. The evening dance at Glamis provided light-hearted amusement and Elizabeth wore 'a rose brocade Vandyck dress with pearls in her hair', another evident echo of her favourite fancy dress theme. Her Palace visits to Princess Mary were resumed in the autumn, providing the occasion when she first privately met Queen Mary, and came under her 'intent, questioning gaze'. The Queen was preoccupied just then with the matrimonial prospects of the Prince of Wales and the possibilities for her second son were beginning to dawn on her.

Lady Airlie has set down a crucial incident in her memoirs: 'I was driving with her one afternoon in the winter of 1920 when she told me that the Prime Minister had advised the King that the country would not tolerate an alliance with a foreigner for the Prince of Wales, and that the Duke of York should also look for a bride among the British aristocracy. "I don't think Bertie will be sorry to hear that," the Queen added. "I have discovered that he is very much attracted to Lady Elizabeth Bowes-Lyon. He's always talking about her. She seems a charming girl but I don't know her very well." I replied that I had known her all her life, and could say nothing but good of her.'

Convinced that mothers should never meddle in their offspring's love-affairs, Queen Mary said nothing more, but Lady Airlie's sensibilities were alert when Elizabeth began calling on her under various pretexts and talked of 'Bertie'. Her confidences were heavy with doubt. She had seen sufficient of the Royal Family to realize how constrained and restricted her life might become if she married into that circle. 'She was frankly doubtful, uncertain of her feelings, and afraid of the public life which would lie ahead of her as the King's daughter-in-law,' Lady Airlie summed up her own intimate view of the situation.

In the spring of 1921, the affair had progressed to the point where the Duke of York felt obliged to consult his father. 'You will be a lucky fellow if she accepts you,' chuckled the King, in his offhand way. There is no evidence that he had met Elizabeth as yet but his judgement of his son's fortunes was sound. The Duke proposed – and was refused.

Sad but utterly sincere, Elizabeth was convinced at the time that her decision was irrevocable. It was not a gambit in a love game; one friend considered the Duke deeply in love but too humble. His response to the refusal could not be wholly concealed. Even Lady Strathmore had to say she felt sorry for him: he looked so disconsolate. 'I do hope he will find a nice wife who will make him happy,' she wrote. 'I like him so much and he is a man who will be made or marred by his wife.' Queen Mary, too, was dismayed, aware now with a mother's certainty that Elizabeth was 'the one girl who could make Bertie happy. But I shall say nothing to either of them.'

Happily, the couple continued to meet. The Duke gathered fresh courage and resolve, especially when he found that his sister would be revisiting Airlie Castle in September and Lord Strathmore similarly suggested that the Duke might like to stay at Glamis for some pheasant shooting, strengthening the pattern of the previous year. When he arrived on 24 September, Lady Strathmore was ill in bed and Elizabeth presided as hostess. 'It is delightful here . . . and Elizabeth is very kind to me,' the royal guest wrote to his mother. And he added a restrained afterthought, 'The more I see her the more I like her.' Queen Mary also decided to renew her own impressions, and came to Glamis for tea before hurrying on to Balmoral. What she saw over the baps and scones deepened her belief that Elizabeth would have been just right for her son and perhaps might still be.

At Sandringham two months later, Princess Mary rushed down a staircase to tell her mother of her betrothal to Lord Lascelles, and the engagement was no sooner announced than Elizabeth was invited to be one of her eight bridesmaids in Westminster Abbey. The bridegroom was fifteen years older than the bride, a difference which may have caused Elizabeth to consider that someone seeming little older than herself, such as Bertie, would surely be perfect. The rush of Christmas was followed by the bride's conferences and dress fittings. The bridesmaids' costumes were of straight-cut cloth of silver, with diadems of silver rose leaves and, in fashionable 1922 idiom, a silver rose worn at the hip with a true lover's knot of blue. Lady Elizabeth was so delighted with her ensemble that she invited the staff and tenants' wives of St Paul's Walden Bury to see it, the first of a happy ritual of previews which, long afterwards, she resumed for the staff at Buckingham Palace.

The wedding took place on 28 February 1922, and Bertie wrote to the Prince of Wales, who was absent in South America, that the bride 'looked lovely in her wedding dress' but he prudently omitted the effect on him of one of the bridesmaids. 'The streets were overcrowded all along the route,' he added, and thus Elizabeth first rode in a State procession through central London and enjoyed a view of the packed street scenes she would one day find so familiar. It was now that she first moved in procession up the Abbey nave which within fifteen months she would herself tread as bride, and again in fifteen years as a Queen to her Coronation. At the Palace, at the family luncheon in the State dining-room, she briefly met or renewed acquaintance with every member of the Royal Family, except the one official absentee, the Prince of Wales. Posed for the first time in a royal photograph, Elizabeth is seen in the back row of the bridal group, her expression pensive, if not anxious. The full view of the whole family with all the pomp and circumstance of the wedding, more than ever persuaded her of the difficulties involved in marrying royalty.

After the wedding, another of the bridesmaids, Diamond Hardinge, responded to Elizabeth's mood by proposing that she should stay with her in Paris, at the British Embassy, no less, where her father, the widowed Lord Hardinge, was ambassador. From that lovely old mansion in its verdant garden Elizabeth gained her first independent view of the splendours and pleasures of the French capital and indeed affectionately regarded the Embassy as her Paris pied a terre forever after.

Diamond was an 'original' quite after Elizabeth's heart, 'a madcap, a tomboy, who delighted in making jokes and playing pranks, as a subsequent Embassy châtelaine, Cynthia Gladwyn, described her. With a 'perfected knack of cracking her jaw with a loud report, it amused her to do so in public places such as the theatre,' and with this lively companion, Elizabeth for her part 'brought enchantment to the Embassy, with her irresistible smile and rippling infectious laughter'. A variety of handsome young attachés were eager to squire her to the cafés or to accompany her on drives to Malmaison and Fontainebleau; and at an Embassy ball one guest considered that 'Lady Elizabeth Lyon was the most charming sight, a bewitching little figure in rose'.

Moreover it was June, and when the formal parties were over, Lady Gladwyn tells us, they went 'with some of the young secretaries to more amusing places, such as the Foire de Neuilly (one of the best fairs of the year) where they all had fun going down the chute in a barrel, escapades about which Lord Hardinge was kept in ignorance'.

One of her Embassy admirers proposed to her that summer – to be gently declined – and two or three others vainly approached the subject in the course of the year. Probably the Duke of York again voiced his hopes. At Bruton Street, some neighbours opposite, the young Pakenhams, remembered him on the balcony of No 17 with Elizabeth, joining with them across the street in the current craze of Beaver, with wild shouts or gestures to score every beard spotted among passersby, until the Pakenhams won the game outright by glimpsing a Greek Orthodox priest crossing Berkeley Square. The Duke had not long returned from the wedding of Princess Marie of Yugoslavia, where he had represented the King, and there are hints in correspondence that Elizabeth may have promised a decision, though we hear nothing more.

'Although the romance seemed at an end, he continued to plead his case and Elizabeth continued to visit me,' wrote Lady Airlie. An effervescent hostess, Mrs Ronald Greville, 'Maggie' to her friends, very deliberately invited the couple to her theatre and supper parties with every confidence of results. The daughter of a whisky magnate who had married his cook, and incredibly rich, Maggie rivalled Mrs James in filling her house with the handsome and celebrated, the royal and the rich, and had, as Osbert Sitwell noted, 'a complete grasp of any situation which might arise'. Above all, she had just brought off the coup of bringing together, 'matching and marrying', Lord Louis Mountbatten and Edwina Ashley (later the Earl and Countess Mountbatten of Burma) and now was ardently eager to play a Scottish Cupid to all the King's sons, preferably with her Surrey home, Polesden Lacey, as a honeymoon retreat.

It turned out to be a case of third time lucky. In September 1922, the Duke of York was yet again invited to Glamis, and Lady Elizabeth once more charmingly acted as hostess. In the evening, a friend records, 'the drawing-room would be dimly lit, except for the pool of light made by the candles on the piano. . . . We would all sing, adapting topical songs to someone with us'. Elizabeth was particularly good at weaving these allusions, her verses greeted 'with great affection and tolerant good humour'. The family fun seemed like a silver cord pulling Bertie from the morass of formality too often engulfing him at the Palace. As Sir John Wheeler-Bennett has written in his official biography of King George VI, 'The happy badinage and affection of a large and closely-knit family were a revelation, providing a climate of ideas to which he instantly responded. His own personality throve and blossomed. He was deeply in love. . . .'

More particularly, his sporting biographer, Aubrey Buxton, detected a significant change even in the Duke's private game-book at this time. 'The tedious repetition of formal entries gives way to a varied pattern of diverse experiences. . . . He discovered suddenly that he knew only one third of his art, and grappled from the outset with his new experiences on the hills and in the bogs of Glamis with unquenchable enthusiasm.'

Elizabeth often accompanied her brothers, Michael and David, with Bertie and at times her lifelong friend Arthur Penn, on these days of rough walking. For the first time the Duke no longer limited his game-book entries to the number and species of birds killed. Remarks and observations crept in, 'an excellent morning's walk. Snipe very wild' . . . 'a good day and birds came well'. One has the impression that Elizabeth set aside her old dislike of shooting, aware that her enthusiasm and observation drew the best from Bertie and stimulated him with her own interest and sense of adventure.

Their ever-quickening companionship continued into the winter. Family letters have told of 'the much-used piano' at the Bury, while outside was 'a garden ready to be enjoyed and work always waiting to be done in it'. After taking an apprentice course at Kew, young brother David was approaching the tasks with real expertise, and a wintry photograph shows Bertie deep in an excavation, coping with tree-roots,

while Elizabeth watches with demure encouragement. The eyes behind
the camera were evidently David's, but when the Duke had departed,
Lady Strathmore herself noticed her daughter's perturbed and abstrac-
ted air. 'That winter was the first time I have ever known Elizabeth
really worried,' she wrote afterwards. 'I think she was torn between her
longing to make Bertie happy and her reluctance to take on the big
responsibilities which this marriage must bring.'

In the New Year of 1923, Elizabeth went to tea with Lady Airlie, as
so often, and instead of talking of Bertie as she had intended her hostess
found herself reminiscing instead of her own marriage, how she had
hated Army life and only tolerated it for her husband's sake, but had
grown to love it. Elizabeth listened sympathetically, but asked few
questions. 'I feared I might have bored her by bringing up a chapter
that closed before she was born,' wrote Lady Airlie. But within days
Bertie was fired with New Year resolve, suddenly so determined that he
arranged a code with his parents at Sandringham for a telegram to signal
success or failure. On Saturday, 13 January the expected message
arrived 'ALL RIGHT BERTIE'.

His 'darling Elizabeth' was finally won over that morning during a
walk together through the leafless Bury woods. One of the family was
to remark, 'courtings are as old as the hills, and just as obvious'. All
the same, everyone was surprised when the pair came back from their
stroll laughing and blushing. The next day saw one of the rare occasions when Elizabeth absented herself from Sunday morning service
and, with everyone else at church, the couple spent an hour or two
alone together and in the evening Bertie hurried back to London. He
had as yet given Elizabeth no engagement ring, for he wished the
choice to be hers. He had few worldly goods to endow, except the
small sum he had saved from his £26,000 Civil List allowance (after
paying various salaries and expenses) since his coming of age. When
he returned to Sandringham on the Monday, Queen Mary jotted
down in her diary, 'we are delighted and he looks beaming'. Bertie in
turn felt that he should put his parents' response on record. 'You and
Papa were both so charming to me,' reads his letter of 16 January
among Queen Mary's papers in the Royal Archives. 'I can never really
thank you properly for giving your consent. I am very very happy and
I can only hope that Elizabeth feels the same as I do. I know I am very
lucky to have won her over at last.' Then his pen was fired with deeper
fervour in an intimate letter to Lady Airlie 'about the wonderful happening in my life. . . . My dream has at last been realized. It seems so

marvellous to me to know that my darling Elizabeth will one day be my wife. . . .'

The *Court Circular* announced the engagement on the evening of 16 January and the news was in the morning papers next day. 'I feel very happy but quite dazed,' wrote Elizabeth. 'We hoped we were going to have a few days peace first, but the cat is now completely out of the bag and there is no possibility of stuffing him back!'

She returned to Bruton Street, indeed, to find her parents' household in a ferment. She had anticipated excitement, but the inundation of cables, letters and callers completely astonished her. Among the reporters crowding the doorstep, one bold spirit, Mr Cozens-Hardy of *The Star*, had the nerve to send in his card and, to his surprise, was ushered into the breakfast-room. 'Mother, leave this gentleman to me,' Lady Elizabeth was heard saying.

With cool presence of mind, she set the stage, and was discovered – Act Two, Scene One – at a little writing desk, answering letters. 'I suppose you have come to congratulate me? How very kind of you. I hadn't the remotest idea everybody would be so interested. . . .' Mr Cozens-Hardy asked if it were true that the Duke had proposed three times. 'Now look at me,' came the answer, with the greatest composure. 'Do you think I am the sort of person Bertie would have to ask twice?' One recognizes the endearing tactical duplicity and her visitor pursued the matter no further. 'Within a few days,' as he tells in his reminiscences, 'I learned from Sir Godfrey Thomas, the Prince of Wales' secretary, that the King had sent an equerry to Bruton Street with instructions that no further interviews were to be given.' Henceforth few were permitted until Lady Cynthia Asquith began her book on the Duchess of York four years later. Yet perhaps the most bemused man in London was the veteran royal portraitist, Frank Salisbury, who had been painting the group canvas of Princess Mary's wedding. To avoid an overcrowded effect the King had suggested that he need not include all the bridesmaids and so the artist had omitted. . . . Lady Elizabeth Bowes-Lyon.

According to Sir John Wheeler-Bennett, the official biographer of George VI, Lady Elizabeth's first visit to Sandringham with her parents was 'an ordeal not to be under-estimated'. But it becomes increasingly clear that she had long since met King George V and his Queen in family privacy, and found no cause for trepidation. 'I was never afraid of him,' she once wrote to the royal physician, Lord Dawson of Penn. 'He was always ready to listen and give advice on one's own silly little affairs. He was so kind and so *dependable*. And when he was in the mood he could be deliciously funny, too! Don't you think so?' Lord Strathmore had also come to know the King and Queen well through nearly twenty years as Lord Lieutenant of Forfarshire, attendant upon every royal visitor to the county. The Strathmores, nevertheless, were astonished when they first set eyes on the crowded little drawing-room of York Cottage, which the King and Queen continued to occupy while old Queen Alexandra lived on at the 'big house'. Lady Strathmore was vividly reminded of her father-in-law's old flat in Grosvenor Gardens, with its poorish water-colours hung upon flock wallpaper and Chinese jars perched upon bookcases from Maples.

The Strathmores were also entertained, however, amid the ornately plastered splendour of Sandringham House itself, where Queen Alexandra awaited them. At Princess Mary's wedding she had perhaps seemed a tiny and unapproachable bejewelled figure in violet velvet. Now, in close-up, the compassionate Elizabeth found her deaf, half-blind, her auburn wig too large; yet there remained, as T E Lawrence said, 'the ghosts of all her loving airs, the little graces, the famous smile, all angular and heart-rending'. There was poignancy in the meeting and the tender-hearted young newcomer was unaware of the impression she was herself creating. 'Elizabeth is charming, so pretty and engaging and natural,' Queen Mary emphasized in her journal, while the King shared his wife's opinion. 'She is a pretty and charming girl and Bertie is a very lucky fellow.' And to her brother, Lord Cambridge, Queen Mary stressed, 'Elizabeth is with us now, perfectly charming, so well brought-up, a great addition to the family.'

Elizabeth wore her engagement ring, a lustrous sapphire set between two diamonds, in time for the weekend, though a hindrance was indicated before wedding plans could be decided. The King and Queen were to pay a State visit to Italy but the government in Rome had not yet stated when they 'really want us to go', Queen Mary apologized. The King's consent to the marriage, required under the Royal Marriage Act of 1772, was formally given at a special meeting of the Privy Council on 12 February with the difficulty unresolved, but the formula must have persuaded the Italians to hurry. 'Now know ye that we have consented and by these Presents signify Our consent to the contracting of Matrimony between His Royal Highness Albert Frederick Arthur George, Duke of York, and the Lady Elizabeth Angela Marguerite Bowes-Lyon. . . .' The Italian date was known within a week and the wedding was announced for Thursday 26 April.

From that moment everything around Elizabeth assumed the double standard of celebrity: her own life and the larger picture of embellished newsprint. She had but to pick up a magazine to find pages spread with Glamis photographs, 'Linked again with Royalty as when a Lyon Wedded Robert II's Daughter' as a headline asserted. A Scottish lass was marrying an English Prince, regardless of the bride's long line of English progenitors or the Danish-Germanic strains of Bertie's parents. Historic precedents bristled: no King's son had married in Westminster Abbey in the 541 years since the young Richard II had wedded Anne of Bohemia in 1382. No prince had married a commoner with consent in the 263 years since James, Duke of York, married Anne Hyde in 1660.

For three months such morsels of information greeted Elizabeth at every turn of the page. In the Archbishop of Canterbury's Faculty Office the marriage license would be engrossed 'by the veteran clerk, Mr Bull, who for three days will stoop over a roll of parchment nearly a yard square, using twenty quill pens of various thicknesses'. With a bright modern flourish the recently-formed British Broadcasting Company offered to broadcast the service by 'wireless', the first broadcasts of 'Grand Opera' from Covent Garden having 'demonstrated the technical possibilities'. In general, the bridal couple would have welcomed the idea and the Dean of Westminster approved. The Abbey Chapter, however, solemnly vetoed the prospect lest 'the Service might be received by persons in Public Houses with their hats on'.

Meanwhile Lady Elizabeth faced her first day of public royal initiation. The Duke of York had been staying at Glamis and on 17 March the couple publicly visited Edinburgh to inspect the plaster model of their four-tiered wedding-cake and to tour a factory known as the Blighty Works, where disabled ex-Servicemen received training in cloth manufacture. That afternoon this was followed by attendance at the England-Scotland rugger match, a game inevitably described as a 'battle of the Thistle and the Rose'. The day owed much to the imaginative planning of Alec Hardinge, Diamond's brother, who was one of the King's secretaries. The cameras clicked at the Duke's spats and Elizabeth's feathered velvet hat, and the old photographs show her in those unbecoming velour fashions, tautly nervous and unsmiling. She was, one recollects, still only twenty-two, and the wooden stands that were rising in the London streets, the warmth of welcoming popularity, the flood of wedding presents, all seemed an unreal dream.

Her wedding gifts already included such unexpected oddities as an improbable mantle of ostrich feathers from South Africa; 1,000 gold-eyed needles from the Livery Company of Needlemakers; and an oak chest from the Pattenmakers, filled with two dozen pairs of goloshes and wellingtons, which she had to acknowledge in a little speech of acceptance at Buckingham Palace. Then there were tartan plaids and knitted blankets and the family joked that she had a life supply of shawls with which, to lessen her liability to colds, Lady Strathmore had supposedly swaddled her from childhood. The jewellery was equipment indeed for a princess: diamond necklaces, tiaras, bracelets and brooches, from the King and Queen and from her own parents, together with 'silver needing a very, very large vault', as David said, with family irreverence.

In public, the couple 'expressed a preference for gifts suitable for furnishing their new home'. These ranged from a magnificent writing-table (the King) to a grand piano and a wardrobe with a superfluity of oriental lacquered cabinets. But indisputably happiest of all in the bride's eyes was the unequalled necklace of diamonds and pearls from the Duke of York, and in his eyes her own gift to him of a dress watchchain of pearls and platinum. The problem of a future home was solved by the grace-and-favour conferment of White Lodge in Richmond Park, where the 'gaga' Lord Farquhar had relinquished his tenancy, and Bertie was particularly attracted by the tennis-court and Elizabeth by the expansive open views. The newspapers were at once full of reminders that the heir to the Throne, the Prince of Wales, had been born there. It was an irony that the real successor to the Throne should begin his married life there. Strangely close to the mark was Elizabeth's throat specialist in Wimpole Street, Mr Irwin Moore, whom she happened to consult one afternoon. A fellow medico, Scott Stevenson, chanced to call in a few minutes later to find Moore in some elation. 'Well, did you see her? You must have met her on the doorstep!'

'Who do you mean? That pretty little girl in blue?'

'Pretty little girl in blue be bothered!' retorted Irwin, with rare perspicacity. 'That's the future Queen of England!'

The select dressmakers of the 1920s were seldom publicized. The temples of Reveille and Worth knew little of the limelight which falls on contemporary couturiers, and Lady Elizabeth looked no farther than the respectably exclusive firm of Handley Seymour to make her wedding dress, trousseau and bridesmaids' dresses, implemented by a little lady described as 'a very fine needlewoman employed for years in the

Bowes-Lyon family'. No designer's name hallmarked the casual artist's sketches: in a sense Elizabeth designed her own wedding-gown by knowing precisely what she wanted. She wished it to be in simple medieval style, with a square neckline, the long sleeves in Nottingham lace, a centre panel of silver lace from neck to hem: one recognizes the Princess Elizabeth theme again, translated in wedding terms. Queen Mary produced a train of old *point de Flandres* lace from her store, which the bridesmaids' ivory and lace-trimmed georgette dresses tactfully matched. Elizabeth had chosen her bridesmaids with geometric social precision: two of Queen Mary's nieces, Lady Mary Cambridge (later Duchess of Beaufort) and Lady May Cambridge; two close personal friends, Betty Cator from her schooldays and Diamond Hardinge; another of Princess Mary's friends and bridesmaids, Lady Mary Thynne, matched by Lady Katherine Hamilton from her own closer circle; and two young nieces, Elizabeth Elphinstone and Cecilia Bowes-Lyon, her brother Patrick's daughter, as bridal attendants.

Only the weather was disobliging, the day dawning cold and wet, the showers soaking the streamers and their motto, 'TRH The Bride and Bridegroom', the raindrops glistening on the silver-painted bells. But the pavements were dry when the bride left her parents' home in Bruton Street, her ermine cloak – a gift of the King – deliberately left open so that the onlookers could see her wedding-gown. Along the outward route the crowds were disappointed to see her State landau escorted by no more than four mounted policemen, in fact a correct formality marking her commoner status for the last time. Her father had never looked more solemn.

'The sun actually came out as the bride entered the Abbey,' the King recorded, and thus it shone on a scene of brilliant uniforms and costumes. The bridegroom waited at the altar in the uniform of a Group Captain of the Royal Air Force, a longish pause with his two brothers, the Prince of Wales and Prince Henry of Gloucester, before the bride slowly approached. An unforeseen delay occurred when one of the clerics in her procession fainted. Then, against the anthem of the choir, there was a rustle of approval as she paused at the flat tombstone of the Unknown Warrior and laid there her bouquet of white roses. It was a remembrance for Fergus, said some. It was an unintentional improvement on Princess Mary, who had placed her bouquet at the Cenotaph in Whitehall after leaving the Abbey, and the emotion of the congregation could be felt as the Archbishop of Canterbury conducted the service. The Archbishop of York, Dr Lang, gave the address. 'You, dear bride, in your Scottish home, have grown up from childhood among country folk and friendship with them has been your native air. So have you both been fitted for your place in the people's life, and your separate lives are now, till death, made one. You cannot resolve that your wedded life will be happy, but you can and will resolve that it shall be noble. . . . The warm and generous heart of this people takes you today into itself. Will you not in response take that heart, with all its joys and sorrows, into your own?'

To the devout Elizabeth his words were a briefing. They mingled with the pealing bells and the cheers, and some onlookers found the bride more serious than smiling. Perhaps the escort of Life Guards appeared to place her at a remove as the wedding coach passed through the tapestry of humanity back along the Mall, through Marlborough Gate to Piccadilly and down Constitution Hill to Buckingham Palace.

Part Three

THE DUCHESS OF YORK

8.   *The Little Duchess*

To Maggie Greville's gratification, the Duke and Duchess of York spent the first two weeks of their honeymoon at Polesden Lacey. In placing her Surrey house at their disposal, Mrs Greville had installed the novelty of a 'wireless receiver', giving them an opportunity to hear their wedding anthems again that evening when the Abbey choir visited the broadcasting studio at Savoy Hill. Polesden Lacey is now a National Trust property, in part a stucco Regency villa much enlarged by Greville money, still basking in wooded seclusion. By no particular wish of their own, the royal couple made their journey by the thirty-five minute steam train puffing from Waterloo, in a special saloon stacked with white roses, white heather, white carnations and lilies of the valley. Crowds waved at every station; and at Bookham there were addresses of welcome and more bouquets when the bride and groom alighted, and drove by car through the long tunnel of verdant trees to the house. The evening was fragrant with the early clematis armandii trained for fifty yards across the south front, and the upper windows commanded a view of the sunset light on the soft Surrey hills. In the dusk the couple strolled in the concealment of the long terrace walk, a pleasance made by no less a romantic than Sheridan, and next morning they dutifully had to occupy themselves with correspondence, writing from the wicker armchairs in the sunroom.

The Duke felt that he could not pass the day without a letter to his mother. 'I do hope you will not miss me very much – though I believe you will, as I have stayed with you so much longer really than my brothers.' A heartfelt message from the King was delivered by a special despatch rider. 'Dearest Bertie – You are indeed a lucky man to have such a charming and delightful wife as Elizabeth, and I trust you will both have many years of happiness together and that you will be as happy as Mama and I after you have been married for thirty years, I can't wish you more. . . .'

On the third day, the world came bursting in. A press photographers' session had been arranged and, to clear any doubts, it was announced that same day that the bride took the rank of a princess, and so the old childish daydream of a Princess Elizabeth came officially true. After the crowded weeks of wedding preparation, the couple relaxed, and Mrs Greville in London kept to herself any private gleanings of the Sunday church-going, the tennis and the golf. No doubt the honeymooners giggled at having Mrs Greville's over-opulent Italian drawing-room to themselves, at the heavily gold-leafed panelling and the sportive cherubs on the painted ceiling. On 2 May, they made a conspiratorial incognito visit to Bruton Street, where David Bowes Lyon was celebrating his coming-of-age. Indeed, Elizabeth had timed her wedding-day so that their big events should occur within a week of each other. In adding his signature to the vellum marriage certificate in the Abbey, among the scrawls of empresses and kings, princes and statesmen, David gleefully reported that he had signed 'very small in the corner'. It was an equally characteristic facet of family modesty that, at the dinner party at Bruton Street after the wedding, the family were unconcerned with Elizabeth's great match but they all emphatically agreed, 'thank God she has married a good man'.

On 9 May the newly-weds arrived at Glamis in appalling weather to find their rooms on the first floor warm and snug, the four-poster bed sheltered by the hangings on which, twelve years earlier, Lady Strathmore had lovingly embroidered the names of all her children (needlework shamelessly snipped in our own day by vandals). By the following week, however, the Duchess was gasping with whooping cough, 'so unromantic on your honeymoon', the Duke wrote to Queen Mary, and the wedding tour later concluded at Frogmore House, in the shadow of Windsor Castle, where the Duchess found an old-fashioned residential suite forlornly isolated among rooms stuffed with surplus furniture, and every corner evoked her husband's boyhood memories.

His parents had lived here as Prince and Princess of Wales: here was the old summer-house where they had tea; here the same inkstains on his old school-desk. 'Nothing has changed at all,' he wrote to his old tutor, Mr Hansell, 'except that it has been lent to us. Old memories come rushing back all the time. . . .' But now the garden and winding lake were charged with romance as he contentedly walked the paths in the evening with his beloved Elizabeth. The couple stayed at Frogmore for only two weeks while the White Lodge, in Richmond Park, was being made ready for them, and yet often revisited it with nostalgic affection.

The young Duchess kept to herself the disappointing first impression that the White Lodge was a royal white elephant which could never be anything but uncomfortable and inconvenient. Built two hundred years earlier, it had been bestowed upon Queen Mary's parents, the Duke and Duchess of Teck, and so similarly shone for her mother-in-law with all the sentiment of childhood. It stood in the heart of Richmond Park – the hunting area to the south-west of London enclosed by Charles I – but its 'airy aspect', as one friend pointed out, merely meant that it was 'open to draughts' and its rehabilitation demanded yards of carpeting and an acre of paint. When the Yorks moved in on 7 June, they concealed their dismay at the formal furnishings and Elizabeth made light of their predicament by some discreet rearrangement in placing her wedding gifts. It was more disturbing for the young Duchess to discover that she could not stir out of doors without the hazard of sightseers and that when the King and Queen first came to luncheon a crowd of people waited for hours at the gates. The Duchess had looked forward to this inaugural joint first visit from her in-laws with some trepidation and had prompted Bertie to warn his mother beforehand, 'our cook is not very good but she can do the plain dishes well, and I know you like that sort'. Delighted to be entertained in her girlhood home, Queen Mary, however, found nothing amiss. 'They have made the house so very nice with all their presents,' she noted that night in her journal.

Apart from the Strathmores, the Prince of Wales – another 'David' within the family – was an early guest, whose honest opinion was that Elizabeth 'had brought into the family a lively and refreshing spirit'. She had also brought an eagerness to serve which pleased the older generation. The Yorks had not concluded their honeymoon before an announcement was made of her first presidency, as head of the Scottish Women's Hospital Association. During the newly-weds' first month in White Lodge, Queen Victoria's third daughter, Princess Christian, died in London at the age of seventy-seven and the majority of her societies and charities turned at once to the newest and youngest member of the Royal Family, endowing her with a ready-made list of good causes. A group of Dr Barnardo girls came to the Lodge in Girl Guide uniform before emigrating to Australia and the Duchess showed them around her new home 'as if we were real friends'. Of her own accord, she gave her early patronage to the Contemporary Art Society and her first 'royal engagement' was to an art exhibition on 18 June to inspect the modish portraiture of Savely Sorin. Her own portrait by Lander was the success of the Royal Academy that year, and the June weddings of two of her bridesmaids, Lady Mary Cambridge and Miss Diamond Hardinge, equally warmed public interest. Admiral Earl Beatty found himself seated next to the new Duchess one night at dinner, 'a perfect little duck, one of the nicest little ladies I have met for years'. The incisive eye of Lady Diana Cooper also detected the Duke and Duchess at a theatre, 'such a sweet little couple, so fond of one another . . . sitting together in the box having private jokes'.

The King and Queen drew them into the ceremonies of Holyrood and as an extra exercise that hot July the newly-weds engaged in a joint first round of duties in Liverpool. In general, the King took the view that the young people 'had just married and must settle down'. In 1923, however, the British throne was not over-decorated with glamorous princesses. No other English prince had married for love in the course of the century, and an extraordinary upsurge of public affection and approval enveloped 'the little Duchess'.

In September, Bertie's game-book shows that he was enjoying a house-party with Elizabeth and her sister Rose at Holwick Hall, a lesser Strathmore property in Yorkshire, when a handsome tribute came from the King at Balmoral. 'The better I know and the more I see of your dear little wife, the more charming I think she is and everyone falls in love with her. . . .' If one could suspect an ulterior motive, it was swiftly forthcoming. White with anger, the Duke had to tell his wife a day or two later, 'We have to pack almost at once for the Balkans.' The first-born infant son of King Alexander of Yugoslavia was to be christened on 21 October, and Lord Curzon as Foreign Minister had advized the King that it was desirable that the Duke and Duchess of York should take up invitations to act as godparents. Moreover, the following day was also to see the wedding of King Alexander's cousin, Prince Paul, to Princess Olga of Greece (elder sister of Princess Marina) at which the Duke and Duchess would represent King George and Queen Mary.

'Curzon should be drowned for giving such short notice. He must know things are different now,' the Duke wrote in exasperation to his secretary, Louis Greig. With less than three weeks to prepare her wardrobe, Elizabeth had reason to joke that her trousseau would have to do. In Belgrade, the intending hosts were in an equal flurry. A large new palace was barely completed in time, and at the height of the festivities the plumbing failed. There was no hot water and the cold supply was clouded with cement. Destined to pass into tragic exile as King Peter of Yugoslavia, the baby was all but drowned at his christening when the ancient Patriarch allowed him to slip into the font, to be rescued only by Bertie's quick presence of mind in scooping him up. Of all the royal Balkan assemblage, Elizabeth had previously met only two, Paul and Olga. Had she caught their eye, she might have quivered at the sight of her bashful husband carrying the screaming naked babe three times-around the altar on a cushion and, scarcely less embarrassing, receiving gravely for this service a traditional gift of hand-embroidered underwear. But amusement was reserved for privacy, and the Duke of York proudly wrote to his father 'they were all enchanted with Elizabeth, especially cousin Missy (Queen Marie of Rumania). She was wonderful with all of them and they were all strangers except two.'

No sooner were the young godparents home than they were guests at another royal wedding, that of the then Crown Prince of Sweden to Lady Louise Mountbatten (sister of Earl Mountbatten). The wedding reception held in the Round Room at Kensington Palace was packed with more royals than in Belgrade: two reigning kings, four queens, six princes, ten princesses, and ducals beyond listing. The Yorks drove there from Buckingham Palace in a car with the King and Queen, and there are memories that Elizabeth was drawn aside from the reception to meet another prince, a two-year-old staying with his nanny Roosie in his grandmother's suite in the private apartments. This was none other than Prince Philip, whose four sisters were Louise's bridesmaids.

It was a November evening of 'dripping mist', perhaps the occasion when a royal chauffeur lost his way in the fog and blundered around Richmond Park for an hour, seeking the White Lodge. The Lodge was colder than the unfinished palace in Belgrade, for the central heating boiler had broken down. In despair that winter, the Duke of York rented 'The Old House' at Guilsborough, forty miles beyond St Paul's Walden, but happily at least in the same direction, and Elizabeth's visits home to her family were then interchanged with Bertie's hunting weekends with the Pytchley. A royal engagement in London often entailed a round journey of 130 miles, but the couple, as a Bowes-Lyon cousin remembered, 'became quite resourceful in borrowing bedrooms'.

In April, 1924 the Duke announced to his mother that the boiler was 'actually finished, and marvel of marvels they worked on Sunday', but this was only in time for the warmer weather. Meanwhile, the Duchess of York was expected to play her pristine part on every royal occasion, her gowns uncrushed by travel, and 17 Bruton Street provided a dressing-room. Then Princess Mary offered her sister-in-law the use of her Mayfair home, Chesterfield House, for the season, and 'the little Duchess' welcomed the novelty, having sighed in despair that even living in the Queen's Dolls' House would be pleasant. Hardened as the Yorks were to the curious royal necessity of living out of suitcases, the capacious wardrobes of Chesterfield House were highly functional during the brilliant and crowded season when the young Duchess attended the Courts at Buckingham Palace and her first State Ball. White Lodge served for garden parties and summer weekends, while Queen Mary's anxiety to 'keep it in the family' was allayed by Elizabeth's beguiling diplomacy.

Over her head, however, there loomed worries far worse than the unwilling boiler or her mother-in-law's possessive regard for white elephants. Powerless as she was to lessen a Bowes-Lyon family scandal, she felt that she was letting Bertie down by the sudden unexpected flux of headlines and Bowes-Lyon gossip, often about relatives whom she had not seen for years. The Yorks were no sooner back from their honeymoon than they were confronted with a shocking news placard, 'Bowes Lyon Shooting Tragedy' and the dreadful inquest details of a young cousin who had shot himself after an unhappy love affair. The suicide of Angus Bowes-Lyon in July, 1923, was moreover followed in June, 1924, by a marriage scandal of less tragic consequence, one not without strains of comedy although it created pages of sensational journalism.

The Duchess had taken it light-heartedly on reading that a girl in an Aberdeen sweet-shop named Connie Bain claimed 'links of royal birth', but the family were agitated to find 'something in it' and heard with alarm that the girl intended to apply to the Court of Session in Edinburgh for a declaration that she was 'the legitimate, eldest, lawful child of Hubert Ernest Bowes Lyon' and thus the Duchess of York's second cousin. No one could tell what would happen. Out indeed into the cold light of court came the truth about cousin Hubert, who was only a year older than Elizabeth's brother Patrick and had certainly never dreamed that his boyish peccadilloes would one day become the concern of the Royal Family and of the world. At the age of twenty, he had countered the boredom of Army life in Edinburgh by setting up house with an 18-year-old charmer named Mary Smeaton. Within two years he respectably married her and they subsequently had two handsome sons. A month before their marriage, however, Mary had also presented him with a lovechild, their daughter, Constance, who to avoid scandal was hastily farmed out to foster-parents. Later, another couple took charge of the child and, taking their name, she became Connie Bain.

In their hurry to hide their 'shame' young Hubert and his Mary failed to realize that, under Scottish law, their subsequent marriage legitimised Connie. The circumstances were not denied and after evidence of identity was given in court, a decree of legitimation was granted. Her point gained, the young lady moreover behaved with quiet dignity, illustrating that she shared other good qualities with the Duchess of York as well as deep blue eyes and a peaches-and-cream complexion. Having proved her name, as she put it, she dropped out of sight and ultimately married a white Nyasaland sugar planter, presumably to live happily ever after. The King, too, quickly set the Duchess's mind at rest and seemed to be more amused than shocked by the storm in a teacup.

Two or three months later, he was also pleased and impressed by Bertie and Elizabeth's successful visit to Northern Ireland, the first official royal visit since he had himself opened the new Ulster Parliament in 1921. The Duke of York reported a 'quiet astounding reception . . . no other word to describe the wonderful enthusiasm. Elizabeth has been marvellous as usual, the people simply love her already. I am very lucky indeed to have her to help me . . . she knows exactly what to do and say to all the people we meet'. The King hardly needed reassuring. He had once 'looked forward with dread to the idea of daughters-in-law,' as he confessed to Queen Mary, and instead he could not but admire Elizabeth's courage, her disarming tact, as well as her stubborn ability to stick to her guns. In his orderly stop-watch household, even his stern insistence on punctuality was not proof against her. The Duchess once arrived two minutes late for dinner and he greeted her apologies with 'You are not late, my dear. I think we are early.'

'If she weren't late she would be perfect,' he later told Dr Lang, 'and how horrible that would be.'

For the winter of 1924–25 Elizabeth also found sympathetic allies to express her viewpoint that her husband had been working very hard and needed a merited holiday. He was to open the second session of the British Empire Exhibition at Wembley in 1925 and it was an effective weapon in her armoury that he had yet seen nothing of the Empire at first hand. Her persuasions were irrefutable and to their delight the Yorks spent Christmas at Government House, Nairobi, having travelled overland through France. At Marseilles they boarded the liner *Mulbera*, and found the capricious Mediterranean colder than Richmond Park.

It was the first Christmas separated from all family ties, other than her husband, that Elizabeth had ever known. Her closest link with home was with Lady Annaly (her former bridesmaid, Lavinia Spencer) who shared the trip as lady-in-waiting. The Duke's comptroller, Captain Basil Brooke, and his equerry, Lieutenant Colin Buist, made up the party. The New Year of 1925 was greeted up country near Meru, and instead of the cool, dry weather that the travellers had expected, the heavens opened and the Yorks had to ford swollen rivers in their truck and lurch through the forest tracks in driving rain. One car had to be left behind, hopelessly waterlogged, while the total party of seven crowded into one small Buick. But then the weather improved and the safari itself was a model of smooth organization. After morning tea at 5.30, the Duchess and 'Lavvy' Annaly, dressed alike in bush-shirt and slacks, were ready to keep up with the men over lava-hard ground although, as a letter home reported, 'it was very hot by 11.30 and we were glad of the mules to ride home on'.

The Duchess, who had practised assiduously with her .275 Rigby rifle, was credited with a rhinoceros, buffalo, waterbuck, oryx, Grant gazelle, dik-dik, hartebeeste, steinbuck, water-hog and jackal, a list one perhaps deprecates from a viewpoint sixty years on, although she preferred to demonstrate her proficiency with a camera. Photographs were captured of a herd of elephants on the move, of ostrich and zebra, and equally of a native cook carried on a stretcher, 'perhaps a strategic malaise'. Late one night the camp was disturbed by a stampede of zebras; another night a sudden storm brought down the tents, leaving everyone in drenched confusion in the darkness. But the Duke and Duchess were young and happy and it was all adventurous fun. Then early in February they came off safari to stay with Lord and Lady Francis Scott on their farm at Rongai when news came of the tragic sudden death of their Christmas host, Sir Robert Coryndon, and the Duke had to return to Nairobi for the funeral. The safari was abandoned but in mid-February the party moved on into Uganda.

They crossed the Victoria Nyanza and saw the source of the White Nile at the Ripon Falls. In Kampala they paid their respects to the young Kabaka of Buganda and then were off again in quest of elephant in the Semiliki Valley. It was not a good time of year, the Duke had to write home, the natives were burning the elephant grass and the ash settled everywhere. But his companions were startled at the aplomb and resilience of the little Duchess. Returning to comparative civilization, 'she would appear in a quarter of an hour,' wrote Captain Brooke, 'looking as though she had never been motoring miles in a Ford over roads which in England would be considered impassable, or creeping through thorn bush and wading waist-high in a swamp'.

After being sorely tried by mosquitoes on a White Nile steamer, the travellers began the last leg of their journey on a leisurely four-weeks' cruise down the Nile on the more comfortable *Nasir*. They paused and camped wherever good sport or good photography were promised; the weather was hot and the river offered the only coolness. At Tonga they motored into the mountains to see the magnificent march past and wrestling games of 12,000 Nubian tribesmen.

At Khartoum, however, triumphal arches awaited them. It was six months since the Governor-General of the Sudan, Sir Lee Stack, had been murdered in Cairo, and the crowds found in the young Duke and Duchess an opportunity to affirm their own potent blend of nationalism and loyalty. With the massive guard about her and the night illuminations of this welcome, the Duchess must have felt that she had seen nearly everything. Even so, floods and bush-fires were capped by a blinding sandstorm stinging from the banks of the Suez Canal before the restful ten-day cruise was completed on the liner *Majola* back to Marseilles.

In the watery sunshine in London on 19 April the royal couple found crowds awaiting them at Victoria Station, but the MCC cricketers were returning on the same train and it was a matter of humorous dispute whether the throngs were greeting the Yorks or the cricket team. With the King and Queen absent on a Mediterranean cruise, it could be said that the 'little Duchess' was in any event actively first lady of the land.

At the heart of London, in the 1920s, a terrace of three or four mansions lay behind the tall iron railings of a cobbled forecourt immediately to the east of Apsley House, where the traffic from the park now pours into the whirlpool of Hyde Park Corner. The homes of Baron Rothschild, Viscount Allendale and others raised impressive stone porticoes and balconies and, at the back, beyond the parlours and conservatories, a fenced enclosure known as Hamilton Gardens provided a shrubby sanctuary for nursemaids and children. In 1924, the Duchess of York heard through the Allendales that one of the mansions, No 145 Piccadilly, was shortly to be vacated and, with her father's eye for an imposing building, she saw at once that the house offered just sufficient accommodation within its four storeys for an appropriate London home. It was also fortunately under the management of Commissioners of Crown Lands, whose spokesmen made much of 'the electric passenger lift' and an oversized drawing-room called 'the ballroom', but over two years of renovation were to elapse before the Yorks could move in.

For ten years, nevertheless, from 1926 to the Abdication débâcle of 1936, 145 Piccadilly was to be a focus of affectionate interest and respect for the monarchy second only to Buckingham Palace. The Prince of Wales' bachelor home at York House, in a secluded courtyard of St James's Palace, was less open to public view, but any passer-by glancing at 145 might catch a glimpse of one or other of the Duke and Duchess of York's many visitors. Though not the most conspicuous royal house in the capital, the solid and dignified façade became a London landmark. It might also be mentioned that it was partnered in this respect by what was formerly St George's Hospital across the way, now a prime suspect for those who still research the enigma of the Queen Mother's birthplace.

The Duke of York has often been depicted as an ineffective younger son whose true strength of character was seen only after he came to the Throne and faced the subsequent steely trials of war, but it would be nearer the truth that, in the 1920s, he mirrored much of the respect and confidence that our own era accords to Prince Philip or the Prince of Wales. Despite the handicap of his stammer, freezing at times into minutes of struggle, he returned from East Africa to open the second season of the British Empire Exhibition at Wembley, and stoically faced stadium amplifiers that gigantically mimicked his every fault. He had the guts to agree to address a Royal Academy dinner; he was a presidential speaker for the Royal Agricultural Society and president of an international congress on aeronautics. He launched into his industrial tours and boys' camps, 'my own private enterprise,' as he said of the camps where boys from public schools and factory lads met and lived together under canvas once a year, and in spite of his verbal handicap he made speeches on topics as varied as trade revival, the police force and the Washington Conference.

Many of these activities were ultimately to centre on 145 Piccadilly, but again the house faced an exasperating series of delays. During Christmas in Nairobi in 1924 the Duchess heard that her eldest sister, May, was to have another baby. It was seven years since Lady Elphinstone had added to the rising number of Elizabeth's nephews and nieces. An Elphinstone daughter, Margaret, was born on 9 June 1925, and still the plans for 145 were hardly begun. Yet perhaps an emotional link may be traced between little Margaret Elphinstone's christening and the sudden fond hopes that Elizabeth confided to her mother at Glamis that September. 'We always wanted a child to make our happiness complete,' the Duke was presently to write jubilantly to Queen Mary, and in December the Duchess precipitately cancelled a promise to view a new frieze by the water-colourist, Gerald Moira, at the Army and Navy Stores. With the workmen in occupation at 145, her pregnancy increased the urgency of finding somewhere to live in central London. Unwilling to budge from the White Lodge situation, the King and Queen apparently offered none of the suitable suites in the Palace, and the Duke arranged to rent 40 Grosvenor Square from a Mrs Hoffman. Then, more happily, Lady Strathmore suggested that the Yorks could move into 17 Bruton Street for the coming event, and Elizabeth accordingly 'went home to Mother', with her husband, after their return from Sandringham at the end of January. Great changes were looming over the King's Norfolk home, for Queen Alexandra had died there shortly before Christmas; and Queen Mary strolled around the big house with her daughter-in-law, noting the faded paper and 'such a bewildering lot of things and pictures' to rearrange. Neither woman dreamed that when the time next came for a change Elizabeth herself would be the châtelaine.

For two blissful months at Bruton Street, the Duchess returned to complete anonymity, enjoying little dinners with Elizabeth Cator and Dorothé Plunket, the Pagets, Spender-Clays and the Vyners. Queen Mary's friend, Hannah Gubbay, an exquisite needlewoman, accepted the task of making much of the new baby's layette, and it was arranged that the invaluable Alah (Mrs Knight) should transfer from the Elphinstone household to be nanny. 'I had her first,' said Elizabeth with ruthless precision, when her sister protested that this might be inconvenient for her own nine-month-old latecomer. At the Palace, Queen Mary chronicled with renewed satisfaction the private comings and goings of 'Bertie and E'.

When the question arose of any necessary protocol for a royal birth at Bruton Street, it was thought that a statutory obligation required the Home Secretary to be present or at least formally represented in the house. 'If there have to be gentlemen waiting outside my bedroom door I hope it's someone we know!' said Elizabeth, and a surprised distant kinsman of her sister-in-law Lady Glamis, a Mr Harry Boyd, found himself transferred from the Foreign Office to undertake 'a lot of waiting about' as Ceremonial Secretary of the Home Office. Through the rainy April day of Tuesday the 20th, he waited and waited indeed, although the Strathmores' hospitality made him 'feel at home'; and in the small hours of Wednesday 21 April, the baby – the future Queen Elizabeth II – was brought into the world by a Caesarean section.

'We were awakened at 4.00 am,' wrote Queen Mary, at Windsor, 'and Reggie Seymour informed us that darling Elizabeth had got a daughter at 2.40. Such a relief and joy.'

The first bulletin missed the early editions of the newspapers and so the 'wireless', still a novelty, was fittingly the medium to give the news in millions of homes: 'Her Royal Highness the Duchess of York was safely delivered of a princess at 2.40 am this morning.' The implication of danger is obvious. That afternoon Queen Mary and King George arrived at Bruton Street to be told that the young mother was alseep. 'We found Celia Strathmore there, and saw the baby,' Queen Mary wrote, and was delighted with her first grand-daughter, 'a little darling with a lovely complexion and fair hair'.

To the young mother, taking her baby in her arms, it was 'a tremendous joy', as her husband wrote the following day. 'It seems so wonderful and strange. I am so proud of Elizabeth at this moment after all that she has gone through during the last few days, and so thankful that everything happened as it should and so successfully.' Whatever the hazards, the medical bulletins spoke of normal and satisfactory progress. Four days later, the Duke of York could write to his father, 'Elizabeth and I have been thinking over names for our little girl and we should like to call her Elizabeth Alexandra Mary.'

One may speculate that if the infant had been a boy, the name David might have been in store, 'such a nice name,' the Duchess had said, and one full of subtle compliments. The young parents were worried lest the name 'Elizabeth' should be disqualified. 'Such a nice name,' the Duke reiterated to his father, 'I am sure there will be no muddle over two Elizabeths in the family and there had been no one of that name in your family for a long time. Elizabeth of York sounds so nice, too.'

The King could raise no objection. The choice of names suitably included his mother and his wife. The name 'Mary' was also in compliment to his daughter. Princess Mary had in fact been one of the first visitors at Bruton Street when the guns were still booming their salute to the newcomer, on the morning of the 21st, proving herself, as ever, a staunch and true friend. And the King had always thought Elizabeth 'a pretty name'.

Ironically, the light correspondence was no sooner concluded than a stern reality confronted the writers in the silent struggle of the General

Strike. The baby's milk depended on the distribution of churns from
behind the sentry-guarded gates of Hyde Park. Some of the residents of
Bruton Street were to be seen peeling potatoes for the volunteers who
manned the food lorries and buses. It was debated whether a policeman
should remain at the door of No 17, but the quiet thoroughfare and the
tranquil nursery in the secure house seemed far removed from the angry
centres where bus windows were smashed and the police drew batons to
charge the crowds.

Two weeks after the strike collapsed, the baby was christened in the
private chapel at Buckingham Palace, with Princess Mary among the six
sponsors. The Duchess similarly sought to compliment the King and
Queen and Lord Strathmore as grandparents, Lady Elphinstone as
aunt, and a survivor of the older generation, Queen Victoria's third son,
the old Duke of Connaught. 'Of course poor baby cried,' Queen Mary
noted. The new baby was third in succession to the Throne *for the time
being*, as *The Times* was at pains to point out. But to the new mother her
intangible distant dream of Princess Elizabeth had become realized at
last with a sweetness beyond her highest hopes.

Before the baby Elizabeth was two months old, the Prime Minister,
Stanley Bruce, of Australia jumped on the bandwagon of the Yorks'
popularity and suggested a visit to Australia in the cause of Commonwealth good relations and trade. The Prince of Wales had toured
Australia in 1920 amid delirious enthusiasm but it was twenty-five years
since King George and Queen Mary, as the then Duke and Duchess of
York, had visited Australia and New Zealand. 'Her smile is commented
on in every paper and her charm of manner is winning golden opinions,'
wrote Lady Mary Lygon, but the letter was dated 1901 and she was
praising not the Duchess of 1926 but her predecessor in the traditional
title early in the reign of bluff King Edward VII.

King George raised the project with Bertie and Elizabeth one day a
luncheon. The key date would be in May, 1927, for the opening ceremony
of the new legislative buildings in Canberra, and inevitably the Duchess
must have made quick calculations on the months of separation from her
baby. More than three years earlier, before the Yorks were married, Queen
Mary is said to have talked gravely to Elizabeth of the responsibilities of
royal status. Clearly one could not always choose for oneself nor always
seek guidance in selecting one's pattern of patronages and presidencies,
each with its roll-call of duties. Yet the outward voyage alone would take
eight weeks and such prolonged and distant travel, snipping away the

sweetest months of motherhood, had never been mentioned.

To an extraordinary degree, the Duchess of York had herself fashioned and moulded her position as a supporting player of the Throne, creating royal duties where none existed, and quickly filling a gap in public life. The monarchy was undergoing a dearth of youthful princesses. Elderly and well-meaning royal ladies were inclined to creak and fluster at public functions, and some of the duller duties were silently neglected. The Duchess of York transformed this flagging scene: her interest in an organization was of flattering intensity. Visiting the North-East she was cheered and subjected to 'endearing epithets' by industrial crowds who mysteriously regarded her as one of themselves, a Cinderella who had pulled it off. A cry was raised which had not been heard for years, 'Oh, isn't she lovely!', a phrase of endearment that has echoed since then around many royal ladies. With new confidence, she became her old free-smiling self again, and clichés about 'radiating charm, grace and dignity' soon abounded. But it was the Duchess of York who burnished the clichés by her air of a continuous personal investment in these now standard royal properties.

What the world did not at once see was her wifely power to soothe her husband's nervous eruptions of quick temper, and her effortless ingenuity in easing tension. She knew precisely what she wanted to achieve as Duchess of York. The dignity of Royal Highness or even the diminutive Ma'am was never meaningless to her, and some early resignations from the Duke's official Household suggest a measure of staff disagreement with the distaff side. The puckish Lady Helen Graham, Lady Annaly, the Countess of Cavan and Mrs Gilmour made an effective rota of ladies-in-waiting, and in 1926 Patrick Hodgson was appointed the Duke's private secretary, though in his first weeks he worked where he could, usually in a spare bedroom. In 1926, White Lodge remained the Yorks' official residence and few knew that in fact they lived at Bruton Street, with Michael and David Bowes Lyon 'dropping in', a community still of family and friends. At weekends, also, they were often to be found at Runton Old Hall, Cromer, which Elizabeth's elder brother, Pat, had rented conveniently near Sandringham.

Bertie rarely stammered in this environment. Across the breakfast table, the impediment became a mere catch in his voice. At the Palace the King found it difficult to listen to him face to face. As soon as his son's facial muscles tightened, he closed his ears to the struggle, with such rough impatience that Bertie wretchedly had to repeat every word over again. The burden of difficult speeches for the Australian – and now

New Zealand – tour was like a nightmare. The Duke had found it useless to consult speech therapists and was sinking into the secret dread of a lifelong struggle when his wife persuaded him to make 'just one more try'.

The last hope was an Australian specialist named Lionel Logue who had won wide recognition among speech consultants in London, and on the Duchess's 'ingenuous insistence', in October 1926, the Duke kept an appointment with Mr Logue in Harley Street. The therapist was confronted, as he later wrote, with 'a slim, quiet man with tired eyes and all the outward symptoms,' and the consultation proved the first step in a prolonged course of successful treatment that mitigated the handicap except when its victim was suffering from excessive fatigue. 'I can tell you what to do but only you can do it,' Mr Logue would tell patients. The Duke began the system of exercises with hope and growing confidence. Not infrequently Elizabeth accompanied him to the consulting room, just to enable her – so she pleaded – fully to understand the treatment and help with it at home. She sat beside him as if enjoying a new game, her finger beating out the tempo of phrasing when rehearsing a speech. 'I really do think you have given me a real good start,' the Duke wrote to Logue at the New Year. 'I am full of confidence.'

Elizabeth herself was much less confident of travelling halfway round the world on the battleship *Renown*. First plans had been for a liner in ordinary service, but the naval battle cruiser was chosen by the King on prestige considerations. Nor was it a consolation that Princess Elizabeth was to spend her time alternately with her Strathmore and Windsor grandparents, though always safe in Alah's hands. 'I felt very much leaving,' the Duchess wrote to Queen Mary from *Renown*. 'The baby was so sweet playing with the buttons on Bertie's uniform that it quite broke me up.' And indeed in the car from Bruton Street Bertie had to tell the chauffeur to drive around a little to give her time to dry her tears.

The patterns of a royal tour, the ceremonies of welcome, the civic festivities, the impossible sightseeing in the midst of massive crowds, the emotional pressures and fatigue of travel were privately a severe trial but equally set new royal precedents. In 1927 the Yorks' 30,000-mile journey was still so novel that three books were written about it, and the slick descriptive phrase 'The Royal Embassy' gained wide currency. Long before Elizabeth II discovered the warmth and gaiety of the Caribbean, her parents were there first, and long before the Queen began her hand-shaking walkabout marathons, her parents greeted the majority of 2,000 guests at Jamaica's Government House. It may be significant that the Duchess did not undertake another overseas tour for twelve years and indeed, as Duchess of York, she travelled abroad only once or twice more and then no farther than Oslo for a royal wedding.

Not that she was a bad sailor. The *Renown* rolled like a barrel both in the Channel and at Las Palmas and the Duchess blamed her uneasiness on her typhoid inoculations. In mid-Atlantic the voyage was clouded by sadness. Word came of the death of her bridesmaid and dear friend, Diamond Hardinge, a sorrow contrasting so poignantly with the jubilant welcome to Jamaica that she felt she could not in good conscience attend a ball on the second night and made her excuses. Again, in the Marquesas, she was crowned with a chaplet of coral, and a day or two later, on 13 February, the news had to be broken that the bandmaster of the Marines had died during the night and was to be buried at sea. The strains of Chopin's Funeral March thudded through the ship. Twenty-five years later to the day another band of the Marines would rehearse that melancholy theme in preparation for the funeral of King George VI.

In every royal progress there comes, early on, some small emblematic incident that seems to set the tenor of the whole. On the first afternoon in Auckland as they moved through the crowds, the Duchess practised a technique of her own which she later described to Mrs Eleanor Roosevelt, the simple method of picking out individuals in the crowd and really looking at them, and of paying attention also to faces at different levels in the throng. People would then say with delight 'She looked at me', infecting everyone with enthusiasm. By chance, a local Communist agitator was singled out in this way. The results were more than could be expected. 'I've done with this bloody Communism!' he announced to the Prime Minister, Mr Coates, next day. 'They're human! I was in the crowd with the wife, and one of the children waved, and I'm blest if the Duchess didn't wave back and smile right into my face, not two yards away. I'll never say a word against them again. I've done with it for good and all.'

It pleased the New Zealand press that she drew the Duke's attention to twins, and played up to the children – it was widely thought that she inspired the Duke's phrase, 'Take care of the children and the country will take care of itself'. It was an additional asset that she also proved herself a keen and adept angler. Trout-fishing in Lake Taupo, she landed a seven-pounder; and trying for schnapper in the Bay of Islands she caught seventeen out of the twenty landed in her boat. In Wellington it was a matter of equal luck that she walked towards a familiar face in the crowd and it proved, of course, to be one of the wounded soldiers whom she had known at Glamis. 'She glows and warms like sunshine,' wrote one of her excited admirers. But the unaccustomed strain of the tour told on the young Duchess and, just as the South Island was reached, she succumbed to tonsillitis and the doctors insisted that she should return to Government House, Wellington.

This verdict was a blow to the Duke, who had modestly thought all along that the crowds were really cheering his wife rather than himself. (Prince Charles today is often under a similar impression.) It was ten days before husband and wife again met and then the Duchess was on the *Renown* in stormy seas near the port of Bluff, watching the perils of the Duke's rough transit from a harbour tug to the ship. 'I was glad to be on board,' she wrote later, 'when I saw my husband being thrown – literally – from the bridge of the tug onto our quarter-deck. It looked most unpleasant, though he didn't seem to mind much!'

Throughout the long journey reassurances and photographs had constantly reached her on the progress of little Elizabeth; she had cut four teeth, it amused her to drive out in the carriage, and so on. At every stop, there were toys, gifts, even coins 'For Baby Betty's money box'. The whole Australian continent blossomed with 'Duchess hats' until every other woman wore a hat with a turned-up brim and feathers to one side.

In every respect, the tour put the final polish on the Duchess's royal graduation. She experienced nearly every occupational hazard of royalty, from the physical pressure of crowds during a broken police cordon to the unexpected peril of fire at sea. On the long haul across the Indian Ocean, when *Renown* was 1,000 miles from the nearest landfall, flames broke out in a boiler-room, and an overflow of oil made the place an inferno. Captain Sullivan gloomily considered plans for abandoning ship, and the blaze reached within a few feet of the main oil tanks before it was finally conquered.

'Did you ever realize, Ma'am, that at one time it was pretty bad?' he asked the Duchess afterwards.

'Yes, I did indeed,' she told him. 'Every hour someone came and said there was nothing to worry about, so I knew there was real trouble.'

When at last Gibraltar was reached, on 25 June, her joy at the thought of home and her baby knew no bounds. The strains of the garrison band came over the water playing 'Now thank we all our God' and the ironic laughter on deck drowned the sound of the music. A good press, however, carried the news of the Yorks' achievements ahead of them, and in London totally unexpected crowds gathered outside Buckingham Palace, cheering, singing and shouting until the radiant Duchess emerged onto the balcony, her baby daughter once again in her arms.

9. *Mother and Daughters*

On their homecoming in 1927, the Duke and Duchess of York moved at once into 145 Piccadilly. Alah and the baby had in fact been in occupation of the fourth-floor nursery for a week, being 'settled down ready for Mummy', and in the view of one friend the joy of the Palace reunion was nothing to 'the happiness of the baby's bath-time, the bidding good-night, the rapture of every minute' after six months' deprivation. On her first morning at home, the Duchess sat down to write a note of thanks to Hannah Gubbay for a surprise homecoming gift of a set of hand-made lace covered cushions in her bedroom. Elsewhere in the house several days were spent shifting furniture that seemed 'not quite contented'. The tusks of the elephant which the Duke had shot in Uganda found a place on either side of the hall, and near at hand was the gold-aproned blackamoor which at present still presides over the stair-case of the Castle of Mey.

Number 145 was the house that the Duchess regarded as the first home of her own, and her wedding gifts and furnishings soon basked in a more congenial environment than at Richmond. The décor was of its day, with the chintz and damask-covered armchairs, the silk-fringed lamps and gilt-framed mirrors, the sofa tables, bronzes, lacquered cabinets and Persian carpets. In the drawing-room, the former so-called ballroom, an immense chandelier hung from the patterned gilt ceiling, and the mouldings of the white-painted double doors were picked out Palace style in gold. But the Duchess made the atmosphere one of home; the double-glazed windows – an innovation at that time – hushed the passing traffic, and it was a house of pleasant sound. A Georgian clock chimed with a serene carillon of sixteen bells and Australian canaries sang near a garden door. Later on, the children's voices drifted down from the nursery landing, echoing beneath the round glass dome.

With an abiding tranquillity amid the activities of public and private life, 145 remained the Yorks' London home for nearly ten years. The couple could hardly imagine circumstances that might force them to leave, although the latent possibilities of the future came alarmingly nearer in 1928. King George V's grave illness with an infected lung in that year brought dynastic reminders that the Prince of Wales, who had been deeply in love for ten years with Mrs Dudley Ward, might never marry and could ascend the throne a bachelor. In that event, the Duchess anxiously realized, her little daughter would be second in line to the Crown. By March 1929, the King was convalescent, but the contingencies still lingered in the public mind. The Duke of York was appointed to serve as Lord High Commissioner to the General Assembly of the Church of Scotland, the first time in three centuries that a member of the Royal Family had been invited to that office, and the Yorks had a lyrical welcome to Edinburgh. 'The only thing I regret is that we have not got Lilibet here,' the Duchess wrote to Queen Mary. 'Not that they would have seen her, but they would have liked to feel she was here. It almost frightens me that the people should love her so much. I suppose that it is a good thing and I hope that she will be worthy of it, poor little darling.'

It appealed whole-heartedly to the Scots that 'Elizabeth of Glamis' should be lodged in state in the royal palace of Holyrood-house. True, there were whiffs of malt from a nearby brewery whenever the windows were opened, and the pantry betrayed a deficiency of glass and linen. But the citizens of Edinburgh delighted in the Duke and Duchess's idea of a children's garden-party so that the 'very young people' could meet them; and one suspects that the Duchess was unaware of her own personal popularity, so taken up was she with the pleasure and pride of her husband's success.

With the King's recovery, the Yorks were able to go to Norway for the wedding of Crown Prince Olav to Princess Martha of Sweden, while Lilibet stayed with her grandfather at Bognor to help cheer him up. 'G delighted to see her,' wrote Queen Mary. 'I played with Lilibet making sand-pies!' The ceremonies in Oslo, incidentally, could be merrily viewed as the hat-trick in an agreeable chain of marriage ceremonies. On 2 February 1928, the Yorks saw Michael Bowes-Lyon married at St George's, Hanover Square, to Elizabeth Cator, the match between her elder brother and her school-friend on which Elizabeth had so long set her heart. There was much family chaff that her younger brother – the only unmarried one – would be next, and on 6 February, 1929 David married the girl of his heart, Rachel Spender Clay, the 'nearest convenient date to a year and a day later'.

When the 1930s dawned, the Duchess of York surely wondered – like her mother thirty years earlier – what the new decade had in store. Within the first week of the New Year a visit to Rome was scheduled for the wedding of Crown Prince Umberto of Italy and Princess Marie José of Belgium, but Elizabeth was laid low by her old adversary, bronchitis, and Bertie had to go alone. In her company he might have found the frantic confusion of the wedding a glorious rag. Without her he could hardly contain his irritability. But on his return his wife confided the wonderful news that she was expecting another baby. Just as Lilibet had so nearly arrived for her parents' third wedding anniversary so it seemed that the newcomer 'might be on time for his mother's thirtieth birthday.'

The Yorks appear to have stumbled at once into the rash supposition that the infant would be a boy. On simple averages the expectation was reasonable, since boys had preponderated in both the Windsor and Bowes-Lyon families. The Duchess moreover rapidly made up her mind that her son should be born under her father's roof at Glamis Castle.

In May, the King evidently agreed to these Scottish anticipations, and husband and wife made light of transporting officials and doctors to Scotland. Old Lady Airlie offered to put people up, and the gynaecologist, Neon Reynolds, leapt at the opportunity of combining his professional services with his passion for fishing and shooting. Only Mr Boyd of the Home Office was alarmed lest anything should be conducted in 'an irregular hole and corner way', as he put it, and he worried so much on that score that he even showed the Duchess a book with passages heavily underscored in red ink concerning the birth of the son of James II and the rumours that a changeling had been substituted in the bedroom, concealed in a warming pan. It only showed, said Mr Boyd, how careful one had to be in dealing with any infant born in the Succession.

The Duchess, however, took her pregnancy calmly, with weekends at St Paul's Walden Bury, a visit to old Princess Victoria at Coppins and sociable occasions with her brother, 'the other David', who in fact was presented by his wife Rachel with a baby daughter on his birthday, 2 May. Despite all the hopes of sex and timing Princess Margaret was, of course, unpunctually born at Glamis on 21 August, making her appearance in the aftermath of a sunset so stormy and splendid that it set the Home Secretary, Mr Clynes, quoting poetry aloud during his wild dash by car to Glamis from Airlie Castle. The anticipated prince was a princess, and the event found the Yorks so unprepared that they had no girl's name in readiness. A week of discussion and uncertainty ensued before the young mother wrote to Queen Mary on 27 August, 'I am very anxious to call her Ann Margaret, as I think that Ann of York sounds pretty and Elizabeth and Ann go so well together. I wonder what you think? Lots of people have suggested Margaret, but it has no family links really on either side.' Three days later, a troubled Queen Mary visited Glamis – 'E looking very well and the baby a darling' – and broke the surprising news that the King thought the name Ann would not do.

Intensely disappointed, the parents had no option but to observe the King's wishes, but it was 6 September before the Duchess managed to couch another letter to Queen Mary in words sufficiently precise and firm, 'Bertie and I have decided now to call our little daughter Margaret Rose, instead of Ann, as Papa does not like Ann – I hope that you like it. I think that it is very pretty together.' The baby protested loudly at her christening in the private chapel of Buckingham Palace in October. The godparents included not only the two Davids – the Prince of Wales and David Bowes Lyon – but also Princess Ingrid of Sweden, Lady Rose Leveson-Gower and the King's sister, Princess Victoria, a spinster who had moped for years after being forbidden to marry the man she loved, a commoner.*

Much later, the Duchess heard with amusement that during late August and September a phenomenal number of girl babies were registered by their surnames only, so anxious were young parents to know the name of the royal baby before christening their offspring.

The Yorks were unaware that the arrival of Princess Margaret heralded the six most settled years of their lives. A serious plan developed indeed for the Duke of York to go to Ottawa as the next 'GG', or Governor-General. In retrospect one realizes that it would have been a highly popular move if the Yorks had resided in Canada however briefly, with their two little girls. The King's advisers, Sir Clive Wigram and Lord Stamfordham, both approved the prospect, but much to the Duchess's relief it was disallowed by Mr J. H. Thomas, the Dominions Secretary of State in the Labour Cabinet. With a sense of reprieve the Duke resumed his hunting with the Pytchley that winter and the Duchess

---

* She fell in love with a member of the Baring family, and later with her father's assistant secretary, Sir Arthur Davidson, but both matches were denied her.

presided happily in her own nursery world with Alah and Bobo (Miss Margaret Macdonald, then an under-nursemaid in the household). The housekeeping at 145 was so personal that on a free afternoon the Duchess would sometimes descend to the basement kitchen to bake baps and scones with another MacDonald, the cook. The weekends, too, brought simple pleasures. The Prince of Wales had begun to plan his new garden at Fort Belvedere on the southern outskirts of Windsor Great Park and Saturday afternoons were often spent in his company hacking at a jungle of saplings and brambles. The sharp billhooks and hatchets caused the Duchess great misgivings and the toilers were besieged with her cries of 'Do be careful! Darling, do mind!'

The 'grace-and-favour' enjoyed by the King's eldest son at Fort Belvedere could not long be withheld from Bertie. The Duke and Duchess of York visited Paris together in July 1931, primarily to see the Colonial Exhibition, but on returning they, too, began house-hunting in the neighbourhood of Windsor and Ascot. It happened that Mrs Fetherstonhaugh, the widow of King George V's racing manager, had but recently vacated the Royal Lodge, Windsor, far deeper within the park than the Fort and hidden within a fenced enclosure of oak coppice and dense yew hedges. King George IV had used the Lodge as a private bower for his friendship with Lady Conyngham. At his command Nash had embellished it with an octagonal conservatory, and Jeffry Wyatt-ville had added a lofty Gothic saloon. Within this thatch-roofed folly, King William and Queen Adelaide subsequently enjoyed picnics and Queen Adelaide draped the conservatory inside with chintz to form a shady marquee. Various tenants had made later alterations and additions. The house had been single-storeyed until Sir Arthur Ellis, Edward VII's chief equerry, added an upper floor and the ultimate result was unsightly.

The Duke and Duchess had to traverse a long glass greenhouse to reach the front door and the best room in the house, the Wyattville saloon, had been divided into three small rooms with ceilings and skirtings that showed dampness. The dilapidated exterior was of a dingy and undistinguished hue. But the Duchess envied the privacy and solitude of the grounds and saw the possibilities of restoring and improving the house itself. 'Having seen it I think it will suit us admirably,' the Duke reported guardedly to the King. Whereupon the King promptly replied, 'I am so pleased to hear that both you and Elizabeth liked the Royal Lodge and would like to live there . . .'

Royal Lodge, as it became known, was to become the York's true family home, and has remained the Queen Mother's country home ever since. The alterations and improvements which she desired were far-reaching and had to be postponed by the 1931 financial crisis. Economy and restriction fell on the nation; the King drastically pruned his Civil List and imposed similar cuts on every member of his family, and the Duke sold the six horses of his hunting stable, no great sacrifice, for he had realized that hunting deprived him of time with his family. The rehabilitation of the grounds of Royal Lodge henceforth became the Yorks' foremost spare-time interest. The clearance of the weeds and scrub of Fort Belvedere was repeated with different emphasis. In the house the saloon was cleared of its internal partition walls and the original splendid proportions restored. With a new wing to replace the conservatory and the drab stucco of the house freshly washed in a shade of pale pink rose, Royal Lodge immediately assumed a pristine air. To the Duchess the presence of a small estate chapel nearly opposite the house seemed particularly homely and welcoming. The family practice of morning prayers was long since discontinued, but there were few times in her life when she missed Sunday morning service, and it was like old times to have a family chapel of her own.

It was pleasant, too, to pop over to the Fort, without straining her brother-in-law's hospitality. One wintry afternoon when the lake in Windsor Great Park, Virginia Water, was frozen over, the three royal brothers, David, Bertie and George of Kent, suggested skating. The Duchess protested that she had never skated before but boots were unceremoniously thrust on her feet, kitchen chairs provided for support, and the Duchess and David's current lady, Thelma Furness, were off on their awkward glides and swoops in gales of laughter. 'The lovely face of the Duchess, her superb colouring heightened by the cold, her eyes wrinkled with the sense of fun never far below the surface, made a picture I shall never forget,' Lady Furness paid her tribute.

For three or four years a steady traffic of fun and companionship went back and forth between the Fort and the Lodge. David and his sophisticates presumably found a 'union of opposites', with Bertie and Elizabeth steeped in their own simple but unstodgy family life. Thelma Furness recollected a day when a pack of unbreakable plastic records arrived at the Fort, a minor marvel when records were usually made of fragile shellac wax. 'Let's see if they really are unbreakable. Come on, David!' cried Bertie, and began a game of skimming the discs across the terrace, where they landed unshattered. Then Bertie devised a boomerang throw, 'the brothers roared with laughter, and had us ducking and dodging like rabbits until we all fled and the game was then hilariously pursued in the drawing room; where a treasured lamp was knocked over and the host called a halt'.

A 1930s snapshot shows a group at the Fort swimming-pool: Mrs Gilmour, Lord Louis Mountbatten, the Duke of York, Prince Gustav Adolf of Sweden, the Princesses Ingrid of Norway and Sybilla of Sweden, and Lady Furness, all in swimsuits. The Duchess of York alone sits smiling in summer frock, with floppy felt hat and pearls. She tolerantly accepted the Prince of Wales' girl-friends in that pre-Simpson era, good-naturedly taking them at their own valuation. The Fort hospitality was returned with Friday evening parties at the Lodge, where Bertie's younger brother, Harry, the Duke of Gloucester, also commenced his courtship of Lady Alice Montague-Douglas-Scott with his hostess's deft encouragement. Under the blossoming and maturing of his life at Royal Lodge, Bertie, too, was discovering himself. He was more surely master of his environment than ever before, yet never ceased to accord his wife the credit for their happiness and would publicly laud 'the strength and comfort which I have always found in my home'.

All three royal brothers – Wales, Gloucester and Kent – envied Bertie the even tenor of his married life, his security in his private realm, as the Duke of Windsor later sadly said, within 'this closely knit fabric of family ties'. During tea in the octagon room, the customary living-room of the Lodge, the talk turned one day towards marriage and the Yorks teased the handsome Prince George who was never short of girls, with 'you should try it'. Within the year he was engaged to Princess Marina, of whom Queen Mary commented to Lady Airlie, 'No bread-and-butter miss will be of any help to Georgie, but this girl will be.'

Early in 1932 the Duchess of York was puzzling over the emerging problem of Lilibet's education when her sister Rose at Rosyth recommended a young governess, fresh from training college, who had been coaching her daughter. The Yorks hoped to find someone young and active who could enjoy playing and exercising with their children and were impressed on hearing that Marion Crawford performed prodigies of walking. They drove over from Glamis to meet her and for the first time Miss Crawford met 'that long appraising stare' of the little Duchess of York. 'She had the nicest, easiest, most friendly of manners and a merry laugh,' wrote the governess. 'There was nothing alarmingly fashionable about her. She sat on the window ledge. The blue of her dress exactly matched the blue of her eyes. My whole impression was of someone small and quite perfect.'

'Why not come for a month and see how you like us and how we like you?' wrote the Duchess a week or two later.

Long afterwards, when she had married and concluded her teaching, Miss Crawford completed – or collaborated in writing – an account of her fifteen years with the Royal Family, and the sheen of feminine journalism imposed on her memoirs created the word 'Crawfie-ism'. If on first meeting the Yorks she found it 'obvious that they were devoted to each other and very much in love', this after nine years of marriage, she can hardly be held guilty of sentiment. 'Crawfie', in retrospect has given us a valuable record of royal domesticity.

To her we owe the authentic picture of the children's high jinks every morning in their parents' bedroom 'no matter how busy the day, how early the start'; the Duchess's games of rummy and racing demon with her daughters every evening from five till six; the hilarious splashing of bath-time; the Duke playing hopscotch on the gravel paths of Hamilton Gardens behind 145 'with great precision of footwork'; and the winter afternoons when the children were learning to dance reels and the Duke and Duchess occasionally joined in. It seemed as if Elizabeth was trying to repeat her own carefree and affectionate childhood, and even to heighten that golden happiness. As with her own mother, she taught Princess Elizabeth to read, acquainted her with the psalms and collects of the old Scottish paraphrased Prayer Book and seemed resolved that rules and discipline should be left to others. If Lady Strathmore had been unable to relinquish authority to governesses, the Duchess evidently made good this failing. 'No one ever had employers who interfered so little,' said Miss Crawford. The Duchess, she found, left much to her judgment and seemed unconcerned with higher education.

Indeed the Duchess spent those fleeting years of her early thirties in a placid dream. In royal duties she never faltered, in the incessant correspondence with her patronages, her charities and societies and the resulting engagements, in the visits with her husband to Wales and Plymouth, Southwold (for his annual boys' camp) and the Midlands. She flew for the first time in 1935, on a visit with him to Brussels. At No 145, the morning interlude with the children was followed by the desk hours with Helen Graham or Mrs Bowlby, Harold Campbell, now technically the Duke of York's private secretary, or Jimmy Cole, who managed the household business and accounts. A sea of photographs, yellowing in the files, enshrines the public activities, but thousands of negatives were destroyed during the blitz, and informal day-to-day records are shrinking fast. In the evenings, the Duke and Duchess sometimes went out, to Ciro's or the Mayfair Club, but more often they sat at home, on either side of the fireplace at No 145, the Duke plying a needle – he made a dozen chair covers in petit point for Royal Lodge – the Duchess perhaps with a book, sometimes at the piano, occasionally playing patience. If the business of tickets were arranged, they could slip out by a back gate into Hyde Park and stroll unrecognized in the dusk to the cinema at Marble Arch.

The Duchess was worried about her mother's health. With her own larger domestic staff – Alah, Bobo and Crawfie for the children alone – the summer visits to Glamis Castle became briefer. Summer holidays were more frequently spent at Birkhall on the Balmoral estate. Birkhall is a stone-built stuccoed Scottish house of 1715, in a dell to the north of Loch Muick. Hospitably extended, it remained the Queen Mother's Balmoral home, with guests constantly coming and going under the broad pine-log porch. In the 1930s it was a paradise of superb Deeside views, and of moorland air tinged with woodsmoke; of Landseers and pinewood furniture, oil lamps and candlelight. Royal Lodge, too, was a haven of quiet comfort, improving each year in domestic perfection. The Duke and Duchess preferred a bedroom suite at garden level, while the children and guests had their rooms upstairs. Edging the terrace, the Duchess caused an elaborate ornamental screen fence to be erected, ensuring unspoiled seclusion. She did not mind taking her children along with her on suitable public engagements and trained them for their public role from an early age. But the terrace fence of Royal Lodge, later replaced by stonework, was a symbol of the absolute reticence of their private lives.

The ideal pattern of the Yorks' family life nevertheless became widely known to the public. 'The home at the heart of the Empire' was one journalistic phrase attaching to No 145, and a little knot of sightseers usually clustered near the pavement railings, as if waiting might evoke some magic at the shrine. As the red London buses rumbled past Hamilton Gardens, top deck passengers craned for a glimpse of 'the little Princesses' at play in the sooty laurels and rhododendrons. Focusing a devoted attention on the Yorks, the public knew nothing of the increasing devotion of the Prince of Wales to a Mrs Ernest Simpson.

On 6 May 1935, King George V and Queen Mary celebrated the Silver Jubilee of their reign. With London full of royalties and Commonwealth premiers, it was a phase fraught with public and more personal entertainment responsibilities for the Duchess of York, herself tangibly a recipient of the tremendous upsurge of loyalty. 'The Duchess was so charming and gracious, the Princesses much interested and waving,' enthused Chips Channon, looking down on the royal procession to St Paul's. The Yorks then represented the King at the pageantry in Edinburgh, and the Duchess and Princess Elizabeth shared in the state drives to the outer regions of London. 'I suppose you think those flags are hung out for you?' said the King jovially one afternoon. 'Let me tell you,' with his hand on his heart, 'they're all for *me*!' At the same time, with a more realistic private appraisal, the King recognized that at the Ascot festivities and Court balls of the year, the little Duchess was the Queen's right hand. He spoke admiringly of her one day in confidences with his old friend, Lady Algy Gordon-Lennox, and added passionately, 'I pray to God that my eldest son will never marry and that nothing will come between Bertie and Lilibet and the throne.'

In November, his third son, Henry of Gloucester, was married to Lady Alice Montague-Douglas-Scott, with Lilibet and Margaret looking 'charming . . . too sweet' among the bridesmaids. In December, in the contrast of events, the King's sister, Princess Victoria, died and the Duchess of York sorrowed greatly for the old lady, who had so often been a trenchant and leg-pulling guest with the King and Queen at Royal Lodge dinner parties. Her sorrowing sympathy for the King, coupled with the fog and chill of the funeral at Windsor, indeed reduced her own spirits to a low ebb and a few days later she fell ill herself with influenza. She seldom went through a winter without a cold, a chill or bronchitis, and some said to her annoyance that it was due to the mist and damp of the Thames Valley, with the Lodge itself in a low-lying frost-trap. But Elizabeth rarely took her ills seriously. It was usually her custom to retire to bed with her own home-made specific. 'What you MUST do is to have a raw egg beaten up well in a little coffee or port or sherry at 11 o'clock every morning,' she once wrote to Crawfie, when the governess went down with flu during a summer holiday. 'It is the most amazing pick-me-up, and if the egg is well-beaten and all those nasty little strings removed, it merely tastes like creamy coffee. Tell your mother this and swallow it like a good patient.' The sovereign remedy nevertheless was ineffective against flu that developed into pneumonia, and the children went to Sandringham with their grandparents while the Duchess remained ill in bed at Royal Lodge.

Christmas dinner was an invalid meal on a tray in a clinical atmosphere of doctors and nurses, but by then she had turned the corner,
and her husband was able to keep her company in her sickroom. It was
the first Christmas they had ever spent alone together, their solitude
and companionship a curious foreshadowing of the future.

A favourable bulletin on the Duchess was not issued until 30
December and in the New Year of 1936 her convalescence was slow. On
16 January, however, a message from Queen Mary said that the King
was unwell and added that she would like Bertie to help with the house-
party. The Duke accordingly hastened to Sandringham, but on
returning three days later he had to break the news to his wife that the
King was gravely ill and might not live. Then he was hurriedly recalled
to Sandringham and, alone and anxious at the Lodge with Lady Helen
Graham, the Duchess heard the solemnly repeated wireless
announcements that the King's life was moving peacefully to its close.
Shortly after midnight the telephone rang. It was her husband to tell
her that the King was dead and, in the morning, the Duchess shook off
her illness to hurry to Queen Mary's side and console her with the
thought that 'his rest came so quietly'.

'No man deserved rest more than he,' she later wrote to her doctor,
Lord Dawson of Penn. 'He was getting so tired, and though occasionally he was his old delightful self, those moments seemed to be getting more rare. I miss him dreadfully. In all the twelve years of having
me as a daughter-in-law he never spoke one unkind or abrupt word to
me, and was always ready to listen and give advice on one's own silly
little affairs. He was so kind, and so *dependable*, don't you think so?'

10. *The Abdication Incident*

The King was dead. In the traditional phrase, 'Long Live the King' . . . the new King Edward VIII. 'David and Bertie went to London for the Proclamation,' Queen Mary noted, and that evening the Duchess of York heard from her husband the surprising fact that Mrs Wallis Simpson had also joined them, watching the ceremony from a window at St James's Palace. She knew, too, of her brother-in-law's 'frantic and unreasonable grief' at Sandringham which, according to Lady Hardinge, 'far exceeded that of his mother and three brothers'. Making every allowance for his over-wrought emotions, she felt sorry for him and could visualize and share the intense nervous strain implicit in becoming King: it was deeply dismaying to realize that her husband was now heir apparent to the Crown.

She clearly foresaw the extra burden both for Bertie and herself that lay ahead. Since David was unmarried, there might be additional feminine obligations to share with Queen Mary. It has become conventional to speak of royal duties. One might rather refer to royal responsibilities, the essays in service which royal ladies undertake by voluntary adoption. Both the Duke and Duchess of York first faced the new era in a spirit of optimism and family co-operation. Within three weeks of his reign, the new King unexpectedly asked his brother to provide a report on how the expenses of Sandringham might be reduced, and it shocked the Duchess that he should think of financial affairs so soon. But with an experienced friend, Lord Radnor, Bertie bent his head to the task and in two weeks produced a highly practical report, for which the new King gave him no encouraging appreciation.

The doctors considered that the east winds of Norfolk in March would be too chill for the Duchess's deferred yet still necessary convalescence, and in the softer clime of Eastbourne she in turn faced a backlog of correspondence.

'I am really very well now,' she wrote to Lord Dawson on 9 March. 'I am only suffering, I think, from the effects of a family break-up, which always happens when the head of a family goes. Outwardly one's life goes on the same, yet everything is different, especially mentally and spiritually. I don't know if it is the result of being ill but I mind things that I don't like more than before. But it will be very good for me to pull myself together and try to collect a little will power. . .'

What was it, then, that she *minded more*? She deeply minded hearing of the King holding a successful 'do' at Fort Belvedere, not four weeks after his father's death, and marching around the table playing his bagpipes. She minded hearing of the King running to fetch Mrs Simpson's nail-file, 'unchanged in manners and love', as Lady Diana Cooper remarked. On every count, religious and ethical, the Duchess of York found herself sharing Queen Mary's disapproval of 'the heightened complications' of the King's private life. On returning to London, she began helping her mother-in-law in planning her impending move to Marlborough House, and in those intimate hours together, sorting out possessions and going through old things, Queen Mary confessed – as she had to Lady Airlie – her concern, even her fear, of being asked to receive Mrs Simpson and her unreadiness to discuss the affair with the King. 'I don't want to give the impression of interfering in his private life. My great hope is that violent infatuations usually wear off.'

Compassionate and charitable as she was, Elizabeth also minded the defiance of old institutions in the King's inability or unwillingness to attend morning service at church. It did not matter that Mrs Simpson had been divorced, but her open association with the King was now becoming known to an ever-widening circle, and it mattered that she was still a married woman, with or without a complaisant husband. 'He gives her the most beautiful jewels,' said Queen Mary, apropos the King. A mere man could notice those startling adornments, 'not only her sparkling talk but also her sparkling jewels', as Sir Samuel Hoare testified. And perhaps above all it mattered to the Yorks that the ready recipient of these favours should be pushed uninvited into their private lives.

The Duchess of Windsor claims in her memoirs to have 'seen the Duchess of York on several occasions at the Fort and in London at York House,' but the meetings evidently produced no conversation of worthy record. Then one weekend that spring, with merely a preliminary phone-call proposing that Bertie might like to see his new American station wagon, the King unexpectedly brought a group of friends over to Royal Lodge to tea. The Yorks met them at the door, and found themselves greeting Mrs Simpson. 'The justly famous charm was highly evident,' writes the Duchess of Windsor, with a miaow, and Miss Crawford, who was present with Lilibet, was aware of the uncomfortable atmosphere. 'A smart, attractive woman already middle-aged, entirely at her ease, rather too much so. She had a distinctly proprietary way of speaking to the new King. I remember she drew him to the window and suggested how certain trees might be moved and a part of a hill taken away to improve the view. I have never admired the Duke and Duchess (of York) more than on that afternoon. They made the best of this awkward occasion and gave no sign whatever of their feelings.'

The crisp-spoken gaucheries would have caused embarrassment in any English home, not least in Royal Lodge, leased to the Yorks as it was by 'His Majesty's grace and favour'. The visitor was nevertheless left with the indelible certainty 'that while the Duke of York was sold on the American station wagon, the Duchess was not sold on the King's other American interest'. The strained atmosphere was equally obvious to a nine-year-old child. 'Crawfie, who *is* she?' Lilibet asked, as soon as they were out of the room. The governess cannot remember her answer.

Shortly afterwards, the King gave a dinner-party for Mr Baldwin as Prime Minister, and the *Court Circular*, that official bulletin of royal activities, concluded the impressive guest list with the words 'and Mr and Mrs Simpson'. As Compton Mackenzie suggested, it was a breakwater to reduce the scandal. But as the cessation of Court mourning approached, the King staged another dinner-party at which, the *Court Circular* stated, the Duke and Duchess of York were present. There were five other married couples, three gentlemen without their wives, including Winston Churchill, the bachelor Philip Sassoon, and the happily married Sir David Margesson, three other ladies, and Mrs Simpson, the obvious partner of the King. According to Lady Hardinge, who was there with her husband, Churchill mischievously introduced George IV and Mrs Fitzherbert into the conversation. The Duchess of York interposed, 'But that was a very long time ago.' Once again she had reason to wonder whether Bertie and herself had been invited to add an additional gloss of respectability to the King's amours.

At the same time, one must remember that the chronicles through the years, the books, films and plays, the documented records and the surmise have intensely dramatized the situation, often beyond a pitch of reality, until the few survivors can rightly claim it was not like that at all. King George V in the last months of his life told Archbishop Lang that he 'feared this affair much more serious than the others', and he warned Mr Baldwin, 'after I am dead the boy will ruin himself in twelve months'. These statements were unknown at the time to the Duke and Duchess of York. The family still followed Queen Mary's hope that the King's infatuation would wear off, rather like the repercussions of Mussolini's attack upon Abyssinia, Hitler's coup in the Rhineland and other unpleasant but inescapable facts. It was equally unthinkable to the Duchess and Queen Mary alike that, in the Queen's phrase, the lady 'with two husbands living' could legally marry the King, and the discreet silence preserved for months by the British press served to foster an illusion that all would come right. At Royal Lodge, throughout these plans and efforts, the Yorks gardened contentedly, and the early summer saw the completion of a glade created from former wilderness, clearly inspired by the green slopes of St Paul's Walden Bury, complete to a copy of the sculpture of Charity. If rain forbade gardening, the Duke set up a drawing-board in his office against any spare moments and he sketched the next stage in the remodelling of the Lodge itself, a proposed guest-wing facing the forecourt which would mask the unsightly domestic ramifications of the saloon. He could pencil draft sketches like an architect and, as one of his architects has drily said, he could read a plan like a builder.

It was in the same lulling mood that the Duke had written to Lady Stair in 'the language of rhododendrons', a letter now well-known to garden-lovers: 'I did so enjoy my visit and you gave me such an Agaepetum (delightful) time. My wife is miserable at having missed the two Formosum (beautiful) days. . . I am glad to tell you she is much better, though I found her looking Microleucrum (small and white). . . . Nice of you to say I deputized well for her but I feel she could have done everything much better, as she has the Agastum (charming) way of Charidotes (giving joy). . . .' Nothing marred the serenity. Woodsmoke often hung on the air, and tractors laden with wire-netting occasionally approached the Lodge, only to veer left and south towards the area where reclaimed marshland was contributing to the lakes and bowers of the newly-formed Savill Gardens.

As late as August 1936, when the King was cruising the Adriatic with Mrs Simpson and others in the yacht *Nahlin*, the evidence is that the Yorks, perturbed as they were by the King's rash indiscretion, still foresaw no insoluble problem which could not be settled within established patterns. If Churchill at the July dinner spoke openly of George IV and Mrs Fitzherbert, Mrs Simpson's intentions of divorcing her husband were then known and the possibility of a morganatic marriage, that comforting chimera, trembled on the air. Whatever happened, it remained unimaginable that the Throne itself could be shaken or forsaken.

While the King was sailing the Mediterranean, the Duke and Duchess of York went to Birkhall as usual and sympathetically invited the Archbishop of Canterbury, Dr Lang, to visit them there. 'A delightful visit,' the Archbishop recorded. 'They were kindness itself. The old house is full of charm and the Duchess has done much with the garden. . . .' But most satisfying of all, the Duchess warmly urged him that he must come again 'so that the links with Balmoral may not be wholly broken'. The fragility of the old ties became all too clear when the Duke discovered by accident that old retainers at Balmoral had been dismissed and old agreements curtly ended without his knowledge. 'David only told me what he had done after it was all over, which I might say made me rather sad,' he wrote to Queen Mary. 'He arranged it all with the official people. I never saw him alone for an instant.'

As early as June, the Duke and Duchess of York had undertaken to open a new Aberdeen hospital on behalf of the King, and the day of the opening ceremony saw the occasion when the King was recognized by many Deeside people at Ballater Station, waiting to welcome Mrs Simpson. The many stories of Mrs Simpson playing hostess at Balmoral are apparently unsupported by any reliable documentation. The Duke of Windsor has put on record that 'naturally Wallis (Mrs Simpson) was included in the party. . . . None of my guests, except brother George and his wife Marina, had ever been to Balmoral. . . . I decided to confine my first house-party to a number of friends to whom I was indebted for hospitality'. The historian, Robert Sencourt, asserts that when the Yorks were invited to dinner at the Castle and found that Mrs Simpson received them, the Duchess (and evidently the Duke) left as soon as they conveniently could. This conflicts with a statement authorized by the Queen Mother that she and her husband were worried and saddened by the overseas whispers and deeply sorry for the King. 'They saw their only duty to lie in showing a serene and confident face in public . . .' said a royal confidante. But on returning to London in October they were plunged into sombre anxiety when the King's private secretary, Major Alec Hardinge – that old friend, brother of Diamond – called at 145 Piccadilly to report a new development. After an interview with the Prime Minister, the King had hinted for the first time of his determination to marry Mrs Simpson come what may.

Elizabeth was firmly persuaded that 'David' would be open to reason. Not to the logical, legalistic contentions of his Ministers, perhaps, nor the pleas of his mother in her seventieth year, but the views of his family contemporaries and especially his nearest brother on whom the consequences of his actions must fall. Getting to see David was very difficult. 'When one does he wants to talk of other matters,' Bertie reported. 'It is all so worrying and I feel we all live a life of conjecture, never knowing what will happen. . .'

On another plane, the Duchess worried about the effect of the tense and anxious atmosphere on her children, and among other innovations the two princesses began swimming lessons at the Bath Club, 'a great diversion that helped to take our minds off the gathering crowds', according to Miss Crawford. The Duchess had come to accept that her elder daughter might one day be Queen; and she could philosophically face the prospect that, in some far distant future, if anything happened to her brother-in-law and he remained childless, her husband might first come to the throne. These were the normal accepted contingencies of life. Only that summer, while at home at 145, she had been alarmed at reports on an assassination attempt while Bertie was at a ceremony with the King in Hyde Park: it turned out that an unnerved man had hurled a loaded revolver between the King and her husband as they rode down Constitution Hill. There were always such risks but, with the approach of autumn, the possibility that the King could voluntarily relinquish his inheritance and thrust the burden of kingship on his younger brother continued to seem inconceivable. 'The Sovereign is not responsible to himself alone,' said Queen Mary, and her steadfast certainty of the obligations of a monarch reassured her daughter-in-law that all might yet be well.

Ultimately, the Duchess and her husband gave much thought to framing a letter to the King in a persuasive attempt to cause him to reconsider the situation. 'Bertie had most at stake,' wrote the Duke of Windsor in his defensive memoirs. 'He wrote that he longed for me to be happy, adding that he of all people should be able to understand my feelings; he was sure that whatever I decided would be in the best interests of the country and the Empire.'

November came and at the end of the month the Yorks had to travel to Edinburgh, where the Duchess was to receive the freedom of that ancient capital and the Duke was to be installed as the Grand Master Mason of Scotland. So far, the media had maintained their policy of silence, the British people were unaware of the inner turmoil of the

Royal Family, and the Duchess had never sustained her husband's spirits or fulfilled her own role more brilliantly than when they faced the tumultuous cheers of the Scots. King George VI's biographer, Sir John Wheeler-Bennett, has mentioned a letter to Queen Mary in the Royal Archives in which 'a member of the Royal Family expresses the hope that her high view of the obligations of Monarchy will prevail'.

'Thank God that we have all got you as a central point,' the writer added, 'because without that point it (the family) might easily disintegrate.' One discerns internal evidence that the author of the letter was the Duchess of York herself. In her humility, she failed to see that in the continuous traditions of the Crown, her husband and herself were fast becoming the central strong point against the shock and strain. On 3 December, as their train drew into London, they were both surprised and horrified as they saw the newspaper placards blazoned with the words, 'The King's Marriage'. So the storm had broken and the British peoples throughout the world were to shake with controversy – for or against the King, the Head of the Church of England, in his violation of the Christian ethic that marriage is indissoluble until death. Squarely in the minds of millions of his subjects was the issue: could the King accept the consecration of the Coronation with a marriage partner who had twice figured in the divorce court?

We come now to the more significant gaps in the personal record of the Duchess of York, the omissions that remain so enigmatic fifty years later. On 16 November, for instance, the King went to dinner with Queen Mary, bent upon telling her of his irrevocable determination to marry Mrs Simpson. With his mother that evening he found his sister, Princess Mary, and his sister-in-law, the Duchess of Gloucester. In his memoirs, the Duke of Windsor has described precisely how his sister-in-law reacted to the situation. 'Never loquacious, she uttered not a word. When at last we got up to leave the table she eagerly seized upon the interruption to protest that she was extremely tired and ask that she be excused.' There is nothing here to block or restrain in the memory, no factors too hostile or unendurable to be expressed. On the more salient occasion of 3 December, Queen Mary asked the King to look in at Marlborough House 'especially as I have not seen you for ten days'. The King drove over and there found the Duke and Duchess of York, who had been dining with his mother. The Duke recorded in a memoranda, 'David said to Queen Mary that he could not live alone as King and must marry. . .'

But was this all? The Duke of Windsor records in his memoirs that he explained to his mother, 'I have no desire to bring you and the family into all this. This is something I must handle alone.' In describing this same exhausting day, he recalls word for word a conversation with Mrs Simpson's aunt and the talks with his legal advisers. Yet of the Duchess of York, there is, one might echo, 'not a word'. If she had made her excuses, as the Duchess of Gloucester had done, one might reasonably expect a passing mention of her presence. If she had no word to say to the brother-in-law who had become so unapproachable, it would have been explicable, though out of key with her spontaneity of character. In a necessarily personal interpretation, one can believe that the Duchess had something to say, and could no longer restrain what had to be said.

Of this conversation with Queen Mary on 16 November, the Duke of Windsor has written, 'The word "duty" fell between us. But there could be no question of my shirking my duty.' Another thought had also dropped into the King's mind, that his younger brother was better fitted by traits of contentment and acceptance to be King. 'I believe they would like someone more like my father,' he had told Walter Monckton. 'Well, there is my brother Bertie. . .'

It is surely valid to suppose that something like this argument was advanced in the Duchess of York's hearing and that frayed nerves caused her to speak in outraged protest, utterly condemning the King's presumption. The gap in the records suggests the unconscious evasion and total repression of the one issue which the central participant could never bring himself to repeat or indeed perhaps face in quiet conscience. The human memory is a fallible instrument, subject to promptings below the level of consciousness and never free from bias, and the Duchess's censure could not be admitted to the crucial flow of the King's thoughts.* As Queen Mary was to write to him many months later, 'You did not seem to take in any point of view but your own . . . I do not think you have ever realized the shock which the attitude you took up caused the family. . .'

With the harsh and searing words of that one passionate outcry – assuming that it occurred – the dreadful conflict was purged. The King returned to Fort Belvedere at 2.00 am next morning. The Duke and Duchess of York went to Royal Lodge as usual that weekend, sadly realizing, as the Duke said, that they would have to do their best 'to clear up

---

* For his play, *Crown Matrimonial*, produced in 1972, the playwright Royce Ryton steeped himself in the documentation and atmosphere of the Abdication and has dramatized his own view of the exchange by giving Elizabeth the lines, 'Everything has to be sacrificed to your vanity, the country, Bertie, the children, your mother, me, the Throne, everything and everyone, so that you can be happy in your private life. You are mesmerized by your own legend.'

the inevitable mess'. Bertie, however, continually telephoned his brother at Fort Belvedere and presently drove over there at his bidding. 'As he is my eldest brother I had to be there to try and help him in his hour of need,' he wrote afterwards, with infinite charity. And of the Monday night he wrote simply, 'I went back to London that night with my wife.' Two weeks were to pass before his wife next returned home to Royal Lodge and then she would no longer be Duchess of York.

Back at No 145, as on other occasions when her constitution was undermined by intensive nervous strain, Elizabeth succumbed to influenza. Her doctors forbade her to leave her room and all the pressing events of the Abdication week were shaped in messages or in her husband's reassurances when he came to her bedside. The physicians would have failed in their duty if they had not warned husband and wife to take precautions less the Duke should catch the infection. Yet he could not relax without her; he was frantic with suspense and the strain of the tasks thrust on his shoulders and we know from his own account that when he went to see his mother he 'broke down and sobbed like a child'. If his wife appeared to some to face the crisis with intense self-control, her secret was not entirely concealed from others. Her maid, Catta Mclean, found her reading her Bible and particularly noticed afterwards that the place-mark denoted St John, 14, the Chapter beginning 'Let not your heart be troubled . . .' and ending 'Arise, let us go hence'.

Shortly after 10.00 am on Thursday 10 December, King Edward VIII signed the instrument of Abdication, witnessed by his three brothers. Technically he remained King until the Declaration of Abdication Bill became law in Parliament. That afternoon Queen Mary went to see the Duchess, remaining with her in her bedroom for an hour and a half. 'The Duchess had sent for me, and I stood outside waiting,' Miss Crawford has chronicled. 'Queen Mary came out and tears were streaming down her face. The Duchess was lying propped up among pillows. I thought that she too had been crying. She held out her hand to me. "I'm afraid there are going to be great changes in our lives, Crawfie," she said. "We must take what is coming to us and make the best of it".' In retrospect, under the reign of King George VI and then his daughter, the Abdication was to seem only an incident in the sustained and brilliant story of the Throne. But that evening, when an upper curtain twitched at No 145, the crowds cheered wildly, convinced that their new Queen had come to look at them. And on returning from Windsor late that night, her husband confided to his diary, 'I found a large crowd outside my house cheering madly. I was overwhelmed.'

Part Four

QUEEN ELIZABETH

11. 'We are not Afraid'

The majestic change of degree from that of Duchess of York to the resounding dignities of Queen was fraught with some perplexity. In the circumstances of Abdication the instant Succession which occurs on the demise of the Sovereign was absent and the decisive transition, so constitutional lawyers argued, was when the Declaration of Abdication Act passed into law with the ancient fiat in Norman French, *Le Roy le veult* – the King wishes it. The new monarch at first resisted the title of King George VI. 'I can't do it,' he told an official, 'I should always be confused with my father.' But on seeking his wife's opinion her feminine judgment prevailed.

Queen Mary heard that Elizabeth's flu symptoms were no better. 'Too unlucky,' she noted, but the sufferer herself welcomed the hours of calm and reflection. On beginning his journey to Portsmouth, the new Duke of Windsor had read a letter from the new Queen to wish him well; and her message led him into a retrospective mood with his travelling companion, Walter Monckton, and he talked of old times and associations as he made his way into exile.

From her pillows and handkerchiefs next morning, Elizabeth heartened her husband with wifely encouragement as, pale and tense, he took his leave of her to attend his Accession Council at St James's Palace. 'With my wife and helpmeet by my side, I take up the heavy task which lies before me. In it I look for the support of my peoples . . .' he told his assembled counsellors. When he returned to 145 Piccadilly, his two daughters had been told by their governess to sweep him a curtsey. 'He stood for a moment touched and taken aback. Then he stooped and kissed them warmly.' This was probably the last occasion of an obeisance in private. The young parents quickly decided that they could not endure this tangible separation from their children, and the courtly old custom was abandoned.

The Queen, as we may henceforth style her, came down to 'an hilarious lunch,' Crawfie relates in her memoirs. The tension of the past weeks was dispersed. While they all sat at table, a message came from Sir Maurice Hankey, the clerk to the Privy Council, to say that the King had just been proclaimed, and the new King George VI looked quizzically at his family. 'Now if someone comes through on the phone,' he said, 'who shall I say I am?' It was as if all the anxious weeks had dissolved into a happy serenity. That afternoon, the King took the two Princesses to join their grandmother at Marlborough House and watch the pageantry of his public proclamation across the way at St James's Palace, while the Queen resumed her correspondence. A King is proclaimed, but rarely his Consort. It was appropriate, she felt, to write first to the Archbishop of Canterbury, 'a long and delightful letter,' as Dr Lang described it, every line in her large flowing handwriting marking her deep sincerity. 'I can hardly now believe that we have been called to this tremendous task and (I am writing to you quite intimately) the curious thing is that we are not afraid. I feel that God has enabled us to face the situation calmly.' And the letter was signed 'for the first time and with great affection, Elizabeth R'.

The new Queen was thirty-six. She had been married for thirteen years, and it seemed a happily auspicious touch that the commencement of the first week of the reign, on Monday 14 December, 1936, was also her husband's forty-first birthday. He had asked that the occasion should not be celebrated publicly but his dedicated interest in the Orders of Chivalry prompted him to commemorate the occasion by bestowing upon his wife the Order of the Garter, the highest and oldest Order he could confer. 'He had discovered that Papa gave it to you on his, Papa's, birthday, 3 June,' the Queen wrote to Queen Mary, 'and the coincidence was so charming that he has now followed suit, and given it to me on his own birthday.' Since Queen Mary was also to attend the family luncheon at 145 Piccadilly that same day, the letter could have waited but Queen Elizabeth had already begun as she meant to continue – the royal task of committing every event and every emotion to paper. Lady Airlie noticed that the Queen, with loving intuition, also constantly sought her mother-in-law's advice 'which pleased her very much'. At an early stage, Queen Mary confided to Lady Airlie that having learned the ropes she intended 'to compile a little book on everything a Queen ought to know and give it to her daughter-in-law' and, says Lady Airlie, 'I saw her carefully making notes for it in that clear orderly handwriting'.

The first British Queen Consort since Tudor times, the new Queen

considered that, just as she had to make much of her own way as Duchess of York, so she had to formulate her own style as Consort. Anson's
Law and Custom of the Constitution asserts that the life and chastity of
the Queen Consort is protected by the law of treason, and that she is free
from the disabilities of a married woman in matters of property and
contract, but the novice would have found this purely academic
reading. The First Lady of the land shares all the protective privileges
of her royal husband, such as exemption from taxation and the privacy
and non-publication of her will: she also has her own separate officers of
ceremony and business officials, her Lord Chamberlain, Treasurer,
Mistress of the Robes, four Ladies of the Bedchamber, four Women of
the Bedchamber and so on. Though interested in the historical niceties,
the Queen felt at once that the limited power of a Queen Consort might
be best defined as the power of doing good.

The role would be largely as she made it: the moral strength of Queen
Mary; the decorative impressment of Queen Alexandra; the charitable
sweetness of Queen Adelaide; the domestic virtues of Queen Charlotte;
each had achieved a different imprint. It can be seen, looking back, how
admirably today's Queen Mother was to blend them all.

The Christmas break at Sandringham – where the King and Queen
were at first technically Queen Mary's guests – served to soften the transition into the new reign, a reminder that the old traditional pattern had
been restored. Strictly, all the Queen's former patronages as Duchess of
York were brought to an end at the Accession, although the majority
were soon resumed. Thus a group of five patronages were first
announced and the net rapidly widened. The Red Cross, the Westminster Abbey organ fund, the Friends of York Minster, the preservation
of old houses, the Royal Horticultural Society, the National Council of
Girls' Clubs, the Victoria League and the Royal National Lifeboat
Institution were among a preliminary few of the two hundred or more
organizations which the Queen was to sponsor, visit, inspect and foster
with close and real interest.

It would have been unthinkable to have celebrated New Year – and
such a New Year – without her brother David's close companionship,
and it amused the King and Queen to devote the first issue of the *Court
Circular* of their Coronation year solely to the announcement that the
'Hon D and Mrs Bowes-Lyon had left Sandringham'. Another private
enjoyment was a visit to Newmarket to inspect the string of royal racehorses at Egerton House, which had passed to the King in his personal
financial settlements with the Duke of Windsor. It remains of interest

that the royal couple visited Aintree that year when the Grand National favourite, Golden Miller, refused a fence and the classic steeplechase was won by Royal Mail, a horse suitably sired by Royal Prince. The King and Queen were Lord Derby's guests at Knowsley and had the added pleasure of seeing the Molyneux Stakes won under the royal colours by the Sandringham-bred Jubilee.

There were other felicities. The first public engagement of the reign saw a drive into the East End on 15 February to open the new concert-hall and cultural centre of the People's Palace. The royal couple moved into Buckingham Palace the following day and that afternoon the Queen performed her own first solo engagement by visiting the textiles section of the British Industries Fair. There were diplomatic receptions, levees . . . so the reign slipped imperceptibly into the old traditional usages, the sturdy established rhythm. The Queen's own impress could be felt. She was not to be a cipher in her husband's shadow. When the first official dinner-party was held at the Palace, the names of the guests were not divulged. There was then to be more privacy, more family reticence, in the new reign than of old. The Queen had divined that one of her functions was to protect the King from the constant blaze of crown, sceptre and orb and to maintain an invulnerable private life of their own. In an early broadcast to his peoples the King had asserted, 'My wife and I dedicate ourselves for all time to your service, and we pray that God may give us guidance and strength to follow the path that lies before us.' Absolute dedication was to have the counter-part of absolute repose, and in ensuring this the Queen asserted one of the first responsibilities of her supporting role.

The move into Buckingham Palace taxed all the Queen's ingenuity and powers of persuasion. 'It was like moving into the curator's wing of a museum,' said one friend, 'except that the outgoing incumbent, Queen Mary, had moved out her own furniture five months before and the walls everywhere in the private apartments bore the scars of her earlier furnishings.' Ironically, the incoming King and Queen were necessarily lodged, as Edward VIII had been, in the ground-floor Belgian suite usually reserved for State visitors, with its rare amenity of modernized plumbing. For a few weeks 145 provided an unobtrusive last-ditch retreat, and the children remained there while the new Queen struggled to create her own sitting-room in the first-floor wing of the Palace as a private sanctum where the King could relax undisturbed. Early in March, one of their first visitors, Lady Airlie, admired the Queen's innumerable personal touches, the lamps and photographs and flowers, and prudently remarked, 'It looks homelike already.' Said the King, 'Elizabeth could make a home anywhere.'

Another early visitor was a stocky young man in his twenties, his outward diffidence soon revealing considerable powers of concentration and drive, who set before them the revised plans for the Coronation. The Duke of Norfolk bore the responsibility as Earl Marshal of supervising all the vast ceremonial of State for the crowning of the King and Queen, though not its religious content. The Coronation date of 12 May, first fixed for the bachelor monarch, remained unchanged and the new King and Queen pleased everyone by the readiness with which they entered into the quickened tempo of preparation.

The designs of Handley Seymour for the dress which would have been worn by the Duchess of York (recognizably in Van Dyck style with square décolleté) needed only ornamental adaptation as the Queen's Coronation gown. The Royal School of Needlework undertook the set of embroidery designs, blending white and gold emblems of the British Isles and Dominions. To the youthful Norman Hartnell, who had won his spurs with the gowns for the Duchess of Gloucester's bridesmaids, went a request to consider the dresses of the six maids-of-honour. With not five months ahead, the plans seemed neither skimped nor hurried. Queen Elizabeth went out of her way to acquaint Hartnell with the head-wreaths worn by Queen Victoria's train-bearers; the King personally led the impressionable young man on a tour of the Winterhalter paintings that had actually inspired some of the Queen's suggestions. Moreover, a new crown was envisaged, in keeping with a long-established tradition of creating a separate crown for the Queen Consort of every reign, and Mr Cecil Mann, the then Crown Jeweller, had an almost daily 5 pm appointment with the royal couple as the intended design was revised and embellished to ultimate perfection. This time, too, the Abbey made no objections when the King and Queen wished the ceremony to be broadcast, particularly anxious, as the Queen put it, that its spiritual significance should be brought home to everyone. At Windsor Castle, at Easter, the Archbishop, Dr Lang, was asked to go through the service privately with them and found them, as he wrote, 'most appreciative and fully conscious of its solemnity'. But when many of the house-party guests had, like the King, retired to bed, the Queen unexpectedly put her feet up on a sofa and sat drinking tea, talking for over an hour to Duff Cooper of the mystique of kingship and 'the intolerable honour'.

Soon all London was in readiness, the stands built and decorated, the 7,700 invitations for the Abbey sent out, the printed card a precious souvenir in itself – the Queen's new arms, with the uncrowned lion of the Bowes-Lyon family occupying the top right-hand corner and the King's armorial bearings to the left. (It was another token of readiness when the Queen's four-poster bed was moved from 145 to the Palace, signifying that the royal private suites were ready at last for occupation.) Nor was it entirely by coincidence that Capt. Ririd Myddleton was appointed Assistant Master of the Household at about this time, a close family friend who had been with David Bowes Lyon at Eton, affording proof to intimates that the Queen would be mistress in her own home.

The royal couple spent the weekend before the Coronation quietly at Royal Lodge with their daughters; and again received the Archbishop of Canterbury back at Buckingham Palace that Sunday evening. It was the Queen's idea that the meeting should coincide with the special prayers being offered for her husband and herself at the evensong services all over the country. 'They knelt with me,' wrote Dr Lang. 'I prayed for them and I gave them my personal blessing. I was much moved, and so were they. Indeed, there were tears in their eyes when we rose from our knees.' This private scene was followed next day by a family lunch when Queen Mary gave the Queen 'a tortoise-shell and diamond fan with ostrich feathers, which had belonged to Mama Alix (Queen Alexandra) and to Bertie and E our gift of a gold tea set'. The evening saw a State banquet for over 450 guests. No single apartment in the Palace could suitably accommodate so large an assembly of statesmen and royalties and so, while the King sat as host in the ballroom, the Queen presided over a more intimate gathering in the adjoining supper-room. She seemed untired and vivacious, although only the previous week the first two Courts of the reign, with their files of curtseying debutantes and mamas, had tested her resilience on two arduous successive evenings.

On Wednesday 12 May, Coronation Day, the testing of loudspeakers awoke the King and Queen at 3.00 am. 'One of them might have been in our room,' wrote the King that evening. 'Bands and marching troops for lining the streets arrived at 5.00 am so sleep was impossible . . . the hours of waiting were nerve-racking.' But it was a Palace innovation that, as for weddings and festive occasions years before at St Paul's Walden Bury, the servants, from the humblest domestics to the steward and housekeeper, were given a first view as the principal figures set out and their Majesties stepped into the Gold State Coach.

Combined with nerves, the jolting ride in the ancient vehicle, sway-ing and dipping on its uneven iron-shod wheels, provided one of the most uncomfortable voyages of Elizabeth's life, leaving her with such distasteful emotions that she ensured the heirloom was radically over-hauled before her daughter used it many years later. Within the Abbey, just as her procession was about to move up the nave, an agonizing halt occurred, when one of her chaplains fainted and at first blocked the way. This was an exceptional coincidence, for a cleric had similarly fainted and delayed her wedding procession; and the incident may have seemed to the faithful Elizabeth almost a personal sign of linking threads in the tapestry. When the procession moved again and the Queen advanced, unflustered, one of the spectators, Lord Mersey, felt the tangible wave of 'widespread affection and admiration'. Another guest thought her 'more composed than usual' and the Archbishop, awaiting her at the sanctuary, considered 'her dignity enhanced rather than diminished' by the tall following figure of the Mistress of the Robes, the Duchess of Northumberland. To Queen Mary, similarly, 'Bertie and E did it all too beautifully'. To others the Queen appeared to move in a trance of consecration as the immense ritual proceeded, minute by slow minute, solemn hour by hour.

By the usages observed for centuries, the Queen awaits her anointing with bare head, and her separate crowning follows that of her husband. The King is crowned while seated in the Coronation chair, its base the ancient stone of Scone; the Queen invested while kneeling before the altar, and she undertakes no Coronation oath. It is well-known that the King was anxious that the crown should be placed on his head with the emerald-studded Cross of St Edward correctly to the front, and to ensure this a red thread was attached, which was missing at the needful moment. 'I never did know whether it was right or not,' wrote the King. A curious photograph shows the Queen, her husband bare-headed in the background, evidently pausing to take her own crown in both hands and carefully examine it. The preliminary prayer was offered, and from their balconied view beside Queen Mary the two young Princesses leaned forward to see what they could of their mother. 'Defend her evermore from dangers, ghostly and bodily. Make her a great example of virtue and piety . . .' Beneath a golden canopy the Queen was anointed with consecrated oil in token of increased honour. She received a ring, the seal of a sincere faith; she received the crown 'of glory, honour and joy . . . with all princely virtue in this life,' the great Koh-i-Noor diamond blazing in its framework.

The Coronation of 1937 also held two passages of memorable and sweeping movement, the first after the King's crowning when, at the shout of 'God Save the King', the peers put on their coronets; the second when the Queen was crowned and the pale, bare arms of the peeresses rose simultaneously to place their coronets. Forty-five minutes elapsed between these two highlights of spectacle, yet to the two central figures there remained a deeper and abiding sense of religious reality. 'The Queen is a person of real piety, who felt her crowning acutely,' summed up the Duchess of Devonshire, her friend of twenty years. The King and Queen felt sustained by some higher power 'the reality of things unseen and eternal', Archbishop Lang testified. And he added, 'They wrote to me afterwards with touching simplicity about it.'

The Queen told her maid, Catta Mclean, that the crown was heavy and gave her a headache, and Lady Hardinge noticed that its weight and warmth marked her forehead, yet Sir John Reith, then firm chieftain of the BBC, discerned little sign of fatigue when he saw the King and Queen in mufti on Coronation night, 'extraordinary to see them now in ordinary easy dress, both in high delight that all had gone so marvellously well'. In the midst of relaxation, the King had to face the ordeal of a broadcast. 'To the Ministry of Kingship I have in your hearing dedicated myself, with the Queen at my side . . . We will, God helping us, faithfully discharge our trust.' The Queen indeed was literally at his side, and had skilfully prompted some rearrangements of the text to avoid the stammering impulse. Henceforward she was with him in speech rehearsals and therapy consultations so often that she unconsciously partly adopted his style of speaking, with deliberate pauses and intonation.

The royal couple made a series of Coronation drives through London with their two daughters, and on successive evenings a State Banquet and a Court Ball saw them called and recalled to the Palace balcony. The Queen's especial occasion was a review of 5,000 men and women of the St John Ambulance Brigade in Hyde Park, not without memories of the little Girl Guide troop at Glamis and Forfar. There was then the glittering dinner-party for a representative group of the princes of India, their one and only meeting as a body with their last Emperor and Empress. There were tours to Wales and Northern Ireland. 'When the staff and I could scarcely stand at the end of the day,' wrote Sir Samuel Hoare, the Home Secretary, 'they would remain alert, talking, asking, remembering names and faces.' In St Giles' Cathedral, during the

Coronation visit to Edinburgh, the King invested the Queen with the Order of the Thistle. 'My wife and I had only one Thistle,' he joked later. 'I wore it one day, she wore it the next.' At the end of their first month of high-pressure engagements, Lady Kennett – the former Lady Scott whom the Queen had shown around Glamis Castle as a child – asked if their Majesties were not tired. 'Not a bit!' the Queen replied. 'We don't look it, do we? We are trying so hard to do it well.'

At Balmoral – or rather during a domestic interlude in Birkhall – privacy was disturbed by preparations for a coming tour of industrial Yorkshire, with lists of schedules and presentations, and the briefing and memorizing of names and careers. There were also tiresome echoes from Austria, where the Duke of Windsor was on honeymoon and set up a plaint that the Duke of Kent, his younger brother, refused to visit him. In reality it was the Duchess of Kent who declined an invitation when travelling nearby, and although the King intervened to suggest that they both might go, the Duchess of Kent – the Princess Marina – felt too bitter an indignation to pay heed.

At least the exiled Duke no longer telephoned the King every few days, 'to see how you are getting along', as he put it. With a stammerer's dislike of the phone, and the difficulties in those days of long-distance reception, the calls had imposed a continuous strain on the King, and the Queen was the first to see that it would be better if the undesired and disturbing conversations were brought to an end. The Duke insistently raised what he termed 'uncomfortable points of business': he is credibly believed to have exacted one million pounds from the King for the property rights of Sandringham and Balmoral, in addition to an annuity estimated to have impoverished George VI's family by £60,000 a year. Moreover, in a European atmosphere ominous with threats of approaching war, the Duke invariably addressed the phone at the top of his voice, heedless of eavesdroppers. Ultimately the considerations of security prevailed, and the King found it imperative to tell his brother that the calls would have to cease. 'The reason must be clear to you,' he said.

'It never was,' wrote the Duke, in one of his defensive excursions into newsprint. 'And those closest to my brother were not displeased.' To the public eye, the gibe included his sister-in-law, the Queen. Queen Mary's diary and other sources offer little evidence of family wedding-gifts to the Windsors, yet guests at the Château de Candé were surprised at the warmth of a well-wishing telegram from 'Bertie and Elizabeth'. In all the disillusion and disappointment that faced the

Duke, there is no firm evidence that the King or an implacable Queen were responsible for the withholding of the status of 'Royal Highness' from his wife. As Queen Mary's biographer, James Pope-Hennessy, pointed out, the Duchess of Windsor was denied the style by a British Cabinet decision of May 1937, and the King's declaration by Letters Patent at the end of that month was no more than the enabling act signed on the advice of his ministers. The King, in fact, was at pains to write to his brother expressing the hope that 'this painful action would not be regarded as an insult'. Taking second thought, the Cabinet had thrown their acid as a rearguard action. Lady Donaldson best summed up their motive in her remarkable biography of Edward VIII. 'Mrs Simpson was an unknown quantity who had already failed to make a success of two marriages: what would happen if she failed in a third? What would become of her? Where would "Her Royal Highness" go? What do? Would there be marriage and re-marriage? More than one Royal Highness? Was there no limit to the possible damage to the throne?'

Staying at Balmoral shortly before the war, a further viewpoint was expressed by Walter Monckton, after urging that the Duke of Windsor was anxious to return to England and perhaps be treated as a young brother of the King so that he could make himself useful. 'But I think the Queen felt plainly that it was undesirable to give the Duke any effective sphere of work,' wrote Monckton. 'I felt then, as always, that she naturally thought that she must be on guard because the Duke of Windsor might be the rallying point for any who might be critical of the King, who was less superficially endowed with the arts and graces that please.' Admittedly this is a partisan view. Queen Elizabeth had by then seen her husband tested in the flame of kingship for nearly three years, and more than ever she shared the view that King George V once expressed to Lady Airlie, 'Bertie has more guts than the rest of his brothers put together.'

'One must hasten slowly,' said the Queen, perhaps a phrase of her parents, but the pomp and diplomatic circumstances of the new reign set the tempo. The resignation of Baldwin as Prime Minister ended an era, and his successor, Neville Chamberlain, was a caretaker in the corridor leading no man knew whither, either to peace or war. The State Visit of King Leopold III of the Belgians, an impending State Visit to France and the prospect of visiting Canada and the United States were signposts of the years 1937–39. The undefined amorphous role of Queen Consort enlarged in every direction, an expanding universe ever more congested with people and events. Overcoming any personal inclinations of laziness, Elizabeth often had to remind herself of another of her mother's maxims, 'first things first', difficult as it was to contrive even that much discipline in making one's way through the tangle of duties and pleasures.

First, then, her life as wife and helpmeet, vigilant for Bertie's health and well-being, protective against the over-demanding, a mutual unflinching partnership. 'They were so particularly together, leaning so much on each other,' said the Queen's eldest sister, Lady Elphinstone. At an early 'command' film performance the King was furious to find that the police had failed to hold back the people on the pavement, and that the Queen in consequence was jostled. But she instantly said 'What a happy crowd!' and his temper subsided. Another time, catching sight of a Hartnell dress design with a head and shoulders pencilled in, he blazed with anger and demanded 'Is this meant to be the Queen?' She hurriedly pacified him. 'Oh, no, dear, I only wish I were as beautiful as that.'

Society, too, buzzed around the young King and Queen, lavish in entertainment and rumour. At the Opening of Parliament Chips Channon considered that the Queen had 'become more matronly' but confided to his diary that 'she showed no sign of her supposed pregnancy'. Sir Philip Sassoon, who was rich as Croesus but equally an old friend, would meet every whim of his guests at Trent Park, from private planes to golf professionals and, for the Queen, Richard Tauber singing on the terrace by moonlight. When seven-year-old Princess Margaret became 'infatuated with a peacock', he thought nothing of sending her two from his gardens, one for herself, one for Lilibet. In such endearments to the children the Queen saw the risk of them being spoiled.

She was constantly trying to emulate her own mother in companionship, yet also persuading Queen Mary more and more to enjoy the relationship, which she knew so well from her own family, of grandmother and grandchildren. Miss Crawford was subtly encouraged to turn to Queen Mary for advice on curriculum and timetables, and the dowager Queen became Lilibet's willing guide in educational excursions around London. As housekeeper or châtelaine, too, with Ririd Myddleton's help, Queen Elizabeth attempted some traditional vigilance. She toured and spot-checked the 'downstairs' of Buckingham Palace as if she were her mother inspecting Glamis, 'consulting with the housekeeper or congratulating a chef', as a staff wife wrote. 'Often before donning her jewels she would walk into the banqueting room, give a final touch to table decorations, rearrange a vase of flowers and express her satisfaction.' During the Coronation, she told Lord Mersey, Buckingham Palace had served 18,832 meals in a week. But she missed the fun of baking scones.

As a Coronation commemorative gift to Windsor Castle it had satisfied her sense of fitness to spend some of her own money in buying a suite of fine early Georgian gilded furniture to embellish one of the duller State Apartments. The Civil List of the new reign followed established precedents in making no separate financial provision for the Queen. In theory, and largely in fact, she remained dependent on whatever her husband privately chose to allow her, and she was amused to find that her bank manager at Coutt's was a Mr George King. While it was publicly announced that she would purchase twentieth-century paintings for the royal collections from time to time, she privately consulted Sir William Llewellyn, then President of the Royal Academy, on where her expenditure would do most good. So it came about that the Queen's purchase of one of Wilson Steer's studies of Chepstow Castle occurred at the moment when the artist was threatened with blindness and encroaching despondency, and Llewellyn visited the ailing old man to cheer him up by telling him of the thought and care bestowed in hanging his painting at Windsor.

With some expert guidance from Lord Wellesley and Sir Walford Davies, she delighted in stealthy acts of grace and rescue. Hearing that Handel's harpsichord was lying neglected in a vault, she had it brought to the Palace and placed into the restoring care of an outstanding craftsman, Henry Tull. Today the instrument is on permanent loan to the National Trust collection at Fenton House, Hampstead, where it can still be played by musicians. She believed also that a Queen should support the feminine wiles of fashion; she gave thought to the ensemble of accessories and, when the 1938 State Visit to Paris came into planning focus, Norman Hartnell was again brilliantly responsive to the Windsor portrayals of the Empress Eugenie in her crinolines.

The State Visit was set for 28 June, and on 22 June David Bowes Lyon telephoned to break the terrible news to his sister that their mother had suffered a dangerous heart attack. In old age Lord and Lady Strathmore had spent much time in a flat in Cumberland Mansions, Portman Square, where they were close to David and their young grandchildren. It had been Elizabeth's custom to visit the old couple at least twice a week; and at 2.00 am on 23 June, with the King and Queen and others of her family around her, Lady Strathmore died.

In France President Lebrun at once called a halt to the preparations of welcome. In the depths of sorrow the Queen nevertheless realized the shadow that her absence might cast, and the increased strain on the King, and the visit was delayed for only three weeks. Soon after returning from the funeral, she sought Norman Hartnell's advice on how the summer gaiety of her wardrobe might be diminished. 'Ma'am, is not white a royal prerogative for mourning?' he suggested. Within the fourteen remaining days her entire collection – evening gowns, after-noon dresses – was altered into white counterparts.

The transformation turned out to be an unforgettable success. Euge-nie herself had never worn anything to rival the billowing skirts com-posed of scores of yards of narrow white Valenciennes lace, sprinkled with silver, which graced the Queen on the first evening at the Elysée Palace. As Lady Diana Cooper wrote, 'Each night's flourish outdid the last.' At the Opera she saw the Queen 'shining with stars and diadem and the Légion d'Honneur proudly worn' walk up the marble staircase preceded by *les chandeliers*, two resplendent footmen bearing twenty-branched candelabra of tall white candles. At the Quai d'Orsay, proto-col security was embarrassing. Beyond the open window, the crowds could be heard cheering and calling, and a guest of the evening, Violet Trefusis, takes up the story. 'The King and Queen consulted no one; they exchanged a look of mischievous complicity, took hands and raced through the room like a couple of children. When they were seen hand in hand, and unaccompanied on the balcony, the people of Paris went mad.' 'France has a monarchy again!' summarized one editorial. 'We have taken the Queen to our hearts. She rules over two nations.'

All the same, the superstitious nevertheless recalled that within four months of a similar visit to Paris by King George V and Queen Mary in April 1914, Britain and France had been at war with Germany. Two months after the State Visit of 1938, Chamberlain and Daladier for Britain and France, Hitler and Mussolini for Germany and Italy signed the Munich Agreement 'as symbolic of the desire of our two peoples never to go to war with one another again'. Mistaken as Munich was, the Queen had reason to suppose that the modest part she and her husband had played in Anglo-French accord had helped to preserve the peace; to preserve it for the time being. Typically, when Chamberlain, sick and weary, retired from the premiership in May 1940, to be replaced by Churchill, she sent the stricken man her own personal letter of thanks: 'During these last desperate and unhappy years you have been a great support and comfort to us both.' It was on the eve of Munich, also, that the Queen went to Clydeside to launch the great liner that was to bear her name, *Queen Elizabeth*. And when she rejoined her husband, he showed her a cordial letter from President Roosevelt containing an invitation to Washington implicit with the reaffirmation of another friendship, another royal mission, in the attempt to stave off war.

During the previous summer Mr Mackenzie King, as Prime Minister of Canada, had first invoked the idea that the King and Queen should pay a visit across the Atlantic, a suggestion quickly linked with an invitation by President Roosevelt to visit the United States, a joint project far more novel then than in these days when royal red carpets have been stretched in nearly every land. No reigning sovereign had ever visited Canada but, in the States, a cross-fire of opposition blazed from those who considered that the burning of the White House should still discount the firmer bonds of a common heritage. 'My husband,' says Eleanor Roosevelt, 'behaved as though we were simply going to have two very nice people to stay.' From the US Embassy in London they had already been reassured by Joe and Rose Kennedy – parents of the future President – that Queen Elizabeth was easy to get along with. 'I found it very difficult to accustom myself to saying "Ma'am" when addressing the Queen and she told me not to bother, putting me at my ease,' wrote Mrs Kennedy. 'She has a very pleasing voice, a beautiful English complexion, great dignity and charm; is simple in manner, stands and holds herself very erect. We talked about the difficulty of sleeping in London, and she was very much amused that I put wax in my ears.'

The Queen was unaware of the strange requirements made in her name in Washington, where a sprung cushion was to be placed in her car to ease continual bowing, a chair for a messenger provided at her bedroom door, and hot-water bottles placed in the beds 'which I did', commented Mrs Roosevelt, 'though the heat of Washington in June must have made them intolerable'. Studying the schedules, the Queen discovered that she, too, had still much to learn. If questioned on British parliamentary institutions, for example, it would never do if she had to conceal that she had never seen the House of Commons. The omission was repaired in March 1939, two months before the tour, when she sat in the Speaker's Gallery to watch a debate. The business before the House was not unamusing, for the witty A P Herbert was asking leave to bring in a Bill to restore public passenger steamers to the Thames.

Once again the invaluable Hartnell was consulted and required to provide five or six changes of costume a day with little repetition. The ever-watching eyes of the press, movie and even the primitive television cameras, silently established new protocol by insisting that a dress worn in Quebec could not be worn in Ottawa without fear of slighting their respective citizens. Outfits had to be suitable for every extreme, from sultry New York to the chilly heights of the Rockies. With the perverse timing of a crowded itinerary, there would be rail stops at smaller halts when the King and Queen would be expected to step onto the observation platform of the royal train at four o'clock in the morning. Should the Queen wear an evening gown or a simple dress for breakfast? Could something be conveniently donned over nightclothes? The indefatigable couturier tells us that he evolved 'a long flowing négligée dress in nectarine velvet touched with a narrow band of sable'.

Within these trifles, Queen Elizabeth was aware of sterner discomforts and hazards. Barely two weeks before the journey Hitler rejected the Anglo-German naval agreement signed only four years earlier. Lord Halifax, the British Foreign Secretary, received a secret Admiralty report that the pace of German aggression rendered an act of piracy and kidnapping against the royal travellers not impossible. On the day of setting sail aboard the Canadian Pacific liner *Empress of Australia*, the Queen was appointed one of five Counsellors of State to carry on the royal power and functions. Since she would be absent from the country, this seemed an anomaly; but the prescription was concerned with the legal possibility of the King's sudden death. As it turned out, the natural hazards of the Atlantic provided the real danger. The ice-fields had come much further south than usual, creating fog so thick the voyage took two days longer than expected.

'For three and a half days we only moved a few miles,' the Queen wrote to Queen Mary. 'The fog was so thick, that it was like a white cloud round the ship, and the foghorn blew incessantly. Its melancholy blasts were echoed back by the icebergs like the twang of a piece of wire. Incredibly eerie, and really very alarming, knowing that we were surrounded by ice, and unable to see a foot either way.

'We very nearly hit a berg the day before yesterday, and the poor Captain was nearly demented because some kind cheerful people kept on reminding him that it was about here that the Titanic was struck, and *just* about the same date!' To which the King added wryly 'I shouldn't have chosen an ice-field surrounded by dense fog in which to have a holiday, but it does seem to be the only place for me to rest nowadays.'

Happily, the ship docked safely and in brilliant sunshine, and in Quebec and Montreal natural curiosity turned into an instant ecstasy. 'We will remember her smile' ran a much-quoted headline, and the discovery that the Queen spoke French and was also the first to translate the Gaelic banners of welcome in a Scottish community gave immense pleasure. A war veteran asked the Queen whether, to settle an argument, she was Scottish or English. 'Since we reached Quebec,' she answered, 'I've been a Canadian.'

'When I induced their Majesties to come out here, I didn't realize I was pulling the string of such a shower-bath,' the then Governor-General, Lord Tweedsmuir (John Buchan) wrote privately. 'The Queen has a perfect genius for the right kind of publicity. The unrehearsed episodes were marvellous. When she laid the foundation stone of the new judicative building I heard the masons talking and realized some of them were Scots – and she made me take her and the King up to them, and they spent at least ten minutes in Scottish reminiscences, in full view of 70,000 people. At the unveiling of the war memorial, where we had some 10,000 veterans, she asked me if it were possible to get closer to them. We went right down among them. We were simply swallowed up! I shall never forget the faces of the Scotland Yard detectives. It was wonderful to see old fellows crying, "Ay, man, if Hitler could just see this".'

Yet the Queen found it difficult 'to know when not to smile', as she admitted to Cecil Beaton. She winced at the plump face revealed in the newspapers. 'It is so distressing to me,' she told Beaton, 'that I always photograph so badly.' Both repetition and the changing climes of opinion have dimmed lesser highlights of the journey, yet it remains remarkable that in Winnipeg the royal train had to move at snail's pace for miles, so vast were the crowds pressing along the track, and at one intended small stop thousands of people were mustered as far as the eye could see. There were times when the Queen all but broke down afterwards under the sheer pressure of emotion.

In Washington, Mrs Roosevelt marvelled that the Queen 'never had a crease in her dress nor a hair out of place. I do not see how it is possible to remain so perfectly in character all the time.' To this degree the royal couple concealed the intense degree of personal strain. The weather was unusually humid, the crowds larger than any Mrs Roosevelt had ever seen, the White House receiving line long and intensive, and one evening the Queen had to confess to faintness and withdrew for a time. One afternoon, vide Mrs Roosevelt, 'the Queen murmured gently in my ear that the heat made her feel very peculiar and did I think she could return to her car'. After that, both the President and his wife noticed how the King and Queen halved the work for each other. During an inspection line, King George stopped at every other person, while his wife spoke to every intervening one. If there were a child in the house the Queen loved being seen by this small audience in gown, jewels and diadem. Starry-eyed, Harry Hopkins' eight-year-old daughter cried in rapture, 'Oh, Daddy, Daddy! I have seen the Fairy Queen!'

In New York an estimated 4,000,000 people lined the royal route, each with some share of that illusion, if the press ovation provides any gauge. At the World Fair, the Queen can claim to have been the first to test the walkabout technique, for an overlong presentation line was reduced to a happy crowd where the royals spoke to many but shook hands with few. The Queen in turn was surprised at the unabashed singing of 'Rule, Britannia!' and 'Land of Hope and Glory'; and next day, staying at the Roosevelts' Hyde Park home and attending the local parish church, she was surprised again. 'The service is *exactly* the same as ours down to every word, and they even had the prayers for the King and the Royal Family,' she wrote to Queen Mary. 'I could not help thinking how curious it sounded and yet how natural.' As to the Roosevelts, she found them 'such a charming and united family, and living so like English people when they come to their country house'. The naïveté that the Queen had curiously retained remains implicit in these words. Neither the King nor Queen had expected such a tremendous and genial welcome in a part alien and republican land. They had faced as great an ovation – and found more demands made on their resilience – than ever before in their lives. On sailing home from Halifax, Queen Elizabeth found herself utterly exhausted although, as Lady Katharine Seymour noted, 'she always brushed off any reference to fatigue'. It took time to place the whole adventure in perspective. 'That tour made us!' the Queen confided to Mackenzie King two years later, 'I mean it made us, the King and I. It came at just the right time.'

12. *Wartime Queen*

In retrospect, it is astonishing that King George VI and Queen Elizabeth resumed their programme of public duties immediately after that arduous North American tour. At Southampton a destroyer ferried the two young princesses to the return ship, the *Empress of Britain*. 'Everyone else kept out of the way for their very joyful reunion,' wrote Miss Crawford, 'the Queen, very slim, said how much the children had grown; the King could hardly take his eyes off Lilibet. There followed an hilarious luncheon, the ship's dining-room festive with streamers and balloons.' And there followed, too, the tremendous enthusiasm of their welcome home to London, the balcony appearances, the many tales to tell.

Wasting no time, the King and Queen drove in state next day to the Guildhall, where the King made an impressive, stammer-free and at times emotional speech on the ideals of the Commonwealth, 'objects that I and the Queen with me set out to fulfil'. 'I have never heard the King speak so effectively, or so movingly,' wrote Sir Alan Lascelles. 'It was very interesting to watch the effect of his words on such hardened experts as Winston Churchill.' And if it was the King's triumph, it was in a deeper, more private sense, no less a triumph for the Queen, 'a change from the old days when I felt speaking was hell', as the King wrote to his old friend, Louis Greig.

Shortly afterwards, between royal tasks various as a civil defence review and a national agricultural show, a fair and good-looking teenage boy came with his mother to tea with the Queen at the Palace. This was an early appearance of Prince Philip, whom she had first seen so long ago when he was a baby at Kensington Palace. A week or two later, Philip was also invited to tea aboard the royal yacht *Victoria and Albert* during the King's visit to Dartmouth, and warmly encouraged by the Queen to get through the plates of shrimps, cakes, sandwiches and a banana split, 'You must make a good meal, I expect it is your last of the day!' 'Lilibet sat pink-faced,' Marion Crawford tells us. The Queen celebrated her thirty-ninth birthday on 4 August at Balmoral and next day invited all the two hundred occupants of the King's annual Boys' Camp to tea at the Castle, urging them to help eat up an enticing assortment of birthday cakes. Two more days and the King had to travel south to review the Reserve Fleet at Weymouth, a gesture that Queen Mary hoped might yet be 'a deterrent factor in Hitler's mind'. With the dismaying news of the German-Soviet aggression pact on 22 August, however, the King hastened to London with war a virtual certainty, while the Queen remained at Birkhall with the children. 'I feel deeply for you, I having gone all through this in 1914 when I was the wife of the Sovereign,' Queen Mary wrote to her from the West Country, and within a day or two Elizabeth could contain her anxieties no longer. 'If things turn out badly I must be with the King,' she explained to her lady-in-waiting, Mrs Geoffrey Bowlby, and straightway hurried south to join him.

On 3 September, after every alternative for peace had failed, Britain was at war with Germany for the second time in twenty-five years. In 1914 Elizabeth had been a schoolgirl of fourteen, her future husband a midshipman in the North Sea, and now she was at the gate of her forties, an active partner in leadership at the very heart of the British nation and the Commonwealth. Like millions of women, she maintained an outward stoical calm, concealing her trepidation for her loved ones, for her brother, David, her own Lyon nephews and the King's family. The plans improvized for her national duties months earlier, whenever she should not be at the King's side, touched civilian life and medical care at every point. A million children had been rushed from London and other imperilled cities into the country and she visited groups of these transplanted 'evacuees' in Sussex, as a propaganda measure to help in moving other children to safety. On the day after the outbreak of war, her first appearance in public was with the King on a heartening tour of civil defence centres and air-raid shelters in London. Day by day, setting an example by carrying her compulsory gas-mask haversack, she inspected Red Cross centres, ambulance trains, government clothing factories, dockland centres and troops in training – and at 6.00 every evening telephoned her daughters in Scotland.

An early personal dilemma lay in the return of the Windsors to London. When this was first mooted some months earlier, her friend, Mrs John Gilmour, had asked the Queen if the Duchess of Windsor would be coming. 'No, certainly not. Wouldn't receive her if she did,' was the answer. 'May I make that known?' asked Mrs Gilmour. 'You certainly may!' The circumstances of war softened that mood not at all. No orders were given for an official car or overnight accommodation when Lord Mountbatten's destroyer, the *Kelly*, brought the pair from Cherbourg to Southampton in black-out darkness, and they spent the night under the roof of Admiral James, the C-in-C of Portsmouth (no relation of the Queen's godmother). Returning from a tour of the London docks with the Queen, the King received his brother alone at Buckingham Palace. 'We talked for about an hour,' he noted in his diary. 'There were no recriminations on either side.' But to the Prime Minister he wrote, 'He seems not a bit worried as to his behaviour in 1936. He has forgotten all about it.' And Lady Metcalfe, who had briefly become the Windsors' English hostess wrote succinctly, 'Their selfishness and self-concentration is terrifying.' The Duke indeed produced a plan for touring the UK Army Commands with his wife, a scheme which the War Minister, Leslie Hore-Belisha, could see distressed the King and Queen alike as they pictured the hostile reception the Duchess might receive in Scotland. But the King shortly decided that his brother's services could best be used by the British Military Mission in Paris and so it was settled.

As it chanced, the Queen's appointment as Commandant-in-Chief of the three women's defence services, the 'Wrens, Waafs and Waacs', was made known on the same day. She had already made up her mind not to wear uniform. She had 'not the figure for it' and, besides, as Hartnell discovered, she 'wished to convey the most comforting, encouraging and sympathetic note possible'. Henceforward she would rarely wear black, nor green which some people consider unlucky. Her preferences later became dusty pink, dusty blue and dusty lilac. '*Dusty* is an apt colour,' she said, 'it doesn't show all the dust on bomb sites.'

It was second nature to offer her harassed husband the softer home atmosphere that she alone could provide. During the peculiar lull of the 'phoney war' – in reality, fraught with intensive preparation – they returned every night to Royal Lodge at Windsor and 'she seemed to drop her cares at the gates,' as one of her Household observed. 'One must do one's best,' she would say, and her best was a factor of encouragement and resilience, helping to set the kind of resolute example that she believed the hour demanded. In November 1939, she took particular care to correctly embody her point of view in a radio broadcast to women. She recalled her previous broadcast just before leaving Canada, a farewell message to women and children given 'in an atmosphere of such goodwill and kindness that the very idea of strife and bloodshed seemed impossible'. Now she addressed the women of France and Poland and the women at home. 'The greater your devotion and courage the sooner shall we see again the happy ordered life for which we long. . . . We put our trust in God, who is our refuge and strength . . .'

If an admiring member of her staff said that 'the Queen never showed that she was worried', it was because her inner, though unboasted, faith was so reliant. Despite the risk of a bombing attack into East Anglia, the family went to Sandringham as usual for Christmas. The princesses were brought down from Scotland, and the first of the King's wartime Christmas broadcasts ended with an impressive and helpful quotation, included on the Queen's prompting: 'I said to the man who stood at the Gate of the Year, "Give me a light that I may tread safely into the unknown". And he replied, "Go out into the darkness and put your hand into the Hand of God. That shall be to you better than light, and safer than a known way . . .".'

So many years later, it appears unconvincing to say that Queen Elizabeth's serenity was a source of strength to the nation, yet it was vitally true at the time. While the adversaries of war silently prepared for the real struggle, she continued to attend concerts and art exhibitions, demonstrating that these civilized essentials were indirect accessories of morale. The treasures of the National Gallery disappeared into safekeeping in the West Country, but pictures from Royal Lodge were included in the exhibitions of British painting that took their place. Later on, during the air-raids, when lunchtime concerts were defiantly given under the sand-bagged laylights of the Gallery and Beethoven and Mozart were heard with such moving effect, the Queen made a point of being present as frequently as possible. When a scheme was set afoot for artists as part of their war service to record the British scene in paintings and drawings while it remained unravaged, she commissioned John Piper to undertake twelve water-colours of Windsor Castle in case it should suffer destruction. That very real risk had to be recognized. 'Now we still have the Castle – and the Pipers,' she said, years later.

As with her peacetime patronages, the Queen was reluctant to lend her name to any movement in which she played no active part. When the air-raids were at their height, Lord Woolton as Food Minister worked out plans for a fleet of travelling vehicles to provide hot meals in blitzed areas where food supplies might break down, and sought permission to call the convoys the Queen's Messengers, since the women in charge, he explained, would indeed be messengers of mercy. 'But why Queen's Messengers?' asked the Queen, 'What will I have done?'

Lord Woolton was moved to speak out. 'But don't you know what you mean to all of us in this country? It isn't only your high position . . . it's the fact that people think of you as a person who would speak the kindly word and, if it fell within your power, would take the cup of hot soup to the needy.' Whereupon, as Lord Woolton tells, the Queen put up her hands and said, 'Oh, my Lord, do you think I mean that? It is what I have tried so hard to be.'

The westward onslaught of the German armies through Holland and Belgium was launched on 2 May 1940, and eleven days later Queen Wilhelmina of the Netherlands was swept to the English shore by defeats and adversities beyond her control. She arrived at Buckingham Palace with no more than she was wearing, and the Queen's maid, Catta Mclean, went out shopping for her, while Queen Elizabeth above all provided the kindly and sympathetic consolation that the distressed fugitive sorely needed. But this was total war. Hitler had drawn up explicit instructions for the treatment of crowned heads and their kinsfolk captured by paratroops; he had hoped to take all the Dutch royal family hostage. Similar ambitions, it had to be recognized, might soon be turned upon the royals in Britain.

It was suggested that Princess Elizabeth and Princess Margaret should be taken to greater safety in Canada, but the Queen declined this agonizing prospect. 'They could not go without me,' she said, 'I could not possibly go without the King, and the King will never go.' The Princesses remained at Windsor Castle, effecting the coincidence that Elizabeth Lyon from the age of fourteen spent her four war years at Glamis Castle and the present Queen Elizabeth II at fourteen similarly began four years at Windsor.

Outwardly, as the enemy armies swept relentlessly nearer, all was calm. On 24 May the Germans entered Boulogne and so gazed as conquerors across the English Channel, and on that day the King broadcast an appeal for a Day of National Prayer to be held on the Sunday, two days later. To the agnostic this would seem a questionable gesture, but to the faithful and to half-believers it was seemly to seek the aid of the Almighty at so dark an hour. It remains notable that the call came from the King, and not firstly from the leaders of religious thought, and many believe that the Queen herself inspired the day as a national rallying point. 'I shall never forget the emotion of that service at Westminster Abbey,' wrote Lord Croft, then Under-Secretary for War, '. . . the King and Queen surrounded by all their Ministers and accompanied by the Queen of Holland and the King of Norway, monarchs of two countries already stricken in defeat. It was with a terrible weight on our hearts that we appealed for the succour of Divine Providence. It seemed almost unbelievable that any but a fraction of our Army could be saved.' Within ten days, 335,000 troops were rescued from the beaches and, whatever the voice of logic, Queen Elizabeth was convinced of the miracle of Dunkirk.

With the German armies mustered across the English Channel and the North Sea, the stage was set for the Battle of Britain itself and the preparations for imminent invasion. The Coates Mission, so-called after its commander, Colonel J S Coates, was drilled and equipped for the safe escort of the Royal Family to a place of safety in the event of German paratroops or land attack. Four houses in different parts of the country – in Dorset, Worcestershire, Scotland and North Wales – were prepared and equipped for their reception, but, notably, the Queen did not bother to see or supervise any of them. 'I should die, if I had to leave,' she told Harold Nicolson. On the other hand, Lord Halifax, the Foreign Secretary, who enjoyed the privilege of walking through the grounds of Buckingham Palace as a short-cut to Whitehall, one morning heard the rattle of rifle fire in the Palace grounds and enquired the reason. He learned that the Queen was practising with service weapons: a .303 rifle and a .38 revolver. 'I shall not go down like the others,' she said, and Lord Halifax decided it would be prudent to cease his Palace walks.

King Haakon of Norway, having undergone the stern reality of invasion, remained sceptical of the security precautions, and the King and Queen took him into the garden one day to show him what would happen when they pressed the alarm – and nothing happened. The police-sergeant on duty had merely told the officer of the guard that no attack was impending 'as he had heard nothing of it'. The earlier air-raid alerts were of small consequence but the King and Queen made their own way to their so-called shelter, a housekeeper's room in the basement, as a matter of example. A lady-in-waiting has told how she saved herself 'with alacrity' from the top floor and 'hung about in the hall, ashamed to be first' until the King and Queen came down unhurriedly, she carrying a small case, he with a corgi in his arms. In the hall 'they had a brief consultation, then the King darted back upstairs to find the other corgi'.

In one of the first air-raids on London a direct hit destroyed their old home – fortunately unoccupied – at 145 Piccadilly, and one afternoon they chanced to be travelling through Rotherhithe during the dockland raids, when the sirens wailed and the police stopped their car and asked them to take cover. As they entered a nearby street shelter those waiting there in the dim lighting could hardly believe their eyes and then raised one of those tremulous, sincere cheers of a small group of people, and eagerly offered seats among them on chairs and benches, and a canteen worker came forward with her strong brew of tea. The King and Queen were never more truly Londoners than at that moment.

The shelter was in Adams Gardens and, incredibly, the Rotherhithe room where Princess Margaret would one day find sanctuary with her husband in the earlier happy years of her ill-starred marriage, was hardly a hundred yards away, 'just around the corner'. Among the East End centres the Queen sought out were the Dockland Settlements, where the bombed-out often slept and were cared for through the shock of homelessness, and the club youngsters had stories to tell of pets and furniture royally retrieved from bomb rubble. No one knew that the grey-haired woman who often headed these adventures and worked among East Enders through the worst of the air-raids was none other than the Queen's godmother, Mrs James.*

In the heart of blitzed Poplar was another direct contact. The Queen's first cousin, Lilian Bowes Lyon, lived in the civilian front line of the Bow Road, heading the local Women's Voluntary Service: working in the shelters, marshalling ambulance and rescue workers where the bombs fell, and at times indignantly telling the Queen herself when supplies were needed or where civil defence failures could be put right. On the day the war ended, she telephoned the Palace to tell of people waiting for hours for bread and potatoes – and couldn't the new American mobile canteens be sent, instead of hanging about in Hyde Park? A Palace aide subsequently thought that the Queen 'fixed it'.

From early September, 1940, as the intensive assault on London began, the King and Queen would be out and about, often together, sometimes separately, frequently before fires had been quenched in the bomb rubble. A woman would take the Queen's arm gasping that her

---

* Mrs James died in 1948 and her will named David Bowes Lyon as an executor, dividing £330,000 in bequests to her many charities and godchildren. She bequeathed paintings by Titian, Reynolds and Gainsborough to the National Gallery and the keepsake of a necklace to her god-daughter, Queen Elizabeth.

little shop was wrecked but that she was still serving customers. 'It is splendid to hear . . . it is sad to see,' the Queen would say, again and again, in different districts. The sight of the small, friendly compassionate figure moving among them was steadying and gave every participant a stronger reassuring sense of individuality and courage. A woman might sob out a story of her children, and the tears that so often glistened in the Queen's eyes raised 'a kind of adoration' from those close enough to see and tell of them.

There were stories about the Queen that spread lip to lip and became part of Cockney folklore. An old woman was in distress because her frightened dog refused to budge from a hole in the debris. 'Perhaps I can try,' said the Queen. 'I am rather good with dogs,' and knelt in the dust to coax him out successfully. A woman with a disabled arm was trying to dress her baby while the local officials accompanying the Queen looked on. 'Let me help,' said the Queen, taking the baby. One eye-witness remembers a group of women exclaiming in rapture as the Queen paused at their bomb-shattered homes, 'Ain't she lovely! Oh, ain't she just bloody lovely!', the cry first heard when she had been Duchess of York.

On 10 September the royal couple returned from a night at Royal Lodge, having heard by telephone that an unexploded bomb had gone off at Buckingham Palace in the early hours. The bomb blast had shattered all the Palace windows to the north and west, and the Queen's sitting-room presented a snowfall of powdered glass. Three days later they were working together with Alec Hardinge during an alert when they heard the sudden roar of low-flying aircraft, the unmistakable whistle of falling bombs and then, glancing across the Palace quadrangle, they actually saw the bombs falling in the split second before the King pushed his wife to the floor. As other explosions followed, they scrambled into the corridor. 'We all wondered why we weren't dead,' the King wrote afterwards in his journal. The raider had released a stick of six bombs, two cutting craters in the forecourt, two in the quadrangle, a fifth wrecking the Chapel and a plumbing workshop and the sixth falling harmlessly in the garden. 'E and I went all round the basement talking to the servants who were all safe. Looking at the wreckage, it is a wonder how they (the plumbers) escaped death.'

A Palace policeman observed, 'a magnificent piece of bombing, Ma'am', apropos the fact that every bomb except one had fallen on open space. Another man noticed that her clothes were stained with the brick-dust that still hung over the rubble. 'That's a comfort, anyway,' said the Queen. 'It makes me feel I can look the East End in the face.'

At Royal Lodge, she had laughed at herself for celebrating her fortieth birthday a day too soon, on Sunday 3 August, in order to be ready for her working programme in London on the Monday. It may be true that her brother, David, who was with the Ministry of Economic Warfare, styled himself the 'economic organizer' of a joint family gift. Her eldest sister, May Elphinstone, was touched at noticing how Elizabeth and the King 'were so particularly together, both leaned so much on each other'. Her other sister, Rose, noticed too how much Elizabeth was sustained by the King. 'The King was a rock to her,' she was to say. 'In all fundamental things the Queen was sustained by the King.' Steeping herself week by week in the human heroism and tragedy of the East End and south London, there were several occasions when she appeared on the scene while rescuers were still tunnelling to free casualties – and the dead – from the wreckage. 'I feel quite exhausted after seeing and hearing so much sadness, sorrow, heroism and magnificent spirit,' she wrote to Queen Mary at Badminton after one of these visits. 'The destruction is so awful, the people so *wonderful* – they *deserve* a better world.'

On the night of 14 November, a Luftwaffe navigational beam was detected aligned directly over Windsor Castle, and into the small hours hundreds of enemy planes streamed overhead despite resistance, their objective Coventry. When the King hurried to the devastated city, the Queen was advised not to accompany him, 'lest her presence should impede the work of rescue,' as she was told at the time, but in reality to spare her the hideous scenes of destruction. When she heard of the wonderful heartening effect of the King's appearance there, she characteristically responded that, after all, she 'should have been there, too'. In one sense she was, for the first Queen's Messenger convoy went into action among the mountains of rubble and fed 12,000 people for three days, and another convoy which she had herself financed was 'back-up' deployed as needed. But the Queen felt her absence so acutely that a train was made ready to take the royal couple to blitzed cities and industrial areas whenever required in the future and, bringing their tangible sympathy and encouragement, they travelled thousands of miles by train and car in the course of the war.

Lord Harlech considered that the visits did incalculable good. 'When the car stops,' he said, 'the Queen nips out into the snow and goes straight into the crowd and starts talking to them. For a moment or two they just gape and gaze in astonishment. But then they all start talking at once. "Hi, your Majesty! Look here!". On the night when St Paul's was ringed with fire, the Queen was planning a New Year respite at Appleton House, near Sandringham. But instead she appeared unexpectedly at the Cathedral among the lay workers and clergy who were helping to clear up the mess, talking to the fire-watchers who had quenched incendiaries on the roof and the bomb-disposal squad who had not long finished digging an unexploded bomb from the foundations.

The Queen constantly felt 'a worrying urge' that she was not doing enough. She visited lonely searchlight units, continually toured hospitals and was tireless – though forbearing in scrutiny – in her visits to women's service units. For spare afternoons a counterpart of the old Glamis wartime sewing parties was held by the wives of Palace staff at trestle-tables in the State Apartments, and items made by the Queen steadily joined the stockpile. During a lull in the enemy bombing campaigns, children began drifting back to the cities, sometimes arousing friction between the parents of evacuee children and the foster-parents who sheltered them. After discussing this problem, the Queen sent out a letter of thanks, bearing her own Coat-of-Arms, to thousands of householders who had taken in children, an essay in royal public relations which caused immense pleasure and renewed the jaded warmth of rural hospitality.

An element that surprised her family was the Queen's remarkably sustained good health, although in the autumn of 1942 Eleanor Roosevelt found both the King and Queen at the Palace living in chilly rooms and suffering from heavy colds, the Queen's bedroom fitted only with fragile windows of thin wood and isinglass. The Queen showed her how the splinters of another bomb had dropped through her former room and lodged in the King's wardrobe. 'We were served on gold and silver plates,' Mrs Roosevelt noted, 'but our bread was the same kind of war bread every other family had to eat. Except for game occasionally, nothing was served that was not served in any war canteen.' Nevertheless, a small birthday cake appeared at teatime with the Queen's apology for 'just missing' her guest's birthday. 'What's in it?' asked Mrs Roosevelt suspiciously, and her hostess laughed and said, 'Probably sawdust!' The Queen confided, too, that her own rationed wardrobe would soon be as sparse as Mrs Roosevelt's fifty-pound travel limit; and when buying gifts at a Red Cross stall, she apologized that she had run out of clothing coupons. Some of the clothes she had worn in 1939 in

North America appeared in public for the next eight years.

Mrs Roosevelt was not told that Palace and gardens became infested by rats after the bombs, until decimated by rat shoots and traps. Nor did she hear of the Queen's 'awful moment' at Windsor Castle one evening when she went to her bedroom and a man suddenly jumped from behind the curtains and flung himself at her feet, seizing her by the ankles. 'For a moment my heart stood absolutely still,' she described the scene afterwards. 'Poor man, I realized quickly he meant no harm.' Knowing that if she screamed he might attack her, she listened as he poured out his grievances until she could move across the room to ring the bell and summon help. He was a deserter, all but unhinged by losing all his family in the blitz. 'Poor man, I was so sorry for him,' Queen Elizabeth summed up her experience.

Wherever the King and Queen travelled in blitzed Britain, they were in danger, from landmines, undetonated bombs and lesser hazards. 'Nobody is immune from it,' wrote the King. Travelling with her husband, the Queen shared the 'occupational risk' and had written letters to her daughters in case anything happened to her. When he travelled alone, she admitted that she worried. In June 1943, when the tide of war was at last turning, the King seized an opportunity of visiting his victorious troops in North Africa, and for the first time the Queen knew the gnawing anxiety of a wife whose husband was serving overseas. He was to fly in Winston Churchill's handsomely-fitted York transport plane, with a refuelling stop at Gibraltar, but in avoiding enemy-occupied France his aircraft would be flying over waters where the enemy had only recently shot down an unarmed neutral plane on a scheduled flight, the aircraft in which Leslie Howard, the actor, had lost his life. The loss of this passenger plane was notified on 2 June, eight days before the King was due to fly, and husband and wife took the potential danger so seriously that the King summoned his solicitor and put his private affairs in order the night before he left.

The King flew out late at night. 'I have had an anxious few hours,' the Queen wrote to Queen Mary. 'At 8.15 I heard that the plane had been heard near Gibraltar, and that it would soon be landing. Then after an hour and a half I heard that there was a thick fog at Gib. and that they were going on to Africa. Then complete silence till a few minutes ago, when a message came that they had landed in Africa, and taken off again. Of course I imagined every sort of horror, and walked up and down my room staring at the telephone.'

The King returned safely two weeks later, tired but sunburned after a tour markedly cheering to the troops who felt that they had merited this recognition. The Queen meanwhile had also basked in a new experience. Before the King's departure she had again been appointed a Counsellor of State and was thus empowered to hold an Investiture at Buckingham Palace. No prior announcement was made, and the King's expected appearance served to camouflage his absence abroad. These wartime ceremonies were held in the Grand Hall of the Palace, splashed with the red and gold of the veteran Yeomen of the Guard, and saw the decoration and occasional ennoblement of thousands of men of the Services and of the Commonwealth throughout the war. Hundreds of relatives and other guests were permitted to watch this great moment of their heroes, and one day in June, the band had as usual played waltzes and minuets and was in the middle of 'A Fine Old English Gentleman' when quietly and unexpectedly the Queen came through the doors onto the dais. No Queen had held an Investiture since Queen Victoria. The first hero to step forward from the waiting file was Wing-Commander Guy Gibson, of dam-busting fame, to receive the VC. Standing close beside the Queen with the decorations, Lord Clarendon found that the ceremony took much longer than usual, so intent was she on conversing with each of the 230 men and women.

As Counsellors of State the following year, when the King visited his armies in Italy, the Queen and Princess Elizabeth both received addresses from the House of Commons and House of Lords and the Queen for the first time had the diversion of signing assent to several Parliamentary Bills which at the touch of her pen became law, Bills more romantic in the assent than in observance, mainly concerned as they were with rural sewage. The Queen also held another Investiture when, in the long rota of the decorated, a certain Brigadier was made a Companion of the Order of the Bath. This afterwards caused a con-tretemps when, on being awarded a higher class of the Order, the recipient was supposed to return the insignia of the lower rank. 'I've lost it,' he asserted, unconvincingly, and added that he couldn't care less what fines the loss cost him: 'That insignia was given me by Her Majesty the Queen and I refuse to part with it for all the money in the world.' The matter was glossed over.

There were the lighter interludes of the Windsor pantomimes, and the Christmas concert at which Sir Dermot Kavanagh remembered the Queen and Lady Mountbatten singing a duet 'A Sailor's Wife a Sailor's Star Must Be', with Princess Margaret at the piano. Yet these were mere episodes interrupting the drab and austere years, the monotonous routine when time was measured only by the fresh campaigns and successive weapons that the enemy hurled towards Britain, the 'flying bombs' and later the silent and thus more terrifying rockets. The pilotless V-bombs trundled over London until the engines cut out and the missile fell and exploded, and they came in such numbers that not all could be shot down over open country or the less populated suburbs, and 2,752 people were killed in the first three weeks. The Queen was one of the few women who knew the official casualties. 'There is something very inhuman about death-dealing missiles being launched in such an indiscriminate manner', she wrote to Queen Mary. In this new phase she often took shelter in a narrow passage behind the Belgian Suite where 'a very large housemaid' was usually to be found. 'We'll hide in there,' she would say. But before the mechanism of the flying bombs became familiar, the Guards Chapel, near Buckingham Palace, was destroyed one Sunday when the place was crowded for morning service. One hundred and twenty-one of the congregation were killed, including many whom Queen Elizabeth knew. The King and Queen were at Windsor when the news came through piecemeal 'the one and only time during the whole war', one of the Household recorded, 'when I saw the Queen really shaken'.

Nevertheless the Household considered that the Queen 'grew used to flying-bombs in a week', which was no doubt true, so adaptable and resilient was the civilian 'Home Front' to the successive horror of each new weapon. On the other hand, the Princesses were coming to London to visit their dental surgeon one morning when a pattern of flying bombs was mapped on their route, and friends knew that the Queen was 'in torment' until she learned that the two girls were safely back at the Castle. Indeed, Lilibet and Margaret were with a group of Girl Guides in Windsor Great Park one morning when a 'doodle bug' thrummed overhead; the girls fell flat, as they had been drilled to do, the Guide captain flung herself on Lilibet, and the bomb exploded a mile or two away on Windsor racecourse. Altogether, more than 200 bombs fell within the park, mercifully with few casualties. One bomb, however, destroyed the two entrance cottages of Royal Lodge, killing a gatekeeper and his wife, and the King and Queen left London as soon as they could to help comfort the survivors. The toll of the war within their personal circle would no longer bear counting. The Queen's Bowes-Lyon nephew, John, son of her eldest brother and heir to the Strathmore title, was killed at Halfaya Pass. Her brother-in-law, the

Duke of Kent, lost his life in an RAF plane crash.

There was a phase earlier in 1944 when Dover and Folkestone bore the brunt of shell-fire and aerial attacks from the German weaponry on the French shore. Winston Churchill's visits to these towns were widely publicised, but Queen Elizabeth decided that these tours of inspection did not answer the needs of the feminine element of the population, who were in fact under shell-fire as the women of England had never been before, and she made her own conscientious and separate visits. Then, in November, a close though not unexpected bereavement occurred in the death of her father, Lord Strathmore, at the age of eighty-nine.

The ashes of the gentle old man were laid to rest at Glamis in the presence of the King and Queen and other family mourners, and Queen Elizabeth returned from the funeral with the sense of loneliness and of a new beginning which we all have on the death of our last parent. The talk now was of the makings of the peace, and to Sir John Reith the Queen was emphatic on one occasion that the Christian ethic should be the basis of post-war policy. There were discussions of a broadcast in which the King might make his own similar views known to the world, and the Queen interposed, 'He really does believe it, you know.'

The unconditional surrender of the German forces was signed in the small hours of Monday morning 7 May 1945. (It was ironic that the sudden death of President Roosevelt had occurred not four weeks earlier.) On the Tuesday afternoon Churchill made the official announcement of victory in Europe and from that moment the multitudes outside the Palace chanted 'We want the King! We want the Queen!' until they appeared with their daughters on the balcony and waved and smiled towards that excited swirling sea. 'We went out eight times altogether,' the King noted. The Queen told Cecil Beaton that the balcony wasn't really safe after the bombing, and it showed. That evening the King broadcast to his peoples, necessarily not the firmer words of Christian post-war policy which his wife had desired. These were to be left to governments, but one may discern wifely influence, and certainly the Queen's full agreement, in his call to an act of national thanksgiving. During the next two days the King and his Queen drove in State through East and South London, moved beyond their expectations by the reception they encountered.

It was the fervour of the Coronation over again, renewed in an unpainted, threadbare, dusty, shabby and makeshift post-war world. As in the Coronation year, the couple made journeys to Edinburgh and

Belfast; and their welcome was nowhere greater than when they visited the newly-liberated Channel Isles in the cruiser *Jamaica* and moved again among the only British peoples who had suffered under the Nazi yoke. Here, above all, the jubilant, loyal welcome turned the Queen's emotions. 'The Queen and I have been overcome by everybody's kindness,' wrote the King from Windsor. 'We have only tried to do our duty during these 5½ years.'

13. *In the Peace*

Queen Elizabeth celebrated her forty-fifth birthday with a Saturday family outing to Ascot races with the King and Princess Elizabeth. Among the runners was her husband's own Hampton-bred horse, Rising Light, and the royal party had the enjoyment of seeing the colt catch up with his rival in a last-second spurt and win by inches in a thrilling finish. For the King, moreover, it was the first horse of his own, as distinct from his leased National Stud string, that he had ever seen ridden to victory.

The very name, Rising Light, seemed propitious, and if the family dinner-party produced jokes about being halfway to ninety, the Queen could reply that she still felt like a rising light herself. To maintain the mood of victory, the royal party again went to Ascot races on the Bank Holiday Monday and had no sooner appeared in the royal box, the King still in uniform, than another of his own horses, Kingstone, obligingly won by four lengths. The Queen found Princess Elizabeth's racing excitement infectious. The Sport of Kings had provided some lighter moments of relaxation during the war, particularly when Sun Chariot won a wartime Oaks in the royal colours, and now racing was to join reading, gardening, walking and the pleasures of human sociability among the Queen's leisure preoccupations. On 15 August, she rode with her husband to the State Opening of Parliament, having helped him to rehearse two alternative speeches in case the war with Japan should end; and the day in fact marked the official end of hostilities in Asia. An impromptu family dinner-party was staged at Buckingham Palace that evening. The following week the Balmoral estate was devoted to a supreme family gathering.

Among the guests were the Queen's sisters, Mary and Rose, her brother David, and many old friends. The Queen had visited Rose, Countess Granville, that summer on the Isle of Man, where her husband was Lieutenant-Governor, giving Rose an illusion of burning her own small candle of deputy queenship. May, as Lady Elphinstone was so often called, was installed with her now grown-up family at Birkhall: her second son Andrew, her fourth child, had returned safely from a German prison-camp and was intent upon entering the Church. And there were Rachel and David's children, Simon and Davina, with just two years dividing them, teenagers as attached as ever David and Elizabeth had been. The house-party included the ever faithful Arthur Penn, Piers Legh and his American wife, the Eldons, Adeanes and others.

The anniversary of the outbreak of war saw the brilliant summer day when the King proposed trying for everything on the game-card and the bag memorably included everything from a stag – shot by Princess Elizabeth – to trout, salmon and an accidental sparrow-hawk. Among the Queen Mother's treasures at Birkhall is a silver mat engraved with the names of the rods and guns. Queen Elizabeth supervized the picnics, and the three sisters revelled in a memorably happy day together at her two-room cottage on the moors. This was of the simplest order, 'one room used as a dining-room with a little table in the centre, and an open fireplace opposite the door; the other evidently the kitchen,' with 'a huge open fireplace with equipment for cooking food', as an earlier guest, Mr Mackenzie King, described it. At the rough wooden table, or on cloths spread in the sun, the moorland feast was of 'cold grouse, a salad, different kinds of sandwiches, bread and butter and cake'.

The holidaymakers returned to Balmoral Castle in time for the ceremony of Beating the Retreat by one of the Highland regiments in the dusk on the front lawn. With this one royal difference, it was like the old days at Glamis: the pipers marching around the dining-table and away, until the music faded in the distance. A new generation renewed the fun of charades. The Game, as it was always called, the game which Churchill 'obviously regarded as inane', was – in the right company – fun of infinite variety, never to be despised. The pastime involved acting out syllables and words to be solved by others. The word 'Crimea' provided a memorable performance: first a crime involving the Queen as a bewildered foreigner; then the last syllable 'ea' as a political meeting full of helpful 'Hear, hears'; and the full word featured Princess Margaret as a Russian spy and the Queen again as Florence Nightingale, using a red chiffon scarf for a blood-stained bandage.

Dressing-up, acting, talking – still at heart the small girl who had held a 'conversation' with Lord Gorell – Queen Elizabeth had little reason to notice the 'horrid milestone' of her mid-forties. The war had snatched a span out of everyone's life, and one felt justified in discounting five years. She enjoyed arguments less than of old, was more subtle and no doubt more practised in caution. Mr Mackenzie King had found the King 'looking older, inclined to be rather excitable', but the Queen 'could not possibly have been more friendly'. This was the common experience. It was equally still the experience of those close to her that her gaiety and cordiality cloaked the real strength of her personality. 'Though she may fight with masked batteries,' Cynthia Asquith said, 'her purpose is nearly always fulfilled.'

Cecil Beaton was beguiled by the Queen's 'slightly hesitant' manner of speaking. 'It gave great point to the delayed word and created a charming atmosphere of shyness and humility . . . "I thought – perhaps – I might wear – a *dress* which perhaps you *know* – with bead embroideries?"' Her friends knew that she had grown accustomed to the aura of majesty without diminishing her endearing sympathy and playful humour. Already, in the memoirs of King George VI's reign, one discerns how often the King's visitors at the Palace 'happened to meet the Queen in the corridor' and how often the Queen offered consolation for Ministers relinquishing their portfolios, or encouragement for diplomats taking up new posts abroad, meetings invariably of useful purpose. Edward Marsh noted that he 'met her by chance in the passage: she was most gracious' but in fact she had been waiting to congratulate him on his KCVO. The chances occurred too often for coincidence. Wit and mischief were never far distant. Meeting Sir John Reith ostensibly by chance, wearing his new ribbon of the GCVO, the Queen said that it was her duty as Grand Master of the Victorian Order to sign the parchment document of appointment and mentioned smilingly that she was always afraid of making a blot. Sir John replied lightly that a blot would enhance the value of the document, and he would hope to find one. Three weeks later it arrived with no obvious blot. But below the signature 'Elizabeth R', was 'a full stop, which was a very large full stop indeed'.

A Consort Queen can rarely express her motivations in public, but Queen Elizabeth liked to speak of the three Ds – Discernment, to judge between the false and true; Decision, to turn judgment into action; and Design, to give practical form to a plan of action. And there was a fourth D, in depths too intimate for speech-making, D for Devout. Perhaps the Ds echo something her mother had said. The house governor of St Mary's Hospital once remarked that it was a miracle St Mary's was never hit by bombs during the war. 'A miracle?' said the Queen. 'That may be so. You know, I include St Mary's in my prayers every night.' A pulic message from the Queen to the World's Evangelical Alliance had contained a significant admission: 'I can truly say that the King and I long to see the Bible back where it ought to be, as a guide and comfort in the homes and lives of our people. From our own experience we know what the Bible can mean for personal life.'

The Palace carpets were threadbare and patched. After that first euphoric post-war holiday, new realities had to be faced. Winston Churchill's leadership had given way to a Labour government. There were new faces from Whitehall, new friendships to be forged, that skill at which the Queen so excelled. In a broadcast the King had warned his people that the 'inevitable consequences of the war would be felt long after we have all forgotten the rejoicings of today'. His wife equally braced herself to the new concept that the six years of war might well be followed by six harsh years of austerity. 'They faced up to their changed life,' said David Bowes Lyon. 'They made the best of it.' The Queen also perceived an impending change at the very heart of her family. The girls were growing up.

Both her daughters had inherited more than a just share of her determination, steeling into obstinacy and, to gain their own way, both at times almost comically employed the same devious stratagems that old Lady Airlie could remember from Queen Elizabeth's girlhood. Princess Elizabeth besieged her father for a year with pleas to be allowed to join the Services, until in March 1945, he no longer had the heart to resist and she undertook training as a Second Subaltern in the ATS. 'We talked of sparking plugs through the whole of dinner,' the Queen told a friend. Princess Margaret had been no less insistent about the first of the Windsor pantomimes, producing drawings, arranging parts, talking pantomime constantly, until at length the King gave way. In the autumn of 1945, similarly, Lilibet suffered a riding accident and was laid up, bruised and aching, for a few days, whereupon Margaret, aged fifteen, begged to be allowed to take over her engagements, especially one involving a public speech that began, 'Now that the long years of war are over and victory is won, we must look forward with glad determination and courage to the tasks that lie ahead.' It occurred to the Queen, as with others, that 'glad determination' were the salient words.

A wartime newcomer, the good-looking RAF equerry, Peter Townsend, noticed 'the astonishing affection generated by that small family', with none of the disputes, sulking or disapproving voices found in other households. The problem of Princess Elizabeth's marriage however increasingly troubled her parents. Prince Philip was in fact only twenty-two when he first broached the possibility of courtship and Lilibet was no more than seventeen. He had paid three or four brief visits to Windsor when on leave, and King George of Greece played a decidedly premature ace in speaking up for his young kinsman. At Windsor the King and Queen perceived 'a situation' both dismaying and astonishing. 'We both think she is too young for that now, as she has never met any young men of her own age,' the King wrote to Queen Mary. 'We are going to tell George that P had better not think any more about it for the present.'

'They want her to see more of the world before committing herself, and to meet more men,' Queen Mary supplemented this information to Lady Airlie, and added lightly, 'I suppose my son is wise. After all he had to wait long enough for *his* wife, and you can see what a success their marriage is!'

Queen Elizabeth nonetheless saw with a mother's watchfulness that there were one or two young Guards officers of ancient family and engaging personality not without appeal to the impressionable Princess. One of them, it was noted, 'fitted in particularly well with the household. He was gentle and poetic and had a delightful sense of humour'. But this paragon became engaged elsewhere and Lilibet took the loss in her stride. Remembering the persuasive influence of Princess Mary's dance parties in the old days, the Queen encouraged Lilibet, and her ever-eager sister, to give gramophone dances at Royal Lodge and the Palace; yet it was Prince Philip's photograph, in disguise with a bushy beard, which gained prominence on Princess Elizabeth's dressing-table. As one friend assessed the situation, neither the King nor the Queen would make up their minds what was best for their daughter. 'They wanted the best for her, and it is never easy for parents to decide what that best is.'

An unexpected complication for the Queen was that the more Philip made headway, the more incandescent became the news publicity. In the autumn of 1946 it became so troublesome that engagement rumours were three times officially – and correctly – denied at her wish. Princess Elizabeth could plead to her mother that an announced engagement would clear the air but Philip was still constitutionally in line to the throne of Greece and difficulties in that country remained to be cleared up. The King received advice that the young couple should wait until after the conclusion of the Royal Family's coming visit to South Africa;

and the Queen noticed that her elder daughter was quiet and subdued as she prepared for the African adventure.

A visit to the then Dominion of South Africa had first been proposed by General Smuts a year or two earlier, and in 1946 the Field Marshal and his son spent a weekend at Windsor Castle discussing the final arrangements. 'I don't mind confessing to you alone that I was rather fearful about it,' the King confided to Smuts months later. Dissensions still actively dragged on from the Kruger republic and it was only five years since the Nationalists had voted for secession from the British Crown. The Queen well knew that the King invariably enjoyed getting to grips with problems at first hand but her own share in reconciling both British and Dutch susceptibilities was summarized in a single widely published remark. A Boer veteran grunted, 'Pleased to have met you, Ma'am, but we still feel sometimes that we cannot forgive the English . . .'. 'I understand perfectly,' she replied. 'We feel very much the same in Scotland, too.'

It was the first tour by the royal family of four – the King and Queen and the two Princesses – and they sailed in the Navy's then newest battleship, *Vanguard*, which Princess Elizabeth had launched some two years previously. By bizarre circumstance, it proved to be the coldest British winter for a century and, as they ploughed towards the sun, the news from home was of unceasing blizzards, of blocked and frozen roads, power cuts and dwindling stocks of fuel, of food ships held up in dock and supply trains halted by the unprecedented snowfalls. For several days the *Vanguard* encountered heavy seas, which the Queen hardly seemed to notice. 'She played Chinese checkers though she had to hold on to the board,' Lady Harlech said later. 'It's like being stroked,' said the Queen, as they entered a warmer latitude and calm waters. But Lilibet unguardedly summed up, 'while we are scorching, we feel rather guilty at being right away from it all', and the Queen wrote home to Queen Mary, 'we think of home all the time, and Bertie has offered to return but Mr Attlee thought that it would only make people feel that things were getting worse, and was not anxious for him to come back'.

When the *Vanguard* sailed into Table Bay the Queen's mail brought an Aberdeen newspaper with pictures of sheep frozen in the fields near Birkhall, and yet a few minutes later the Queen stepped out on deck to the happy view of school-children massed on Signal Hill in brilliant sunlight, their white outfits forming a living slogan, 'Welcome'.

By car, train and plane, the Royal Family were constantly on the move through South Africa and the Rhodesias from 17 February to 24 April, yet the full and overpowering schedules were not received aboard *Vanguard* until two days before the travellers disembarked at Cape Town. The Queen wrote to Queen Mary that she feared the tour would be 'very strenuous', although Princess Elizabeth put it with more youthful and reckless verve, 'my heart rather sinks when I think what is ahead . . . it is absolutely staggering how much they expect us to do and go on doing for so long at a stretch. I hope we shall survive, that's all . . '

The tour party was as congenial as the Queen could wish. Apart from the King's secretaries, the Queen had her own secretary, Major Harvey; her two ladies-in-waiting, Lady Harlech and Lady Delia Peel, with Lady Margaret Egerton as lady-in-waiting to the Princesses; and then there were 'the two Peters', Wing-Commander Peter Townsend and Lieutenant-Commander Peter Ashmore as equerries, both often agreeable riding and dancing partners to the Princesses. Peter Ashmore was a bachelor and like Prince Philip, who was the same age, he had served on destroyers, which created a common interest with Princess Elizabeth, while the older and married Peter Townsend was already a sympathetic friend and counsellor to Princess Margaret.

The pattern had formed before *Vanguard* docked and, in the first hours ashore, the banquet in City Hall provided an unforeseen minor complication: seven lean years of war and austerity had left the visitors unaccustomed to lavish menus, and all the royal party felt an uneasy queasiness. An American correspondent described the tour as 'an endless procession of official receptions, tedious reviews, soporific speeches and tiresome dedications'. But it was a fact that the Queen attempted to charge each solid unremitting duty with new significance; and succeeded in winning friends with every introduction, every handshake, every smile. 'The King owed so much to the gracious – and tenacious – support of the Queen,' wrote Peter Townsend. 'She was indefatigable . . . Even the hardest republican hearts melted before her radiance.'

The unique phenomenon of the royal journey was the ivory-and-gold White Train with its fourteen coaches, a third of a mile long from locomotive to baggage tender, a snaking caravan intended to be as efficient and restful a travelling home as could be devized. Yet the Queen always made a point of sitting 'in the hot seat' by the window on long runs, to be there ready to return the wave of some isolated farmer. Whenever the

The Queen, Empress of India, broadcasts to the women of the Empire from Buckingham Palace. A wartime study by Cecil Beaton, 1939. POPPERFOTO

A work-party at Buckingham Palace, 1940: the Queen (third from left) sewing. CATHCART ARCHIVES

During the Battle of Britain. . . 'He says his hands are dirty!' POPPERFOTO

A flashback to the royal visit to South Africa, 1947. With General Smuts in the Natal National Park.
PRESS ASSOCIATION

King George VI and Queen Elizabeth on their Silver Wedding drive, April 1948.
POPPERFOTO

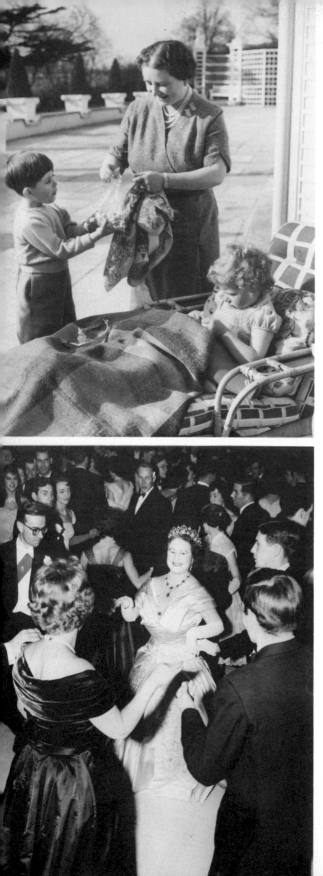

The Queen Mother at
home at Royal Lodge
with Prince Charles and
Princess Anne, 1954.
RADIO TIMES-HULTON

At the Castle of Mey
with her friends
Commander and Lady
Doris Vyner. JOHN ADAMS

Dancing an eightsome
reel at a London
University Ball.
ASSOCIATED PRESS

*Her zest for racing. . .
With the Queen and
Princess Margaret at the
Derby, 1959.*
ASSOCIATED PRESS

*A stroll at Royal Lodge
for a 70th birthday
photograph.*
CECIL BEATON
CAMERA PRESS

The happy grandmother — with Prince Charles, Princess Anne and Prince Andrew.

REUTERPHOTO

A medal for mother-in-law: the Duke of Edinburgh presents the Albert Medal to the Queen Mother for her services to art. PRESS ASSOCIATION

Four generations: the Queen Mother with her first great-grandson, Master Peter Phillips, 1977. PRESS ASSOCIATION

Tribute of flowers:
the Queen Mother outside Clarence House
on her 80th birthday
with the children of the realm.
POPPERFOTO

*A solemn moment
at the wedding of Charles and Diana,
St Paul's Cathedral, 29 July 1981.*
POPPERFOTO

royal train spent the night in a siding near a vineyard or farm, one or other of the party invariably walked to the house next morning to express thanks for the owner's hospitality. This, too, was an effective exercise in public relations. The schedules of the White Train were often delayed after the listed presentations while the Queen made her way towards some small group at the back of the platform. After listening to a Bantu choir, she spent an extra forty minutes going round the ranks of singers on a chatty walkabout.

On the other hand, the sheer tension of the tour caused the Queen a fright in an incident she termed 'the worst mistake of my life'. Touring by car through the jubilant crowds of the Reef towns, the King was on edge with fatigue and the Queen trying her best to soothe him when suddenly a huge Zulu burst from the throng and rushed at terrifying speed towards the slow-moving open car, shouting and gesticulating with every apparent ferocity. His fingers clutched the car and he hung on with something shining in his free hand while the Queen beat him off, whacking him with her parasol until it broke in two. The police knocked him senseless, and within a second the Queen was waving and smiling, as captivating as ever. She had quite thought she was fending off a potential assassin. In fact he was clutching a ten-shilling note loyally intended as a birthday gift for Princess Elizabeth.

The tour extended into Rhodesia as far north as the Victoria Falls, burnishing the Queen's love affair with that tormented country. In Salisbury her husband opened Parliament as King of Rhodesia, and near Bulawayo the party walked up the granite hill slope to the grave of Cecil Rhodes until the Queen found she could hardly undertake another step in her high-heeled cutaway shoes. Lilibet lent her mother her sandals and continued the climb in her stockinged feet. 'It was so like Mummy to set out in those shoes,' said the Princess. It was so like Queen Elizabeth, climbing a mountain while on duty, so far from home, always to wish to look her formal best. 'People dress up to see me,' she once said. 'I must dress up for them'.

The King and Queen returned to London on 12 May, the tenth anniversary of their Coronation. Despite the physical demands of the tour, they noticed the sense of relaxation after the untroubled cruise home. Lilibet danced a little jig of joy on the *Vanguard*'s deck when she sighted the English coastline, deliriously happy that the difficulties of her engagement were at last to be smoothed away. The King could joke that they had all reduced their weight, but the Queen was horrified to discover that her husband, never with a surplus ounce, had in fact lost seventeen pounds. 'If as I firmly believe it has, our visit has altered the conception of Monarchy to some South Africans and has given them a new viewpoint, then our tour has been well worth while,' the King wrote privately to General Smuts. The plural was not the royal 'We', but the unity of husband and wife. None could divine that within four-teen years South Africa would become a republic. It was a more apparent irony that within four months of the *Vanguard*'s return India became a self-governing nation and, on 15 August 1947 the King effectively ceased to sign as 'George R I'. 'The I for Emperor of India left out, very sad,' Queen Mary noted. But Queen Elizabeth had never signed herself as more than Elizabeth R, and she ceased to be Empress of India with but the smallest pang. It would perhaps lessen the con-stant work on Bertie's desk.

At the end of Royal Ascot week at Windsor the Queen gave a dance for 100 young people, all friends of her daughters, at which the Princess and Prince Philip – now Lieut Philip Mountbatten, RN, a naturalized British subject – danced nearly every dance together. On 8 July, the young man was invited to Buckingham Palace for dinner, and he and the Princess were a little behind-hand in entering the dining-room together. The Queen immediately noticed that her daughter's right hand covered the fingers of her left hand, and at once went and kissed her. 'It's too big!' said the Princess, laughing and displaying her dia-mond ring, which was loose on her finger and had to be returned to the jewellers for fitting next day. On 10 July the engagement was made known to the world.

Queen Elizabeth knew no phase more crowded with gossipy happy events nor with the sweetness of memory than when she prepared for her daughter's marriage. Friends suspected a maternal desire to defer the wedding-day till the Spring because of the promise of better weather, but it was difficult to thwart youthful impatience even long enough to make the arrangements for wedding guests. Norman Hart-nell had arranged to visit the United States to receive a dressmaker's award, the Neiman-Marcus 'Oscar' of couturiers, and cancelled his journey in order to make the wedding-dress in time. 'I roamed the Lon-don art galleries in search of classic inspiration,' he wrote, 'and fortu-nately found a Botticelli figure in clinging ivory silk, trailed with jasmine, smilax, syringa and small white rose-like blossoms.' The Queen and her daughter approved the design only on the eve of leaving for Balmoral, and for herself Queen Elizabeth approved 'a dress of apricot and golden brocade, gracefully draped and trailing'.

The wedding of Princess Elizabeth took place on 20 November 1947. There were the inevitable wedding-day crises, usual in any family. As a bride's perquisite of 'something borrowed' the Princess had selected her mother's sunray diamond tiara, and as the piece was being set upon her head, the old wire frame snapped. 'We have two hours, and there are other tiaras,' the Queen calmed her, as a jeweller rushed the piece to his workshop for repair. The bride also wished to wear the double string of pearls her parents had given her as a wedding gift, which had been placed among the wedding-presents on show at St James's Palace, and Jock Colville, her recently appointed private secretary, had some trouble in bringing it back through the police cordons. At the last moment, too, the bridal bouquet disappeared, but happily came to light presently in a cupboard. As one of the dressers noted, 'the Princess had her head in the clouds', and it was the Queen who smoothed these difficulties. One of her staff on this day of deep but checked emotion had never more admired her self-control. It was the Queen's idea, similarly, that each plate at the wedding breakfast had beside it a bunch of white heather, sent down from Balmoral.

'What a wonderful day it has been,' she said afterwards and, philosophically, 'they grow up and leave us, and we must make the best of it.' The first disconsolate blank in her motherly world was lightened however by a letter from Lilibet on her honeymoon saying that, after all, the long wait before the engagement and the wedding had been for the best. 'I was so glad you wrote and told Mummy . . .' the King had occasion to reply. 'I was rather afraid that you had thought I was being hard-hearted about it. I was so anxious for you to come to South Africa as you knew. Our family, us four, the "Royal Family" must remain together with additions of course at suitable moments! I have watched you grow up all these years with pride under the skilful direction of Mummy, who as you know is the most marvellous person in the World in my eyes . . .'

14. *Light and Shadow*

In the retrospect of her middle years it can be seen that the Queen Mother – the then Queen of England – passed through a seven-year phase of alternate rejoicing and anxiety, joy and grief. In April, 1948, five months after Princess Elizabeth's wedding the King and his Consort set aside a day of national thanksgiving and rededication for their Silver Wedding. The precedent of a semi-state drive to a thanksgiving service in St Paul's Cathedral had been established by King George V and Queen Mary in 1918. Under the dreary monotony of austerity and shortage which thirty years later followed the long struggle of another war, the British people found the observances of national pageantry all the more welcome, 'a flash of colour on the hard road we have to travel', as Winston Churchill had said earlier. One felicitous observance was the issue of a special Silver Wedding postage stamp on which the Queen herself appeared, posed in profile with her husband, wearing the necklace of diamonds and rubies that had been his wedding gift.

For the King and Queen, with Princess Margaret, the day began with the private observance of Holy Communion. Later that morning observers were unanimous that Queen Elizabeth had never looked more serenely beautiful than in the drive in the open state landau through the two miles of cheering spectators to St Paul's. With a congregation of 4,000, the service was broadcast to the world.

In the white and gold State dining-room of Buckingham Palace, seventy guests were entertained to luncheon. To count the Queen's blessings after twenty-five years, six of her eight bridesmaids were at the Palace, each with remembrances, each with a renewed sense of affectionate dedication to her, as the one-tier cake was cut. Lady Katherine Seymour *née* Hamilton, Lady Nunburnholme *née* Mary Thynne, Lady May Abel-Smith, the daughter of the Earl of Athlone, the Duchess of Beaufort, formerly Lady Mary Cambridge, the Queen's sister-in-law, Mrs Michael Bowes-Lyon, formerly Betty Cator and

Mary Elphinstone, all were there. It was a sadness that the youngest bridesmaid, the former Cecilia Bowes-Lyon, had died the previous year in Switzerland. Another guest was Lady Doris Vyner, who had been a Gordon-Lennox, sister of the 9th Duke of Richmond, a friend so dear that she would certainly have been a bridesmaid in 1923 if her own wedding only a few days earlier had not made her a bride. Around the table, though some were gone, there were still brothers and sisters-in-law to share the fun. She could see beloved nephews and nieces and so many old friends.

In the afternoon the long-wedded pair drove in an open car in the April sunshine through twenty miles of the shabbier streets of London, receiving everywhere an affectionate ovation. Returning to the Palace, the King and Queen were called repeatedly to the balcony and then the crowds fell silent to hear over the loudspeakers the 'Silver Wedding broadcast', first from the King and then his wife. The King spoke of the day 'of deep significance to ourselves as man and wife', of his heavy burden, at times 'almost too heavy but for the strength and comfort which I have always found in my home'. The honesty of truth necessarily shines through the formality of public speeches, and the Queen then spoke of her deep thankfulness 'for our twenty-five years of happiness together, for the opportunities of service we have been given to our beloved country, and for the blessings of our home and children . . .

'There must be many who feel, as we do,' she continued, 'that the sanctities of married life are in some way the highest form of human fellowship . . . Looking back over the last twenty-five years and to my own happy childhood, I realize more and more the wonderful sense of security and happiness which comes from a beloved home. Therefore at this time my heart goes out to all those who are living in uncongenial surroundings and who are longing for the time when they will have a home of their own.'

These words were truthful, compassionate and homely, and precisely what the people wished to hear. Before the day closed, Michael Adeane showed the Queen Mother another considerable pile of the well-wishing letters and messages that were pouring in from all parts of the world. 'We were both dumbfounded over our reception . . .' the King reported to his mother. 'So many nice letters from all and sundry, thanking us for what we have tried to do all these years. It does spur us on to further efforts.'

In the stocktaking of their happy married life, she and her husband could now privately anticipate their first grandchild. Princess Elizabeth expectantly brought out the old pram 'to get my hand in' one morning, and her mother spoke wistfully to Lady Granville of how much Alah would have enjoyed the preparations, the flood of gifts.* A deep fulfilment mingles with sweet incredulity in the anticipations of one's first grandchild, but the family happiness was darkly edged for Queen Elizabeth by an unforeseen anxiety for the King's health. He had been aware for some time of a tendency to cramp in his legs until, in the autumn of 1948, he had to admit to his wife that the pain often kept him awake at night. On 30 October – only two days before the birth of Prince Charles – four doctors undertook a full-scale examination, and what they had to tell the Queen was distressing. 'In layman's language,' the King wrote to his Balmoral physician, Dr Middleton, 'the doctors have found the cause of the trouble.' And he gave details of an obstruction in the arteries causing a risk that his right leg might have to be amputated.

Under the intense shock of this discovery, husband and wife were agreed that Lilibet should not be told until safely after the baby's arrival. Marion Crawford, who was still with the Household as governess to Margaret, mentions that 'the Queen was quite distraught with anxiety until the operation was over'. The Princess had insisted on having her baby at home 'in my own room, among the things I know', but in fact the Buhl Room on the first floor of the Palace was made ready as a surgery. On 12 November the King underwent investigative surgery to relieve the obstruction and on the evening of 14 November Prince Philip hurried to the Queen at her husband's bedside with the joyful news that a grandson had been born, and the Queen went down in the lift to the Belgian Suite to take the seven pound six ounce baby Prince Charles in her arms.

Meanwhile the cheers and songs of the waiting crowds could be heard deep inside the Palace, a tumult renewed for the arrival of Queen Mary, then in her eighty-second year, 'delighted at being a great-grandmother' as she noted next day. Presently the crowds had to be asked for 'a little quietness, please' and gradually the crowds dispersed, unaware that the request had been as much for the King's sake as for the Princess. The first bulletin on his health was not made public until nine days later. By then his improvement had surprised the doctors, and on 15 December he was able to attend his grandson's christening in the gold and silver Music Room of the Palace. One looks through the photographs of that

* Clara Knight had died at Sandringham two years earlier. 'I feel that so much of my life has gone with her,' the Queen had said.

private family gathering, and finds for one moment the Queen, in her dress of gold tissue, and her brother, David, alone together: David with the flower of a godfather in his buttonhole standing as if protectively behind the little Elizabeth Lyon of long ago, and on the Queen's face is the look of anxious care that her family had noticed in the months of self-questioning before she decided to wed.

By the end of the year, the King's health had so much improved that the threat of amputation was past. As a grandmother should, the Queen had the very real pleasure of mothering her daughter's child, for Princess Elizabeth fell ill with measles at Sandringham and had to remain in isolation. On the Royal Family's return to London, the Queen next enjoyed an early view of the renovations at Clarence House, the Nash mansion a stone's throw from Buckingham Palace, which after mouldering in disrepair for years was being restored as Princess Elizabeth and Prince Philip's future home. In February it seemed to the public a good augury that the King was able to hold his own Investiture of the New Year Honours. This involved only a small deception. The King had mentioned that the necessity of standing would be the trouble, and the Queen urged that, with an apology to the assembly, he could remain seated. Her optimism bounded again, but sadly, in the following month, the doctors had to tell her that they were not yet satisfied with the King's condition, and on 12 March her husband underwent a further operation to improve the circulation of his right leg.

As both wife and mother, the Queen strove to keep her worst fears to herself. To provide an extra distraction for Princess Elizabeth she asked her old friend, Peter Cazalet, who had become a professional National Hunt trainer, to look about for a steeplechaser of quality which she might own in partnership with the Princess. The Queen had readily understood how the zest and uncertainty of racing could absorb her elder daughter and, a curious twist, this attempt to divert the Princess from worrying was the beginning of the Queen Mother's own ardent interest in steeplechasing. But it was early summer before Mr Cazalet acquired Monaveen. By then the King had again made a good recovery and the actual purchase of the horse, as it turned out, was in its own small fashion to help interest and comfort the Queen herself in a further private sadness, namely, the death at a comparatively early age of sixty-five of her eldest brother Patrick (the 15th Earl of Strathmore) who had been so blithe a guest at her Silver Wedding.

Thus went the flux of light and shadow.

It fell to a Scotsman, Professor James Learmonth of Edinburgh, one of the foremost vascular specialists in the country, to break it to the Queen that her husband's life would have to be very different in the future. The King was soon in sufficient health to receive all seven of his Commonwealth Prime Ministers but henceforward would steadily have to avoid exertion. 'He may pay more heed to you, Ma'am, than to his doctors,' was the tenor of the advice to the Queen. She had feared worse, and her sense of relief and of fun obviously lay behind a ceremony in the King's bedroom, just after Professor Learmonth's final examination, when his patient asked him to pass him his bath-robe and slippers and then suddenly produced a sword from beneath the pillow. 'You used a knife on me,' said the King. 'Now I'm going to use one on you,' and, bidding the surgeon kneel, he bestowed the accolade of knighthood.

As an instance of the new regimen, the King attended the Trooping the Colour ceremony seated in an open carriage, while Princess Elizabeth took the salute as his deputy, and a variety of public engagements were henceforth unobtrusively transferred to his wife or elder daughter. The Queen's mention in a speech of 'the person who once prayed to be granted, not a lighter load, but a stronger back' was meaningful. Loath to give up his shooting at Balmoral that August, the King improvised a harness with a long trace attached to a pony, which pulled him uphill. 'I've only got to *move* my legs without any exertion,' he explained. Should the pony ever bolt, the difficulty had been foreseen and a quick-release mechanism would detach the King in his harness. But the Queen preferred simpler measures and a set of happy snapshots shows her, wearing one of her favourite old felt hats, sprawling in the heather with her husband for a picnic, with Philip and Lilibet, David Lyon and others in the background. 'Fine, SW wind, 263 grouse, 2 golden plover', noted the King in his game-book.

Life was quiet at the Palace after Elizabeth and Philip had moved into Clarence House, and quieter still whenever the Princess joined her husband in Malta. A happy sequel in the New Year of 1950 was her delighted news that she was expecting another baby, with a reasonable prospect that this second grandchild might arrive on the Queen's birthday. 'Or perhaps mine!' said Princess Margaret, who already enjoyed being styled 'Charlie's Aunt'.

The stork judiciously divided the honours. On 4 August the Queen celebrated her fiftieth birthday with her husband in London amid family festivities and on the 11th, for the first time, the King travelled north alone for his Balmoral commitments, while the Queen remained in town to await events. *The Times* had commented on the Queen's birthday in a leader, 'it would be impossible to over-estimate the reinforcement that the King has derived from the serene and steady support of the Queen. She has sustained him in sickness and in health, at all times taking her full share in the burdens of royal service', and through the next ten days newspapers noted the ever-swelling crowds around Clarence House. On the morning of 15 August their cheers welcomed the Queen to Clarence House at 11.45, and a daughter was born to Princess Elizabeth five minutes later.

The Queen had vivid memories of the difficulties when she had wished to name her own second baby Ann, but now she and her husband were charmed by the names Anne Elizabeth Alice Louise. With the King's returning strength, there ensued a period of calm when Lilibet was able to absent herself from late November into February, 1951, with her husband in the Mediterranean. The Queen's task lay largely in preserving the serenity of her own domestic scene and in softening her husband's occasional irascible outbursts – though never with her – that so tried his nerves. In the international field, the lowering shadows of the Korean war, where British naval forces and troops were involved, and the oil nationalization crisis in Anglo-Persian relations both ultimately combined to depress him.

'The incessant worries and crises got me down properly,' he later wrote to a friend. Then optimism was renewed with the prospect that his doctors were for the first time prepared to consider reasonably leisurely plans for a royal visit to Australia and New Zealand in the following year. The Queen expectantly arranged for a semi-holiday with her husband in June, when they intended to visit her sister Rose in Northern Ireland, where Earl Granville was Governor-General. On 24 May, however, the King retired to bed with influenza.

This time the doctors discovered a small area of catarrhal inflammation in the left lung and he was still confined to his room while Princess Elizabeth acted as his deputy for the second year at the Trooping the Colour and during a State Visit from King Haakon of Norway. 'I have a condition known as pneumonitis,' Bertie wrote to his mother. 'Not pneumonia though if left it might become it. Everyone is very relieved at this revelation and the doctors are happier. . .' The Queen camouflaged her anxieties when, as he said, he was 'unable to chuck out the bug'. By August however, she celebrated her fifty-first birthday, sunning with him at Balmoral in a happier frame of mind.

The two months' rest had restored his confidence and, early on Princess Margaret's twenty-first birthday, he was able to go rabbiting for a few hours with Prince Philip, Lord Plunket, and his old friend Sir Harold Campbell.

The sunshine and the shadow . . . the weather turned wet and cold and the King developed the symptoms of a chill. According to Peter Townsend, who had been appointed assistant Master of the Household the previous year, 'it was the Queen who, suspecting now that the King was suffering from something worse, made him send to London for his doctors'. She was told that a blockage of the bronchial tubes would necessitate 'a lung resection'. 'And what is that?' the King asked, and was warned that it might involve the removal of his left lung. The Queen learned the fuller truth of a malign growth, and was warned also of cardiac complications. She had to face a risk that the King might die of thrombosis on the operating table. Returning from Scotland, it was one of the rare occasions when she felt she could not face the scrutiny of the public and ordered her car to drive into Buckingham Palace by a side gate.

Perhaps husband and wife each kept their misgivings from the other. The King's biographer, Sir John Wheeler-Bennett, found that 'they paid minute attention to the wording of the (pre- operative) bulletins issued to the public . . . the King's considera- tion was for the suspense which the Queen and his daughters would be undergoing'. Elizabeth and Philip had been due to sail to Canada on the liner *Empress of France* for an official visit on 25 September. Instead they gained time by flying out on 8 October, after several reassuring bulletins, although the Princess carried with her a sealed envelope which she knew contained a draft Accession Declaration against the event of her father's death.

The lung resection had taken place on 23 September, and the Queen was emotionally moved and comforted by the messages that poured in not only from governments, but also from ordinary people in every part of the world. 'One must have no self pity,' she had written privately to her sister Rose, but all went well. The Queen especially took the King's duty rota of nurses under her wing. Two of the sisters were her companions that year at the Royal Variety performance, and the audience rose to give them a standing ovation. As a rarity, the brooches which the King gave the nurses bear the Queen's initials as well as his own. 'I shall never forget their gentleness, the skill and devotion,' the Queen Mother said, years afterwards.

Through the long anxious days, the Queen spent hours sitting quietly at her husband's bedside – reading, working, talking – until, in mid-October, he was sufficiently recovered to sit in his chair. Constitutionally, she had been appointed a Counsellor of State, with her daughters, the then Duke of Gloucester and the Princess Royal. Of the nurses, one had begun her training in Edinburgh, another had passed her preliminary nursing examination while still at school, a third was devoted to a sister who ran a nursery school. The Queen soon knew all their different stories, and the confidences which she in turn entrusted to them have never been betrayed. At the end of November – with the General Election settled and Winston Churchill again at the head of government – the King was able to return to Royal Lodge. 'As we drove through the gates we felt at once the calm of this place,' he wrote to a friend. The Queen had not set foot in the Lodge for four months and in the little chapel in the grounds she joined in the national thanksgiving for the King's recovery.

When Princess Elizabeth and Prince Philip returned from Canada after a most successful visit, Royal Lodge was the scene of a family reunion. At last Queen Elizabeth felt the lifting of the oppressive clouds that had burdened her for so long. The young couple took over the plans of a tour to Australia and New Zealand instead of the King, while an invitation came to their Majesties from the Prime Minister of South Africa, Dr Malan, placing a house at their disposal so that King George could recuperate in the warmth and sunshine there. The commencement of this holiday was arranged for 10 March.

The tour to Australia was to take Princess Elizabeth and her husband through Kenya, and it was a time for both the King and Queen of looking back through old photographs and souvenirs, recollecting and eagerly telling their daughter of their own adventures when they were still a newly-married young couple. At Sandringham, too, over Christmas, the sentiment of thirty years of pleasant and nostalgic experiences gathered around them. Some four years earlier, the King had set plans in motion for an enclosed garden of the Scottish pattern such as his wife had always known. The new garden was but a step from his own temporary bedroom near the north door; there were pleached lime walks to keep the wind at bay and, with memories of Glamis, husband and wife were able to stroll there for a little each day. One morning, the King put a stick to his shoulder, as if cocking a gun, and murmured, 'I believe I could shoot now,' and his wife experienced an overwhelming if illusory surge of confidence that all was well.

In the company of Prince Philip, with the royal secretary Michael

Adeane and others, the King resumed shooting on New Year's Day, 1952, and, two weeks later, the Queen was so reassured that she played truant with Princess Elizabeth to go to the races at Hurst Park, and on 30 January the whole family went to London for a theatre party. It was a happy *bon voyage* evening for Elizabeth and Philip, who were flying out to Kenya as the first leg of the intended visit to Australia the following day. The King chose the musical show at Drury Lane, *South Pacific*, with its songs of distant islands, and the following morning the King and Queen were both at Heathrow airport to bid the young people farewell.

Five days later the relentless span of time had crept round to 5 February 1952, the last full day of King George VI's life. He always keenly enjoyed a shooting day with his tenant farmers, police, keepers and so on, shooting hares, rabbits and so forth, cleaning up the land; and on this particular day the extraordinary total of 480 hares and two rabbits was obtained. Meanwhile, the Queen and Princess Margaret went to lunch with the artist, Edward Seago, at his riverside home at Ludham, some thirty miles east of Sandringham. Philip and Elizabeth had made that pleasant excursion, and Seago in turn was invited to Sandringham summer and winter. His paintings were often gifts to the Queen on her birthday and at Christmas, and her many private purchases of his work exemplified her discerning and friendly patronage. After enjoying the studio that day, the Queen and Princess Margaret went with the artist to Barton Broad, where he had hired a motor-cruiser to take them through the ever-changing waters for an hour or so, and so on to tea with a friend at Barton Hall.

Rejoining her husband at Sandringham, the Queen then devoted a little time in the nursery to sturdy three-year-old Charles and little Anne. The King greatly admired the landscape paintings and sketches the Queen had brought home, so redolent of his beloved Norfolk atmosphere, and they both viewed them again after dinner. Relaxed and contented, they listened together to a radio commentary of Princess Elizabeth and Prince Philip in Kenya before the King retired to his room to work at some papers. And so with friends, with art and a little pleasurable sight-seeing, with her grandchildren, her younger daughter, and with her husband, the King, the former Elizabeth Lyon also passed her last day as Queen of England.

In the morning Queen Elizabeth's maid, Gwen Suckling, brought her tea as usual. A few minutes later a message was brought in from the equerry-in-charge, Sir Harold Campbell, requesting to see Her Majesty. She had known Sir Harold for nearly thirty years and now it was his tragic task to tell her that the King had died peacefully in his sleep; a task that she made curiously easy.

She went to the King; and presently received the unavailing doctors, and in the King's study she gave the orders for the day, as she had always done whenever her husband was unwell. Her staff would have relieved her of these responsibilities, but she wished to work on, and she gave instructions for a vigil to be kept at the King's open door, quietly saying, 'the King must not be left'. Pale but outwardly composed, not yet clad in mourning, she began writing letters and tried to encourage Princess Margaret to follow her example. She prepared food for the two corgi dogs, as was her custom, knowing that the anodyne of occupation snatched each slow passing minute from her agony. 'I never knew a woman could be so brave,' wrote Harold Campbell to his wife that night. Within the week she had prepared a message of thanks to the 'multitude of people' who expressed their sympathy and affection. 'I want you to know how your concern for me has upheld me in my sorrow, and how proud you have made me by your wonderful tributes to my dear husband, a great and noble King. . . My only wish now is that I may be allowed to continue the work that we sought to do together.'

In privacy and desolation after the funeral, her thoughts dwelt on the day at Ludham, and she wrote to Edward Seago:

'I have been longing to write and tell you what real pleasure your lovely pictures gave the King . . . I got back to Sandringham rather late and, as I always did, rushed straight to the King's room to say that I was back and to see how he was. I found him so well, so gay and so interested in our lovely cruise; and then I told him that you had sent the pictures back in my car and we went straight to the hall where they had been set out. He was enchanted with them all, and we spent a very happy time looking at them together.

'We had such a truly gay dinner with the King, like his old self, and more picture looking after dinner. Thank you with all my heart for giving us the heavenly pictures and particularly for the pleasure you have given the King on Tuesday, 5 Feb. One cannot yet believe that it has all happened, one feels rather dazed . . . Later on I shall write and thank you for the enchanting day that Margaret and I spent with you. But I did want to tell you about the King enjoying the pictures.

Yours very sincerely,
Elizabeth R.'

Part Five

QUEEN ELIZABETH THE QUEEN MOTHER

15. *Beginning Again*

'One must feel gratitude for what has been,' said the widowed Queen, 'rather than distress for what is lost', a maxim from which Princess Margaret as well as her staff drew comfort as they awaited the return of the new Queen Elizabeth II from Kenya. The Rector of Sandringham, the Rev H D Anderson, was struck by the fact that the Princess and her mother each separately sent him a message asking him to pray for the Queen. On her first day of bereavement Queen Elizabeth went as usual to see the children in the nursery. She bore in mind the lines of William Blake, *Labour well the Minute Particulars, attend to the Little Ones; And those who are in misery cannot remain so long*. 'I have got to start sometime, better now than later,' she told Harold Campbell.

The young Queen flew home by the fastest possible route but private grief yields place to royal procedures and it was not until after her Accession Council on 8 February, the third day of her reign, that she could be reunited with her mother and sister at Sandringham. The funeral of King George VI was held at St George's Chapel, Windsor, on 14 February, and on the eve of that day his widow fulfilled one of her tasks of transition and announced that she wished to be known as Queen Elizabeth the Queen Mother, an apt and fortunate phrase.

It has been said that her guiding beacon was the thought of what her husband would have wished her to do, but in the first two months of the new reign the Queen Mother effaced herself from public life. It could not be otherwise. The return to her rooms in Buckingham Palace where she was now technically a guest; the homecoming to Royal Lodge, where each familiar morning sound betrayed a different pattern, unavoidably each waking day emphasized her desolation. Old Princess Marie Louise attempted to compliment her on her composure. 'Not when I am alone,' the Queen Mother said sadly.

Queen Elizabeth* was still only fifty-one, and the happiness of her marriage had spanned almost twenty-nine years. She had blessings to count, her two daughters and her two grandchildren, Charles and Anne, and, apart from the Royal Family, the deep turmoil of sorrow was alleviated in its degree by the consoling texture of family and friends. Her nearest Lyon brothers, David and his wife Rachel, Michael and *his* Elizabeth; the Elphinstones, and especially her sister Rose; her firm friends, Lady Doris Vyner, Lady Lavinia Annaly, Lady Katherine Seymour, Lady Ruth Fermoy, Lady Jean Rankin and their husbands, were all quickly at her side. She may have asked in thankfulness how she had earned so many friends and so much affection; and as the widowed Queen thought of the future she characteristically began to fret about any hazards to her staff. Within the month a new red leather despatch-box was brought to her desk emblazoned in gold with the words 'HM Queen Elizabeth the Queen Mother' and her cypher. The new Queen had insisted on the makers hurrying it through as a symbol to her mother of renewed purpose.

The Queen Mother believed with genuine modesty that her usefulness derived only from the late King. As a family friend, Lady Cynthia Colville, wrote with discernment, 'Whereas everybody recognized how much the King had owed to his wonderful Consort, few people realized how much she had relied on *him* – on his capacity for wise and detached judgment, for sound advice, and how lost she now felt without him.' Four years earlier, as a young bride, Lilibet had continually turned to her mother for guidance and advice. Now the very ring of resurgent youth in the immediate popular phrase 'the new Elizabethans' may have given the Queen Mother pause in considering retirement.

At this juncture the new Queen first gently drew her back into the sunlight. Just as the Queen Mother had once sought to divert Princess Elizabeth from worrying over her father by providing the racing interest of Monaveen, so her daughter turned with identical strategy to the therapy of mundane matters and urged her into an expedition to Beckhampton to see the five royal racehorses which Noel Murless had in training there. Shortly afterwards the Queen Mother attended the confirmation of the schoolboy Duke of Kent in the private chapel of Windsor Castle, a ceremony implicit with the preoccupations of young life springing up all around her and, early in May, as Colonel-in-Chief of the Black Watch, she picked up the threads of duty in making a

* The Queen Mother was known as Queen Elizabeth to her Household. Queen Elizabeth II is usually referred to as the Queen in further pages.

special journey to Scotland to inspect the 1st Battalion on its departure
for the battle-front of Korea. Then, later in the month, an enlivening
and impromptu adventure befell her.

The world's first jet airliner, the Comet, had recently made its
inaugural overnight flight to Johannesburg after trials based on the De
Havilland proving airfield near Hatfield and, lunching at Hatfield House
with her lifelong friends, Lord and Lady Salisbury, the Queen Mother
complimented Lady de Havilland on the achievement. 'Why don't you
try it, Ma'am?' Lord Salisbury suggested. Amid merriment his guest
enquired, 'You mean they have a Comet to spare?' A 'phone call arranged
a flight for a few days later, and thus it was from Hatfield, where Queen
Elizabeth I held her first Privy Council, that another Queen Elizabeth set
out for her first jet-flight, as if to prelude a new phase in her life. One could
hardly find a better illustration of what the British mean by continuity.

The flying picnic party included, with the Queen Mother and
Princess Margaret, Sir Geoffrey and Lady de Havilland, the Salisburys, Group Captain Peter Townsend, Sir Miles Thomas and, at the
last moment, two of the Queen Mother's chauffeurs were invited along
so that they, too, could enjoy the experience. They lunched over the
Alps, skirted the Mediterranean towards Bordeaux and touched down
back at Hatfield after a four-hour round flight of 1850 miles. At one
point, the Queen Mother took the test pilot John Cunningham's seat at
the controls. 'Entering into the spirit of the thing,' wrote Sir Miles
Thomas, 'Cunningham showed Her Majesty how to take hold of the
controls professionally, and how to trip out the automatic pilot . . .

' "Could we go faster than the Meteor jet fighter?" she asked, and under
Cunningham's direction she eased the control forward, the Comet
gathered speed, Cunningham gave her a little extra throttle, the mach
needle crept towards the coloured danger sector, and suddenly the Comet
began to porpoise. We had reached the limit of her aerodynamic stabi-
lity . . .' Miles Thomas wrote, 'That trip was, of course, before the
cataclysmic crashes the Comets later suffered through structural weakness.
Had that porpoising gone on the wracking on the structure could well have
precipitated a rupture . . . I still shudder every time I think of that flight.'

But the Queen Mother landed in exhilarated mood. Her sense of fun,
bubbling afresh, prompted her to send a telegram to No 600 Squadron
of the RAF, of which she was Hon Air Commodore. 'Today I took over
as first pilot. We exceeded a reading of 0.8 mach at 40,000 feet.' The
commanding officer replied to the royal message with correct aplomb,
'Your squadron overwhelmingly proud.'

The following month the Queen Mother went to stay with her close friends, the Vyners, at their poetically named Scottish home, the House of the Northern Gate, high on Dunnet Head. A daughter of the 8th Duke of Richmond and Gordon, Lady Doris was the impetuous friend who would probably have been one of her bridesmaids if she had not married Lieut Clare Vyner of the Royal Navy not a month beforehand. The two women had always kept in touch. From earlier visits the Queen Mother knew and admired the pastoral Caithness landscape and the friendly incurious local people, but now the Vyners had news of great future consequence. A few miles along the coast towards John o'Groats, Barrowgill Castle was fo sale. The sale particulars cautiously described the grey pile as having 'all the external dignity of an ancient Highland residence', and as soon as the Queen Mother drove down the long avenue of stunted trees and saw the cannon mounted in the forecourt, as at Glamis, she was captivated with the idea of possessing it.

The estate was being divided and sold up under the auspices of the then owner, Captain F B Imbert-Terry. An earlier viewer had thought it 'gaunt and windswept, the castle shabby and neglected, with dark, cramped rooms furnished with cluttered drabness'. The Queen Mother thought this unfavourable account was 'rather unfair on the owner'. There were, in fact, five white-tiled bathrooms, a measure of modern heating and – a foremost virtue in the hospitable Queen Mother's eyes – no fewer than fifteen bedrooms, apart from a staff wing. And indubitably it was a castle, a Scottish tower house, with romantic turrets and walls of masonry six feet thick. Built by the 4th Earl of Caithness in 1570 – shortly after incurring the gratitude of Mary, Queen of Scots, for serving on the jury which acquitted her lover, Bothwell, of murdering Earl Darnley – and the Earls of Caithness had lived there for 300 years.

As at Glamis, vaulted arches rose to support the massive tower structure, a double stone stairway led to the drawing-room and dining-room floor, and on one side tall windows commanded magnificent coastal views of the Pentland Firth. As at Glamis, also, there were alluring stories of ghosts and bricked-up rooms for the imaginative, and even the merit of a swinging trapdoor resembling the Glamis pattern admitting to a so-called dungeon beneath. In the grounds the twenty-five acres included an alleged deer park, a walled garden, neglected trout ponds, and a roughly constructed sea-water bathing-pool adjoining a sandy beach. Queen Elizabeth inspected the estate as if trapped in a dream and reported to southern friends that she had seen mermaids – or were they seals? – splashing on the rocks. Outwardly she told Capt Imbert-

Terry that it would be pleasant to think about and after two more visits that June she talked diffidently of a survey. In August, she found that the castle had not yet been sold, and in making up her mind she finally came five times within a week.

When asked the following year why she had bought the place, the Queen Mother explained that it was because 'it was a lovely little castle which was in danger of becoming derelict'. 'Roofless!' she had added, in a poetic flight, and indeed the ink was no sooner dry on the contract than the autumn gales blew slates from the roof. There was also the element that on her brother Patrick's death four years earlier, her nephew, Timothy, had inherited Glamis as the 16th Earl of Strathmore, imposing a sparse regime which firmly ended the old way of life. But clearly the Queen Mother shrewdly purchased her Caithness castle, to which she restored the old name of the Castle of Mey, chiefly because it filled a spare niche in her generous heart and opened appealing fresh vistas of private life, of friendly hospitality blended with solitude and time to think.

The new interest of Mey assuaged the slow transitions of widowhood. So much renovation was found desirable that three years elapsed before the Queen Mother's personal standard – the Royal Standard impaled with the black archers' bows and blue lions of the Bowes-Lyon family – was flown from the flagstaff. Damp had so penetrated the structure that the thick walls had to be 'oiled' and repointed to defy the rain; mains electricity presently banished the oil-lamps, and the gardens were rejuvenated, until eventually every detail of décor and furnishing directly expressed the new owner's standards of comfort and taste. With Doris and Clare Vyner's unfailing hospitality, Queen Elizabeth browsed through the Caithness antique shops collecting local prints and happily followed every clue to the castle treasures scattered through an auction in Victorian times. The saddle-backed Georgian chairs were restored to the dining-room, enhanced by the Queen Mother's cypher, and the Sword of State of the Earls of Caithness was traced through successive owners to a Glasgow museum, from which the City fathers gallantly presented it to her. The papier-mâché costumed blackamoor that once stood in the entrance hall of 145 Piccadilly came into use; and instead of the mournful case of stuffed birds that greeted the Queen Mother on her first viewing with the Vyners, another decorative kneeling African figure supported a large oyster-shell bowl of flowers.

Such decorative fancies set the theme of the Castle of Mey: the drawing-room with its white-and-gold Chippendale, tapestried walls and yellow upholstery; the boudoir high in the tower cosy with rush matting and tartan rugs; the bedrooms each to a different colour scheme, inviting with chintz and muslin, warm mahogany and pile carpeting. The women of Caithness once made a rug for the castle, embracing fleur-de-lis of blue and gold upon white. Each member of the scattered twenty-nine Women's Institutes worked upon the gift, and Queen Elizabeth's characteristic response to this happy sentiment has been to place the rug in her own panelled bedroom.

In spring and autumn as well as high summer, when the Queen Mother drops out of sight she is often to be found at Mey with friends or with her grandchildren or with other kinfolk seldom in the public eye. Her brother David's son and daughter, Simon and Davina, soon provided her with great-nephews and nieces, a younger generation with whom she maintained affectionate contact. The Castle of Mey was seldom deserted.

Into her mid-eighties, in fair weather, Queen Elizabeth has enjoyed fishing the Thurso river, perhaps less than of old or with no more reward than an afternoon in her green waders watching the placid eddies of the stream, though she usually helps to fill a basket. Moreover, the Lady of Mey takes part in the life of the neighbourhood – her birthdays occasionally find her at an agricultural show, presenting prizes for the best sheep and poultry and home-bottled fruit. Her benevolences also extended to the repairs of Kirkwall Cathedral in the Orkneys or the funds of the Caithness annual ball; and her hairdresser, Mr Robert, has only to telephone the housekeeper whenever he seeks a Scottish holiday.

King George VI was fond of claiming that he and his wife were 'much attached' to the domestic hearth, and he more than once delighted in giving her a fire-surround or chimney-piece as an anniversary present. One of these gifts, a small white marble surround carved with the medallion of a heart and the gentle inscription *Patientia Vincet* (Patience Conquers), was soon installed in her boudoir in the old tower of Mey, her serene sanctum of sanctums, and the white marble fireplace in her bedroom at Buckingham Palace was similarly transferred to Clarence House.

It has been the common fate of dowager Queens to be uprooted. The young Queen Victoria was regarded as highly considerate when she permitted her bereaved aunt, Queen Adelaide, to move her bedstead from Windsor Castle. Nearly a century later, Queen Mary confided to her journal 'I took leave of my lovely rooms with a sad heart' before her move to Marlborough House.

As the home of the Queen Mother, Clarence House has held its place among the pleasant landmarks of London for well over thirty years, but it had emerged from the 1939–45 war in sad dilapidation. Many rooms lacked electricity, old gas brackets sprouted from the walls and the only bath then to be found was a rusting antique in a bedroom cupboard. Designed by Nash as a mansion for the Duke of Clarence, brother of George IV, it was linked by corridors with the state rooms and diplomatic quarters of St James's Palace, a highly convenient facility. It subsequently became the residence of Queen Victoria's second son, the Duke of Edinburgh, and later of her youngest son, the Duke of Connaught. But 'Clarry' was little occupied until its brilliant transformation for Princess Elizabeth and Philip, and the Queen Mother counted its fresh modernity among her blessings. She asserted her own colour schemes, with her own money, and Parliament was required to defray the cost by only £8,000. Watching progress attentively, Queen Mary inspected the house approvingly, particularly delighted to note the care accorded the integral plaster-framed portraits of George III and his family in the State dining-room. But the old dowager Queen did not live to see the completion of the works and died on 24 March 1953.

Queen Elizabeth the Queen Mother formally moved into Clarence House on 18 May of that year, only two weeks before her daughter's Coronation. With her was her faithful but reconstituted staff, with Sir Arthur Penn as treasurer, young Captain Oliver Dawnay as private secretary, Group-Captain Peter Townsend as intended comptroller and the Lady Hyde, a friend of precisely her own age and a veteran of her own Coronation, as her first rota lady-in-waiting. With the younger Earl of Airlie as her Lord Chamberlain, these formed the firm nucleus of her entourage, supporting her in the hospitality and entertainment with which she supplemented the Coronation festivities. In the televised ceremonial of the Coronation the Queen Mother was of course both a participant in the processions and a spectator of her daughter's crowning. It had not been the custom of Queen Dowagers to witness the coronation subsequent to their own until, in 1937, Queen Mary had set a constitutional precedent by sitting with 'the little Princesses' to see her son and daughter-in-law separately crowned King and Queen. Now the Queen Mother and Princess Margaret processed effectively through the Abbey and had a space left between them in the royal gallery for the four-and-a-half-year-old Prince Charles, who presently made his appearance between his grandmother and his aunt, a small figure in white silk.

The little boy lent a happy domestic touch to the pageantry, now asking his grandmama questions, now scrambling to retrieve a handbag from beneath her chair, now heaving sighs, but often watching absorbed, head cupped in hands. In the streets, during the long processional ride, the Queen Mother as usual received an overwhelming ovation and for her, as always, a deep stirring of emotion had to be held in check. Through London's own festivities, moreover, she enjoyed one personal viewpoint known to few. At night, from a platform under the dark trees against the garden wall of Clarence House, she could look down into the radiant silver-arched avenue of the Mall and for several evenings she stood there, quite unobserved or unrecognized with David, with Rose, with Arthur Penn and other friends, enjoying the fantastic spectacle of the singing, dancing crowds.

16. *Mother and Grandmother*

To the Coronation guests in Westminster Abbey Queen Elizabeth the Queen Mother had seemed a serene and untroubled figure. Only her innermost circle knew of the private distresses and difficulties behind her smiling composure. A month before the ceremony grief had come in the early death of her elder brother, Michael, aged only fifty-nine, a sorrow deepened in that his widow was her old school friend, Elizabeth Cator, and their twin daughters, Mary and Patricia, had but recently come of age. Again, the grave illness of her brother-in-law, Earl Granville, Rose's husband, gave anxious concern; and only three weeks after the Coronation, the Queen Mother found herself sorrowing for her sister in sharing the deep inner loneliness of widowhood. Beside these anxieties the difficulties surrounding Princess Margaret's ardent wish to be betrothed to Peter Townsend weighed more heavily on her mind.

As a realist, the Queen Mother had only recently cautioned the portraitist, Denis Fildes, 'I expect you will need to show me a little older. One does not stand still.' Like a mother, she blamed herself for not anticipating the developing situation between her younger daughter and the pleasant, often self-effacing Peter. (Born in November, 1914, Peter was closer in age to the mother than to the daughter.) It is in the nature of royalty that in their own complete dedication they often unthinkingly accept an illusion of total dedication among those around them, and Group-Captain Townsend was unhappily to illustrate this dilemma.

As a young airman, a nerve-ridden fighter ace of the Battle of Britain, he had married after a few weeks' courtship and in due course had fathered two sons. In 1943, the King imaginatively decided to create a new band of Equerries of Honour from among young men with exceptional war records; and with a string of citations mentioning his 'leadership, unflagging zeal, skill and determination' Townsend was one of the first to be chosen. Supposed to last three months his term of duty was extended and he was still at the King's side eight years later.

Both men had qualities in common to forge and strengthen a bond between them. Both held a high sense of duty deepened by personal religious philosophy, each still possessed a slight stammer buoyed by social gaiety, and Peter had something of the King's early diffidence, direct honesty and quizzical humour. His early duties, he was to find, ranged from assisting the King at Investitures to taking the two young Princesses to the cinema. Later he lent lightness of heart to the royal tour of South Africa and in 1948 he was attached to Princess Margaret's small entourage attending Queen Juliana's Inauguration in Amsterdam. Then, as Assistant Master of the Household, he became an essential cog in the King and Queen's social and recreational life, almost one of the family and all but indispensable.

In the summer of 1952, while the Queen Mother was with the Vyners, the Queen, Prince Philip and Princess Margaret gravitated naturally to Saturday afternoon tea at the Townsends at their cottage in Windsor Great Park. Yet within six months Peter was awarded a decree *nisi* in the divorce court, and at Sandringham a member of the staff dauntingly recorded, 'We watched what seemed to be a ripening friendship. Our view was that it would be regrettable if a man in Townsend's position allowed Princess Margaret's interest to grow into anything stronger than friendly feeling.'

The Queen Mother understood the psychological effect of a father figure on a bereft girl in her early twenties and noted her own reliance as a widow upon a close and sturdy friend, but for Peter and Margaret the situation seemed utterly different. 'We had discovered another world which belonged, jointly and exclusively, to us. We longed as never before to remain together and never be parted,' Peter Townsend chronicled in his memoirs. Princess Margaret confided her emotions to both her sister and her mother. 'They did not flinch, but faced it with perfect calm. I imagine that the Queen Mother's reaction was that this simply cannot be,' wrote Townsend. But 'she never once hurt either of us through the whole difficult affair.' Certainly a foremost consideration in her heart was that the King would never have permitted it.

It was the old question of divorce and the Church, the dilemma of the Duke of Windsor visited upon a younger generation, with different overtones. The Queen was advised that she could not validly give her consent to Margaret's marriage to a divorced man. The Queen Mother behaved, as Townsend says, 'with a regard for us both . . . thoughtful as ever for the feelings of others'. She had cause to hope that Margaret's love would prove a passing infatuation. She perhaps assumed at times the rather vague manner so familiar to her intimates, first adopted as a defence against her husband's occasional testiness, and for two months the two royal ladies, Queen and Queen Mother, wavered in a sea of discussion.

The subject was pursued at the Palace and even in Downing Street, with Tommy Lascelles, the Queen's private secretary, their friends, the Nevills, and others, until with infinite maternal tact, the Queen Mother prevailed on Margaret to allow herself time and patience, and accept the counsel that Peter's absence abroad would be better for the time being. Group Captain Townsend had been due to accompany the Queen Mother and Princess Margaret on a visit to Rhodesia. Instead, Lord Plunket, with his courtier-like devotion, was substituted, while Peter accompanied the Queen and Prince Philip on their Coronation visit to Northern Ireland before being transferred as an air attaché to the British Embassy in Brussels.

One love affair was deferred, if not broken, but another resumed. With her visit to the then Rhodesia, the Queen Mother took up again an affection for the African scene first begun when her two friends and kinfolk, Lord and Lady Francis Scott, first settled in Kenya. A courtship by correspondence, so to speak, it developed into reality during her tour with her husband as Duchess of York, when she and the Duke had stayed with the Scotts at Rongai, and again when she visited Rhodesia with the King. Now her aircraft was the first jet-plane to land at Salisbury. A biting wind at Bulawayo laid Princess Margaret up with a chill, but the Queen Mother fulfilled an exacting and successful programme, with encouraging spurs to the future.

Four years later, she was eagerly back there again to do whatever she could in strengthening the new-formed Federation of Rhodesia and Nyasaland. In Southern Rhodesia she held a tribal parley or Indaba to remind the chieftains of their sixty unbroken years of peace. In Northern Rhodesia she descended 1400 feet to the rockface of a copper mine, a feat so prodigious for a woman in her fifties that strikes and riot squads were forgotten in the African anxiety to see her. In Zomba, now flourishing as the capital of independent Malawi, she appeared in full royal rig of tiara and white chiffon to receive token of loyalty from 140 chieftains eager to demonstrate the goodwill that was to seal Malawi into the Commonwealth. Then again, in 1960, she visited the Federation to open the Kariba Dam and tour the Copper Belt. At one point, as she stood on the edge of an opencast pit, a truck with a full load was coming up the track below her and, as I noted nearer the time, 'she saw that it was driven by an African and waved her hand. The driver, surprised, recognized her and took one hand from the wheel to doff his red mining helmet, giving her a flashing smile. The incident was nothing, yet it was everything.' But alas the incident belongs to the broken dream of Federation and not the disillusioning later discords.

But the Queen Mother was full of hope and optimism, her taste for travel whetted and renewed, while in Britain she found herself enjoying a personal renaissance such as she had never imagined. When Elizabeth as Queen made her sweeping 1953–4 tour of the Commonwealth, absenting herself from London for six months, the Queen Mother became a deputy monarch as no past Consort had ever been before. Of the five Counsellors of State appointed to transact the royal prerogatives, the Queen Mother was the most prominent in royal authority; and Clarence House, with its glittering candelabra and chiming clocks, its delicate paintings, flowers and painted furniture, became for a time the cynosure of Government Ministers, diplomats and statesmen. The French Ambassador, René Massigli, was charmed by a stand-in Head of State who enthusiastically showed him her French Impressionists, and especially a Monet, *The Rock*, which the artist had presented to Clemenceau. The Queen Mother disposed of the Queen's New Year Honours List in six Investitures at Buckingham Palace, pleasantly embellishing hundreds of conferments and knighthoods with unhesitant conversation, and what did it matter if she invariably ran considerably behind time? In bestowing the accolade upon Epstein, she deftly mentioned Princess Margaret's readiness to sit for him if he should wish. The graceful tribute led to the only royal portrait bust among his works.

With Princess Margaret, she held a Privy Council at Clarence House and indeed transferred the formal reception of foreign diplomats to her first-floor drawing room in order to give the police and others at the Palace extra opportunities for leave. British ambassadors newly appointed overseas came to her to kiss hands on taking up their posts; new foreign ambassadors gravely presented their credentials. One morning the skirl of bagpipes disturbed the early morning calm of St James's. She had adopted a new idea, and the Queen Mother's personal piper, a pipe major of the London Scottish, was henceforth to add his distinctive ceremonial touch to the scene whenever she was in residence. The Queen had directed that her mother should receive from the Lord Mayor of London the same privileges accorded to herself or to a foreign Head of State. On entering the City to receive the freedom of the Grocers' Company – the first woman to be made free of Grocers' Hall in eight centuries – the Queen Mother was therefore greeted by the Lord Mayor in his richest crimson and gold. In the autumn Princess Margaret moved into Clarence House with her, occupying the eastern garden suite on the ground floor, sociably close to the temporary First Lady of the land.

When the Queen and Prince Philip returned from their 173-day circuit of the world and the Commonwealth, they sailed with great réclame into the Pool of London aboard the new royal yacht *Britannia* and five months later the Queen Mother embarked, not without trepidation, on her own first solo travels. A handsome sum to commemorate King George VI had been collected in the United States and it had been urged that the Queen Mother should receive the resulting cheque (for a fund for training Commonwealth students in America) at a dinner in the grand ballroom of the Waldorf Astoria. The possible emotional hazards of a royal widow on a mission of remembrance filled her with dread: what questions might be thrust at her during that American institution, the press conference? What unexpected demands on even her well disciplined self-control might arise from among 5,000 guests at a Commonwealth ball?

Little occured quite as expected. On 21 October she sailed on the liner she had launched and named in the dark days of Munich, *Queen Elizabeth*, and through the next five days of a stormy Atlantic crossing, applause rippled out whenever she emerged from her suite on the main M deck. The ship's officers went round with her polite message asking people 'please not to bother', though with little effect. Prolonged outbursts of clapping occurred in the dining-room and the cinema. In New York, her host, Sir Pierson Dixon, showed her the editorial in the *New York Times*: 'Of all the many reasons for welcoming Queen Elizabeth the Queen Mother the pleasantest is that she is so nice . . .'

She was of course a traffic-stopper, and in one view 'a quick-change Queen of all Hearts'. Her first official engagement was a banquet at the Waldorf to celebrate the bicentenary of the founding of Columbia University under a charter of George II. Probably in all that academic assembly none knew that, twenty-five years earlier in New Zealand, the conjuring smile of their royal guest had caused a convinced communist to undergo a change of heart and mind. Nor did they realize that, in their own midst, it happened again . . . rather as if that royal arch-critic William Hamilton had faced conversion on meeting Prince Charles.

John McGovern, a left-wing MP for the tough Shettleston division of Glasgow, who had led the Scottish hunger-strikers in the grim depression era and had been twice arrested and imprisoned in unemployment riots, considered it a slur on his principles to be invited to meet the Queen Mother at the Waldorf.

'I have never recognized royalty,' he wrote. 'I had never been to a royal garden-party or a luncheon or dinner attended by royalty. Royal personages were untouchables to me. I knew that the republicans, Bevanites and fellow-travellers would attack me if I went to the dinner.' Yet the Queen Mother's conquest was swift and total. 'My wife and I cheered her heartily. I completely lost my proletarian snobbery. It was amazing that it had to be on American soil that I first recognized royalty . . .' So marked was McGovern's new conviction that two years later he readily associated himself with a speech of welcome in the House of Commons on the return of the Queen and Prince Philip from Nigeria.

Obviously, the visitor played her cards well. At the English Speaking Union dinner she entered preceded by a trio of pipers, two of the Black Watch and her own Pipe Major in full accoutrement. Bigger and better, 5,000 guests packed a Commonwealth ball at the huge Park Avenue armoury where, despite the handicap of a flag-decked royal box intensively floodlit through most of the evening, her smiles and high spirits were irrepressible. The presentation line had been limited to ninety, each stop-watch timed with American efficiency to 37 seconds, but she foreseeably spent an hour and a half thus profitably occupied. As ever, it was the unexpected that caught her emotion. She went to a theatre to see a light-hearted musical, and as she entered the packed audience rose to applaud her, an ovation continued so insistently after she had taken her seat that she had to rise and turn in acknowledgment, touched and nearly in tears at the unforeseen welcome. Throughout much of the performance crowds waited outside in the hope of seeing her.

Encouraged by her friend, Lady Jean Rankin, she had planned to do much private sightseeing, but crowds gathered wherever word spread of her, and her glimpses of Manhattan were at best fugitive entrancements, usually with inescapable cavalcades of observers. Lady Jean Rankin had praised the phenomenal costume jewellery at Saks, and the Queen Mother went there to find an immovable wall of watchful humanity standing with their backs to the showcases, and she had to content herself with seeing a few pieces brought to her in a separate

boutique. Her staff recall whizzing up and down in elevators to find
some quieter corner of the store but every floor revealed a vista of
excited sales-girls and customers stampeding to see her. At the United
Nations Building she improved the shining hour with an animated and
extended friendly conversation with the Soviet delegate, Mr
Vyshinsky. In the Metropolitan Museum she walked untiringly
through twenty-four rooms to seek out 'old friends' among paintings
and exhibits. Then the Museum hierarchy entertained her to tea, and it
turned out that the elderly butler who served her tea had been one of the
younger footmen in her father's employ in her girlhood. It made a small
world.

In Washington, as the guest of the Eisenhowers at the White House,
she caught up with long-desired visits to institutions as varied as the
Smithsonian, the Library of Congress and the Pentagon and, well-
informed in that vast warren, she gratified her wish to tour the limitless
drug-store, 'an amazing shop'. Now in mood and spirit an unmistakable
royal tourist, she visited Annapolis, and Richmond, Virginia, and was
lodged overnight in Williamsburg, dining at the King's Arms Tavern
and driving through the meticulously restored period streets next day in
a horse-carriage 'quite amazed', as she noted, 'at the skill and patience
with which the serene Colonial atmosphere has been brought back to
life'. Moreover, on Armistice Day, 11 November, the girl from Bruton
Street knelt at prayer in George Washington's pew in Bruton Church.
Again, in a sense, a small world, its events strangely synchronized.

An ensuing week in Canada was in no sense a mere sentimental journey. A visit to Ottawa expanded mysteriously into French Quebec,
where the November rain failed to quench the cries of 'Vive la Reine!'
The Canadian press went to town in discussing the Queen Mother as
potentially the next Governor-General to succeed Vincent Massey.
Such headlines opened an intimidating prospect of exile, in a friendly
sister country, but exile from family and friends. The prospect was
publicly broached to the Queen in London who replied with instant
diplomacy, 'Oh dear, we couldn't spare Mother'.

In other ways the crowded journey could not disperse private preoccupations. Lady Annaly fell ill, the Lavvy Annaly who had sponsored
her first public waltzing with the Duke of York, and within three hours
of returning to London the Queen Mother was at her old friend's hospital bedside. Princess Margaret, too, had undergone a strain, not only in
separation from Peter Townsend but in discovering what life was like
without Mother. Queen Elizabeth's absence was brief in the context of

present-day royal travel, yet devoted mother and daughter had never before been parted for so long. If Margaret flew off by helicopter for one of her working days in the provinces, the Queen Mother invariably went down to the hall of Clarence House to meet her on her return. Working separately at their desks, the Princess in her ground-floor sitting-room, the Queen Mother upstairs, the two exchanged notes at times on so telepathic an impulse that their footmen met halfway. Ever since an episode when a woman staffing the switchboard had been found to be a drug addict, written messages had seemed safer than the telephone. The Queen Mother was far from possessive. She knew – and was allowed to know – that Margaret wrote to Peter Townsend nearly every day. This was within the terms of the 'agreement' and after a year when Peter had some business occasion to visit London, Queen Elizabeth invited him to tea.

To defeat the press this involved Peter in a cloak-and-dagger meeting in Harrod's book department with Sir Norman Gwatkin, of the Lord Chamberlain's office, who then drove him to Clarence House, without a soul suspecting, and having made him welcome the Queen Mother left him with Margaret talking over the teacups. When he came the following year, however, every newspaper produced its biggest-type headlines. On the Princess's twenty-fifth birthday celebrations at Balmoral, the minister of Craithie, the Rev John Lamb, had thought it kindly to pray for her 'that, trusting in Thee, she may find fulfilment of her heart's desires'. In the little granite kirk, his words were quiet and intimate, but the media blazoned them around the world. 'In any ordinary family,' I wrote at the time, 'a daughter can suffer the illusion of love without all western civilization baying at her heels. A mother may reason, cajole or quarrel, with scarcely a ripple beyond the family circle.' But the Townsend drama was whipped into a whirlwind.

In October, 1955, a crisis seemed imminent in the situation. Peter was again in London and he and the Princess spent the weekend – as separate guests, it was carefully emphasized – at the home of John and Jean Wills. Jean was the Queen Mother's niece, May Elphinstone's daughter, a staunch friend if ever there was one, and for three days her quiet home in Berkshire was under siege.

Revealing no hint of a mother's persuasions, the Queen Mother busied herself at the Castle of Mey. 'Meg sips tea with Peter. Mom makes it a crowd' ran an American headline. On returning to London, 'Mom' however joined the couple for tea. By ordinary standards, the Princess could retire into private life, relinquish royal duty and thus marry a divorced man. The Church of England's then inflexible dictum against divorce remained the one objection, though many believe that the issue was morally resolved on 21 October, the day when the memorial statue of King George VI in the Mall was unveiled by the Queen. 'Much was asked of my father in personal sacrifice and endeavour,'she said, in her address. 'He shirked no task, however difficult, and to the end he never faltered in his duty.' The Queen's script had been prepared days in advance, but the family truth seemed as inescapable as the chill rain itself. It was also one of the rare occasions since the Abdication when the Queen Mother met the Duchess of Windsor, according her a steely politeness.

At the end of the month Peter Townsend and Princess Margaret were again guests in the country, this time with the Rupert Nevills at Uckfield. Both had separately decided that the situation was untenable and Peter had claimed that he chiefly drafted the statement, 'mindful of the Church's teaching . . . and conscious of my duty to the Commonwealth . . . I have decided not to marry Group Captain Peter Townsend'.

The script was first seen by the Queen and the Queen Mother, and the resulting flurry of messengers between Uckfield, Windsor and Clarence House together with the several journeys of Oliver Dawnay, the Queen Mother's secretary, unmistakably suggested Queen Elizabeth's preference that the issue should be allowed to drop without a public statement. But the Princess closed the chapter in her own way, 'a great act of self-sacrifice', as Harold Nicolson, a biographer of George V, wrote in his private journal.

There were to be other meetings, notably in 1958 when the Queen Mother invited Peter Townsend to tea at Clarence House and to lunch at Royal Lodge. The American public have been entertained rather than enlightened by the reminiscences of a footman against whom the Queen Mother gained a legal injunction to restrain him 'from publishing matters known to him by reason of having been in her service'. But he overheard the Queen Mother say nothing more fervid than 'good afternoon, Peter, it's been a long time. It's so very lovely to have you here again', and in the following year Peter Townsend married Mlle Marie-Luce Jamagne, the daughter of a Belgian tobacco manufacturer.

Whenever the Queen was away on one of her overseas tours, in the Arctic Circle or the Antarctic or anywhere between Malta and New Zealand, the Queen Mother took up some of the happiest interludes of her middle-age as grandmother and guardian to Prince Charles and

Princess Anne. 'Ever since I can remember, my grandmother has been the most wonderful example of fun, laughter, warmth, infinite security and, above all else, exquisite taste,' wrote the Prince of Wales. 'For me she has always been one of those extraordinarily rare people whose touch can turn everything to gold.' As a small boy, his first hours at Hill House day school were spent happily painting because, he told the headmaster, his grandmother had already taught him to draw. At seven he was seen confidently standing beside her in the shallows of the Dee taking his first angling lessons. In his first homesick days at Cheam School it was his grandmother who with his Aunt Margo encouragingly came to visit him to see 'how wonderfully he was settling down'.

At Clarence House, in a schoolboy's memories, there was always chocolate cake for tea. In his most tender years, he had found his grandmother's handbag always worth examining for candies. A traffic policeman, recognizing the Queen Mother in a car, was startled when she threw him a toffee and then realized that the laughing boy beside her was Charles. Providing 'unashamed appetizers' was part of the privilege of grandmothering, a craft to which she clearly devoted much thought, even to taking a refresher lesson in conjuring and sending an equerry to Hamley's store to buy some ready-made tricks.

Some of the best private film sequences of Charles's boyhood owed much to his grandmother's cine-camera. In his first term at Gordonstoun she specially travelled up to Birkhall, a round trip of 1,000 miles, to comply with the school rule that new boys could be visited by, or spend their third Sunday with, relatives. Before long, young school friends were invited to share these pleasures, and the Queen Grandmother injected her own novelties into the perennial treats. Other boys had obliging relatives to invite them to lunch at a local hotel. Queen Elizabeth arranged a rendezvous at the local railway station so that Charles and 'her young friends' could have the fun of lunching with her in the royal coach of her train. Prince Charles's interest in music and his enthusiasm for the cello were similarly inspired. At Royal Lodge she was prodigal with time in listening to records with him, showing the fun of 'sharing in records' by accompanying the discs of Sinatra or Crosby on the piano. In sickness as much as in health, whether Charles was in hospital with whooping cough in Aberdeen or appendicitis in London, she turned up as a reliable and encouraging visitor. The bedside, she once said, had been one of her favourite spots ever since the Glamis Hospital.

If she made a wish at the font as one of Princess Anne's three godmothers, it surely derived from a day of mingled duties and pleasures in Kent shortly before Anne was born, when she was Queen Consort and had paid a visit to see her steeplechase horses in training with Peter Cazalet at Fairlawne; the duties, a pleasure itself, included a visit to Benenden School, which she never afterwards ceased to champion. Disappointed that Charles did not go to Eton, as David had done, she expressed her views more strongly when the later phase of Anne's education came up for discussion and urged the proximity of Benenden – to Fairlawne, Eridge and Uckfield and the Nevills, to Ashford and the Princess's Mountbatten-Knatchbull cousins.

Princess Anne's riding career derives from her grandmother's enthusiasm as well as that of the Queen. The first time she ever rode a horse other than her pony or during riding lessons is said to have been during a weekend visit to Eridge with the Queen Mother. 'An active grandmama, never on the sidelines,' sums up one view of her family influence. Prince Charles's sense of kinship for Australia was kindled, he thinks, 'by her effervescent enthusiasm.' Too young to remember his mother's first visit to the vast continent, he was all the more stirred as a receptive schoolboy by his grandmother's racy impressions.

The success of her solo visit to the US and Canada had enhanced her confidence, and for 1958 she took up the long-deferred plans to revisit New Zealand and Australia first projected and even announced for the King and herself ten years earlier. With the difference of travelling eastward rather than west, it was essentially the tour embarked upon by Elizabeth and Philip in 1952 which had ended so tragically six days later when her daughter had become Queen Regnant. Now the Queen Mother's Household checked back to the original draft itinerary, reviewed the file of invitations and subsequent amendments, and discreetly drafted a route complying with her obvious challenge to herself to go over much of the ground toured with her husband in the early happy years of her marriage.

Friends were dismayed to discover that in six strenuous weeks she permitted herself only one day free from official duties. She felt it was what her husband would have wished. Every strategic decision clearly rested on what he would have done. 'Well, I made it,' she said to Sir George Holland, the first in line to meet her in Canberra. The reference was not to the fatigues of the tour but to her long-standing promise to open the headquarters of the Servicemen's League. 'I hope I'll get there,' she had reaffirmed, 'before I'm in a wheelchair!'

In 1927 the young Duke and Duchess of York had sailed through the Panama Canal and visited Fiji before landing in Auckland. Now the Queen Mother, in her fifty-eighth year, stepped out of her aircraft at Montreal in a snowstorm, made another appearance in Vancouver in pouring rain and, despite the fatiguing ever-lengthening time changes, was alert at 4.30 am Honolulu time to enjoy a drive to Waikiki Beach while her plane refuelled. In Fiji, watching the same display of native dancing after thirty years, she enjoyed a vivid illusion of recapturing time itself. From Auckland, although her North Island tour took her to hitherto unvisited small towns, so many incidents of her first tour seemed to repeat themselves that she became apprehensive lest she should fall ill in South Island as she had before – and in fact a picnic near Wellington was cancelled and she retired to bed on the willing advice of her doctors. But this precaution was sufficient and her fears were over.

A new generation of young news cameramen demonstrated that photographically she had improved beyond recognition from some of her early photographs. (Her speeches in fact are prepared in larger typescript to avoid wearing glasses and she occasionally feels unsteady on high heels.) The major difference in the tour rose from her expressed preference for informal open-air gatherings at which she could mingle and talk with as many people as possible. In Sydney she faced huge crowds in blazing sun, 125,000 children being assembled at one event. From Brisbane she travelled hundreds of miles in heavy rain, often with long detours to avoid floods, while never failing to stop to receive drenched bouquets from the umbrella-grouped throngs. In the downpours one or two small towns were somehow missed, blanketed from view by the rain, and the cavalcade of royal cars retraced its course to go through them again. 'Disorganized?' said her Australian press aide, as the rain lashed down, 'we can't be sure what day it is'.

The 1927 tour had nearly come to a disastrous end with the fire aboard *Repulse* in the middle of the Indian Ocean. Flying home over the same course in 1958, Queen Elizabeth was not at all surprised when the Qantas air captain confessed that the cylinder head of one of the engines had cracked but could be nursed along on three engines, although the need of a new engine and cowling would entail a delay of a day or two in Mauritius. Unperturbed, his royal passenger pretended she would be glad of the rest. In retrospect, she recalled the journey less for its misadventures than for the bitter disappointment to the Australian air crew who had hoped to bring her home in record time.

A relief plane rushing a new engine was delayed by storms, and when it arrived the fitters worked through the night hindered by torrential rain. The royal party then safely reached Entebbe only to face another prolonged stop: the replacement engine had developed ignition troubles. A relief aircraft was actually standing by at Nairobi but by now it had become a personal issue between the Queen Mother with her air crew against the malignant gremlins. Flying delays have become familiar in our day and age but this was an occasion when the engineers, struggling in the small hours and using every blanking word in the book, found their remarkable passenger beside them warming them with her sympathy, echoing much the same language and completely unruffled. At Malta another delay arose from hydraulic trouble until, nearly three days late, she was forced at last to transfer to a relief plane. But her glowing messages of thanks to the crew left an ineffaceable impression. Disregarding the disappointments, she became the first member of the British Royal Family to fly around the world.

Another soft-pedalled fact was that the delay would have doubled to nearly a week if an intended visit to Kenya to open the new Nairobi airport had not been cancelled en route, not without her promise to pay a visit the following year. As events proved, this journey, too, was darkened by circumstances and her staff were aware of two personal confrontations with sorrow. The first was the death of that other Elizabeth Bowes-Lyon, her namesake and sister-in-law, Michael's widow, whom she had first met at the Misses Birtwhistle classes so long ago. And in alighting from her aircraft at Nairobi on 5 February she could not forget that it was just seven years since her last waking day with her husband at Sandringham.

The very purpose of her journey was in pursuit of his ideals of a Commonwealth of free nations, and against obstacles, too, as he might have wished. The African elected members of the Kenya Legislative Assembly had decided to boycott her visit since 'conditions do not permit full participation by African people in events of joy', and yet the cheering welcoming crowds could not have been happier. In the background babble of loud-speakers the voice of Cairo Radio demanded hostility to 'this visit of the leader of the imperialist dogs'. Fortunately, the pervading reality saw a group of Arab sheiks waiting to greet her and she replied to their welcome with the reminder that their friendship had stood the test of time. For the news reporters a good story hinged on a tribal gathering of the Masai who had been praying for weeks for rain on their sun-scorched plateau. As Queen Elizabeth faced the elders, she expressed her hope that they would be blessed with rain, and the first drops fell before she reached her car, then rain so heavy that it delayed her aircraft take-off. In London, the phrase 'Queen Mother Wins Over Terrorists' made an irresistible headline, founded on the news from Kitale, in western Kenya, when hundreds of Suk tribesmen gathered to show their allegiance and an anti-white movement, Mau Mau in character, reversed gears into loyalty.

In private correspondence with friends, the Queen Mother's repetition of the word 'nostalgic' told of deeper emotions. At one point, she had met the old man who had been gun-bearer to Bertie when he shot his first lion, a shy old man but strong and youthful thirty years earlier. Near Murchison Falls she told Jean Rankin of being on recognizably the same path trodden with her husband in 1925. And for light relief she could write to Charles to boast that she had crossed and recrossed the Equator fifteen times that morning on the elbow bends of a mountain-railway.

In mid-tour the Queen Mother also spent a night at Tree Tops, the observation hotel in the tree branches where her daughter had become Queen. The original rough look-out had been destroyed by fire — suspected as Mau Mau arson — and rebuilt on a different site nearby, but the experience of watching rhinoceros, buffalo, bush buck and forest hogs coming to the water hole remained unchanged. From camp up country she could write to her grandson of the five elephants that had awakened her crashing around the verandah, the wallow of glorious mud in which scores of snorting hippos frolicked, and for fuller proof of adventure she brought home her cine-films and photographs: the one she took within yards of a lioness that had just killed an antelope, the hungry crocodiles washing against the launch, the spectacular rush of the Nile . . .

17. *New Avenues*

At the gate of her sixtieth year, Queen Elizabeth the Queen Mother had the happiness of knowing that Princess Margaret had fallen in love with Antony Armstrong-Jones. But would it last? The deepening friendship suggested a romance which she approvingly fostered and furthered by every stratagem known to a mother. 'They are two of a kind,' summed up her view, and she watched the strengthening currents of affinity and affection with unalloyed pleasure.

The Queen Mother first remembered being photographed and amused by the young man after Lady Anne Coke's wedding to Colin Tennant at Holkham Hall in 1956. A personable morning-coated figure ducking about with his camera with amusing speed and agility, he was the eldest son of the Countess of Rosse, as she learned, an old Etonian – though not so old in an age sense – in a newly-respectable profession. A few months later she heard of Tony Armstrong-Jones again when he had taken some exceptional portrait photographs for the young Duke of Kent's twenty-first birthday and the Queen Mother added her own recommendation shortly before the Queen commissioned him to photograph Charles and Anne at Buckingham Palace. Even now one cannot always analyse the subtleties of a royal lady who played her cards close to her heart. It may be relevant that Princess Margaret first met Tony Armstrong-Jones at a dinner-party at the Cheyne Walk home of Elizabeth Cavendish, whose mother had been another of the large company of Elizabeth Lyon's girlhood friends.

The evening 'went with a zing', and Queen Elizabeth noticed with motherly alertness that Tony featured increasingly in her daughter's table chatter, his know-how on cameras, his fashion sketches, his 'car going like crazy', his photographic scenery for the Crank revues, and the witty book of photographs he was planning on the contrasts of London. What was the very opposite of a dockers' strip cabaret if not Mme Vacani's exclusive dancing class? Or what stronger contrast to cleaning the small-paned lamps of Whitehall than the glass roof of Paddington Station? Lord Snowdon will still not tell of those days, but it would be surprising if the Queen Mother did not contribute her own contrasts on so inviting a theme.

Below the carefree superficial play of conversation, Queen Elizabeth worried about her younger daughter, never very strong, highly-strung, powerless and brittle against severe migraine, impulsive yet often unexpectedly level-headed. In other ways the Queen Mother saw her younger self mirrored in Margaret, even the recurrent bouts of flu, her hatred of being coddled and, in deeper purposes, her anxiety to do right and her fret against uncertainty.

Queen Elizabeth believed in desirably smoothing the way without apparent intervention. At Clarence House mother and daughter usually joined the Household officials in the library for luncheon, but the evening would often find the Queen Mother placidly content to don her reading glasses and settle down with a book while the slam of car doors and the young laughter announced the turbulent flow of the Princess's friends downstairs.

Before the Tony love affair, Margaret had been briefly engaged to 'dear, faithful' Billy Wallace but on discovering his earlier romances, she changed her mind. And now Tony whirled Elizabeth Cavendish and the Princess off to his old cottage in Sussex, expeditions from which Margaret always returned in high spirits, full of astonishing stories. The Queen Mother would dearly have liked to explore his Pimlico studio and basement flat, so wondrously transformed from old shop premises. But apart from the risk of undesired publicity, a deterring feature was a spiral steel staircase, and having recently hurt her hip in a fall on the concrete steps at Hurst Park races, the Queen Mother made do with a photograph of Tony, smiling and debonair, descending the stairway with a loaded tray.

Then, one afternoon, Margaret visited one of the Dockland Settlements in the East End – of which she was president – and returned home breathless with stories of Tony's room in Rotherhithe, a low-beamed, white-painted room right beside the river: one could feed the swans from the window. The Queen Mother enjoyed the picture conjured up of her unpredictable daughter arriving incognito for drinks with Elizabeth Cavendish and others in an old house 'almost falling into the Thames'. Yet the Room – the capital emphasis gradually crept in – was later to provide one of the most remarkable episodes of Queen Elizabeth's own private life, and the setting was indeed romantic and extraordinary – down on the Thames among the moored barges, tugs and occasional great ship, looking towards the huge portal of Tower Bridge, with the dome of St Paul's beyond.

In his book on London, which was early on Queen Elizabeth's desk, Tony Armstrong-Jones wrote of the local circles of London people 'relaxed when they're inside the circle and a bit guarded with non-members', the private circles in which people were 'most themselves – their most normal, and in a way their most strange'. He was judiciously first invited into the private circle of Royal Lodge, that inner family sanctuary, when he had just returned from his first visit to New York, feverish to describe his impressions, but by then he was already a frequent visitor at Clarence House, under a mother's appreciative survey. He was only five months older than Margaret and but a few inches taller, a welcome trait after many over-tall escorts. The son of a barrister, a Queen's Counsel, his father had been twice divorced but, as one of Tony's uncles, a High Court judge, summed up, 'one does not visit the peccadilloes of papa upon the children'. The young man's light, pleasant voice threw ideas about like a juggler; his immediate laughter was infectious; his very nature seemed warm and dependable.

A close observer was later to write of Margaret and Tony, 'At a deeper emotional level, both have had disadvantages to overcome. Both are sociable yet paradoxically solitary'. The pair were as alike as the Chelsea china peapods that Margaret and Lilibet had once given their mother as an anniversary gift, and any cautious note went unnoticed in Queen Elizabeth's ever-growing confidence that all would be well.

There came a pause when Margaret drew back to consider the totally unforeseen new direction that her life might be taking. Her mother was about to fulfil some duties in Rome and the Princess arranged to join her. To her hostess, Lady Ashley Clarke, the Queen Mother spoke with conviction of being 'dazzlingly optimistic of clear skies ahead'.

Queen Elizabeth had never visited Rome, having never travelled farther south in Italy than her girlhood visits to her Strathmore grandmother near San Remo and her Scott grandmother in Florence. She hoped to spend some days as a tourist, and the Lord Mayor himself was a perfect guide to the Capitol and the vistas of the Forum. Both ladies called on the jovial new Pope John and then chiefly followed their separate devices. Margaret to explore some of the churches, cameramen permitting, and her mother to seek out the Villa d'Este. The Queen Mother lunched one day with one of her oldest friends and mentors, Sir D'Arcy Osborne, brother-in-law of her eldest brother, whose insight and shrewdness seemed to have sharpened with age. Mother and daughter, indeed, separately sought out trusted opinions, with a satisfactory outcome.

In July, Mr Antony Armstrong-Jones was among the announced guests at a luncheon party at Clarence House given by the Queen Mother for the High Commissioner of Rhodesia, Sir Gilbert Rennie; and Lady Rennie wondered a little about the handsome young man who 'cast an occasional deeply mischievous glance along the table towards Princess Margaret'. Remarkably, Tony was so well accepted as a royal photographer that the press paid him little attention in any other context. In May, he had approached the Queen Mother for 'a serious talk', but seriousness was for others and an understanding was established in a mood of light gaiety.

Princess Margaret was then third in succession to the Throne and, as recorded in my biography of Lord Snowdon, 'the Queen on her own initiative decided to consult her Ministers on the conjectural situation that might arise if her sister should wish to marry a commoner'. As hopes drew so close to realization, the Queen Mother had never been happier in all her years of widowhood. There was the added pleasure that the Queen returned from a tour in Canada to confide that she was expecting another baby, perhaps in January.

A few months later, on 13 January 1960, a requisite note of romance was no doubt struck when Queen Elizabeth headed the Royal Family to the wedding of Pamela Mountbatten and David Hicks at Romsey Abbey. The ceremony was filled with grand-motherly pleasure in watching Princess Anne as a bridesmaid for the first time, 'intent and purposeful', and there was the fun, too, that the Queen Mother had no sooner arrived at the wedding reception than all the lights failed, and the festivities continued by candlelight.

The Queen had agreed that Princess Margaret's engagement should be officially announced seven days after the advent of the new baby, and a pleasant lull ensued until Prince Andrew was born at Buckingham Palace on 19 February. On 24 February, the Queen Mother and Princess Margaret attended a Bowes-Lyon wedding, that of her niece Diana to Peter Somervell in the Henry VII Chapel of Westminster Abbey. But on Sunday morning, the 21st, came the tragic and totally unexpected news that the Countess Mountbatten, who had left shortly after Pammy's wedding for a duty tour of North Borneo, had died during the night. She was only fifty-eight. In deference to Earl Mountbatten, Princess Margaret agreed with her mother that her engagement announcement should be further postponed. It was, in fact, made known on 26 February:

> *It is with the greatest pleasure that Queen Elizabeth the Queen Mother announces the betrothal of her beloved daughter The Princess Margaret to Mr Antony Charles Robert Armstrong-Jones, son of Mr R O L Armstrong-Jones, QC, and the Countess of Rosse, to which union The Queen has gladly given her consent.*

By a happy chance, Queen Elizabeth had undertaken to attend a gala ballet performance at Covent Garden a day or two later and the brilliantly-lit theatre, with the television cameras trained on the royal box, became the scene of the couple's first appearance in public. 'I expect I shall manage the stairs,' the Queen Mother said, still in some pain and difficulty and receiving physiotherapy months after her Hurst Park accident. It strikes one now that she was delicately setting an example to Tony. She ascended the staircase – notorious for its length – without a soul realizing her handicap. Tony followed her and mounted the stairs without setting a hand on the balustrade . . . and only Margaret and his future mother-in-law knew he had been suffering from the recurrent and intractable pain of a polio-stricken left leg, the legacy of a long boyhood fight with infantile paralysis.

The wedding took place in Westminster Abbey on 6 May, the Queen Mother having fondly immersed herself in the intricate arrangements while the unofficial betrothal was still secret. One had to return to Victorian precedents for any guidance on a wedding sponsored by a widowed royal mother, but Lord Airlie came up with the ambiguous solution, 'The Lord Chamberlain to Queen Elizabeth the Queen Mother is commanded by Her Majesty to invite' etc, etc. For her form of service, the Princess chose the vows of the 1662 prayer book, the wording that her mother had used in 1923, and throughout the wedding preparations one readily detects the tug of private affections which carried such weight in the Queen Mother's affairs. The very date of the wedding was chosen because it coincided with Rose's seventieth birthday. No higher compliment could be paid to the aunt and god-mother after whom Princess Margaret Rose was named.

The street decorations were agreed on a theme of spring flowers and roses; and Norman Hartnell had already evolved his supreme design for the semi-crinoline wedding-gown, the bridesmaids' dresses and for the Queen Mother's own superb gown in white and gold. Queen Elizabeth indeed found great pleasure in marshalling all the thousand details of the wedding; and the provision of television monitors in the Abbey for the first time, to enable everyone in even the farthest recesses of the nave to share fully in the ceremony, was one of the fruits of her direct attention. When arranging to deputize for the Queen at the Abbey Maundy ceremony that year, she had advanced the matter so cogently to the Dean, Dr Symes Abbot, that he felt he had no alternative.

Princess Margaret and her husband sailed in the royal yacht *Britannia* on their Caribbean honeymoon and the following week, the Queen Mother herself flew off on another tour of the Rhodesias and Nyasaland. For her sixtieth birthday, photographs necessarily taken in advance, she dandled the five-month-old Prince Andrew on her knee and so gratified the British public who had seen few pictures of the baby until that moment . . . and were soon of course eagerly and prematurely awaiting signs of more grandchildren to come.

In July 1960, Margaret and Tony moved into their new home, 10 Kensington Palace, a trim pocket-size Georgian house on the northern flank of the Palace community, which resembles a village in its variety of buildings, and it did not occur to the Queen Mother that she was now technically alone. Both her children had now left the nest but maudlin notions of solitude never entered her head. On the day of moving-in, Margaret hurried from Clarence House to surprise her husband at Kensington, where from early morning he had been hanging pictures, while Tony at the same time left Kensington Palace to greet her at 'Clarence', and the Queen Mother spent an agitated half-hour at the telephone striving to unite them. In the second week she formally observed her parental status by going to lunch, enthusiastically admiring everything and characteristically going downstairs afterwards to congratulate the cook and meet the staff generally. 'Isn't it such fun,' she exclaimed, 'to be in at the beginning of a new house!'

Meanwhile, she enjoyed the social overtures with the new in-laws; the pleasure of entertaining the Rosses at Clarence House and being entertained in turn. Amusing, too, with Tony's sister, Susan, the Viscountess de Vesci, to enquire after her mother-in-law, whom she already knew well as a lady in waiting to the then Duchess of Gloucester. For even the unquenchably sociable Queen Elizabeth, the spadework of truly making new friends hardened with passing time; and in her early sixties the Queen Mother had become painfully conscious of lessening ranks among her closer companions and relatives. At Christmas, to her distress, her valiant lifelong friend, Sir Arthur Penn, fell seriously ill, and she repeatedly went to see him in hospital. He had always said that he would serve her for life and he died on 30 December, the day before he was due to retire. Early in February another personal sorrow came to the Queen Mother in the death of her eldest sister, Lady Elphinstone. Above all, she was most concerned at the possible effect of this bereavement on her widowed sister, Rose, who was seven years younger than May Elphinstone but already in her seventies.

Many of the year's plans were in fact redrafted for Rose's special benefit. It had been arranged, for instance, that Queen Elizabeth should pay an official visit to Tunisia in April, and for Rose Granville this became an invitation for a pleasant seven-day cruise outward on *Britannia*. The two sisters revisited Gibraltar together; and Lady Granville rested aboard while Queen Elizabeth energetically explored the ruins of Carthage. Then to the appropriate sound of a 21-gun salute as the royal yacht left Sousse harbour the first officer brought a coded message with the heartening news to the sisters that Princess Margaret was expecting a baby in November.

As so often, sunshine and darkest shadow fretted around Queen Elizabeth for the rest of the year. It was 'a nuisance' that she suffered a fall during the Ascot house-party at Windsor Castle, and cracked a small bone in her foot. Even so, she was characteristically determined to launch the liner *Northern Star* at Tyneside, 'with a wheelchair or full stretcher party', she had joked. A wheelchair was considered advisable but, realizing that the crowds could not see her as she was trundled along, she disregarded the doctors and the pain and walked down the ramp from the launching platform. A subsequent engagement necessitated her foot resting on a cushion, whereupon each of the 'presentations' were invited to sit beside her and talk for a few moments. Her phrase for it, of course, was 'delightful, most pleasant fun'. A week or so later, after flying by helicopter to Cambridge for an agricultural show, she used the wheelchair between the tents and enclosures, but 'restfully sat or stood about', so she reassured her friends, while 'looking or talking'.

In 1956 the Queen Mother had been the first member of the Royal Family to travel by helicopter, taking a flying leap, indeed, from Windsor to Biggin Hill, and she was credited with saying that the 'chopper' transformed her life 'as it did that of Anne Boleyn'. It was both time-saving and exciting, making nonsense of overland distances, enabling scheduled engagements to be spread over farther horizons. It endowed her with a special entrance, stepping from the red-painted machines of the Queen's Flight, a little figure with feathery millinery, pastel mink and three-string pearls, she radiates a droll sense of contemporary fun and excitement; and Prince Charles recollects his enthusiasm while at Gordonstoun for his grandmother's arrival by chopper, and his sense of adventure, too, in lurching away from the fields and woods and touching down in no time at Birkhall or Mey.

At one time, the Queen Mother was said to be as 'chopper-minded' as Prince Philip. In a friendly rivalry, indeed, she eclipsed her son-in-law by being the first to fly by helicopter from Sandringham to the Palace. In June 1961, for the wedding in York Minster of the Duke of Kent to Katharine Worsley, the festive atmosphere of the royal train, crowded with wedding guests, proved irresistible. But she had also undertaken to attend a gala performance at Covent Garden that evening, an engagement achieved by leaving the wedding reception after an hour, returning by plane to Heathrow and taking a four-minute helicopter flight from airport to Palace. It was part of the story, too, that at the Queen Mother's suggestion the newly-wed Kents flew by a Queen's Flight aircraft to commence their honeymoon at Birkhall, a romantic innovation followed two years later, at her invitation, by Princess Alexandra and Angus Ogilvy.

In September David Bowes-Lyon joined his sister at Birkhall, as so often, hopeful that the Deeside air would help his asthma and as anxious as his wife Rachel to see every improvement around that dear old Jacobean house. He confessed to feeling tired but would not admit that he had been overdoing it: it was the best defence that, like his sister, he liked to keep busy. Then, in the midst of this summer contentment, there came one of the saddest shocks of Queen Elizabeth's life, for on 13 September David died of a heart attack. Three days later he was buried at St Paul's Walden in the moan and chill of a great gale that swept across Britain, and his sister in her deep grief could scarcely realize that all the span of his life had been enfolded within her own.

Princess Margaret and her husband were at the Queen Mother's side when the Royal Family returned to Balmoral and to Birkall. It may be no more than coincidence that the problem of a title for Tony was brought forward during the following days, as if to help occupy Queen Elizabeth's mind and ease her sorrowing thoughts, and before the end of the month it was made known that Princess Margaret would have her baby at Clarence House. Biography is hindsight, it has been said, and one detects in these details filial generosity and compassion. Tony Armstrong-Jones had earlier demurred at a title, but the Queen had enquired if he would accept the gift of an earldom. In the last analysis any lingering disinclination was overcome probably less because his wife wished it so, but because the idea was also at once acceptable to the Queen Mother whom he has never ceased to admire. Princess Margaret presented him with a son at Clarence House on the morning of 3 November, and six weeks later the baby was christened at Buckingham Palace with the Queen Mother's three favourite names, David Albert (for Bertie) Charles. As the Earl of Snowdon's first-born son he also took his father's subsidiary title, Viscount Linley of Nymans. He was Queen Elizabeth's third grandson and fourth grandchild, the one baby so far born under her roof during her tenure of Clarence House. Indeed, he was only two months old when his parents decided that a second honeymoon in the warmth of Antigua would be in order, while the infant David remained in his royal grandmother's devoted care at Sandringham.

18. *Adventures*

On 11 December 1961, Queen Elizabeth found herself the centre of a family commemoration unobserved by the public, although the flurry of bouquets delivered at Royal Lodge and Clarence House showed that it had not passed unheeded by her kinfolk. The newspapers focused attention on the passing of a quarter-century since the Abdication and mostly failed to comment on the Silver Jubilee of the Queen Mother as a Queen. Her amusement at this lapse was equalled by her pleasure at the family dinner given by the Queen on Sunday evening the 10th at Windsor Castle, at which twenty-five are said to have sat down at table.

The nearest to a public celebration was not until her silver anniversary as Colonel-in-Chief of the Black Watch in 1962, marked by a regimental review at Perth in September. This, too, came second in news coverage to the centenary of the Black Watch of Canada in June when, similarly as Colonel-in-Chief, she flew to Montreal for the celebrations. She pronouced her stay in a twentieth-floor hotel suite as 'highly enjoyable' and within ten days also crammed in visits to Ottawa, Toronto, the St Lawrence Seaway and the new pioneering spectacle of Upper Canada Village. She had, however, expressed a preference to avoid regimental and public expense, and it was an innovation at the time that she flew the Atlantic on an ordinary Trans-Canada scheduled passenger flight, filling the first class cabin with her suite of nine and winning applause with her unhurried explanation and acknowledgment of the 'economy' section. The expensive tradition of Guildhall welcome-home banquets had recently been discontinued at the wish of the Queen. But perhaps Queen Elizabeth was also bearing in mind Lord Snowdon's dictum that there was so much more adventurous fun in ordinary life.

Franta Belsky, the sculptor, has told of her sittings at his cluttered Kensington studio when, in rest periods, 'in tiara and full trimmings she poked around the plaster casts and dusty glassfibre pieces on the shelves, and filled the kettle and put it on the gas-ring, revelling in slumming'. To attend quiet country weddings, often of grand-nephews and nieces, to have tea with lifelong intimates in small country cottages, to climb Kensington stairways to visit old friends in topmost flats, all rank among the pursuits which give Queen Elizabeth keen pleasure. After Lord Snowdon had parted with his Pimlico studio, she regretted having never seen it except from across the pavement in a car. And on returning from Canada 'updated for a few more years', as she said, the Queen Mother undertook the strangest adventure of all.

When the story of Tony's 'hideaway' Rotherhithe room became known shortly after the engagement, the astonished world took it for granted that the romantic couple had flown, never more to return. 'Don't let anyone in,' Tony had asked his landlord friend and, remarkably, the room remained inviolate, and yet was still visited, an intrinsic part of the Snowdons' happiness, for another three years. Margaret always had fresh stories of narrow escapes from discovery. During the spring tides a Thames excursion steamer had come closer than usual, with the loudspeaker bawling, 'that's where it happened, right where that couple is sitting', and the passengers had hardly bothered to look. The Queen Mother felt that she knew it from Tony's photographs as if it were her own, the white-painted walls and rush matting, the huge painting of a fierce old Admiral peering from behind the upright piano, the alcove shelves with their array of bargains found on street market barrows by the Princess disguised in Tony's old mac. Noel Coward enthused on a superlative evening in the room with Princess Margaret and Tony and Margaret Leighton and submitted to Queen Elizabeth that 'one should see for oneself'.

One summer evening she could withstand the temptation no longer. Most remarkable of all, the landlord upstairs was a young journalist who of course knew and yet valiantly maintained the Snowdons' secret, even the extraordinary episode of the Queen Mother's visit. It was not until the house fell victim to an official demolition order and the brick dust subsided over paradise irretrievably lost, that the Fleet Street knight errant, William Glenton, published his impression of the Queen Mother at large in the East End. 'I failed to see how anyone could not recognize the unmistakable figure . . . My tension grew with each step she made along the pavement in her inimitable, slow, gracious manner . . . The cat had left a visiting card in the hall, but although the Queen Mother could not have failed to notice, she gave no sign and smiled all the while . . .'. And before long he noticed that 'she was shedding some of her royal aura and becoming more jolly'.

A meal was served, glasses clinked, the swans gliding by on the Thames were fed and Margaret played a galaxy of popular tunes, old and new, 'the Queen Mother singing gaily'. The crew of a passing Dutch freighter were saluted from the bay window with the Marseillaise, the striped Netherlands flag having been mistaken for the tricolour, with all the royal group 'waving wildly from the window'. At midnight, the Queen Mother wandered under the gaslight into the nearby St Mary's parish churchyard, looking for the graves of some of the crew of the *Mayflower*. Her search was in vain, but the main adventure of the evening was unforgettable. 'I haven't enjoyed myself so much since I was a girl of twenty,' Queen Elizabeth said on taking her leave.

The birth of a son (George, Earl of St Andrews) to the Duchess of Kent was one of the happy events of the '62 summer, and the preparations for his christening at the Palace on 14 September may have softened the sad anniversary echoes of her brother David's death in the Queen Mother's thoughts. With the Queen and the Snowdons she flew down from Scotland for the ceremony, but back at Birkhall next day, her 'mind on other things', she stumbled while in the house and, for the second time within fifteen months, suffered a small fractured bone in her foot. Within the week, her old friend, Ruth Fermoy, also had an accident, slipping on a marble floor and breaking her hip, 'so much more aristocratic', and the two commiserated with one another by 'phone. As soon as she could wear a surgical supporting shoe, Queen Elizabeth cheerfully hobbled into the London Clinic 'to help get the patient up'. But it was most vexing, and she limped through her winter engagements, bravely touring a museum exhibition without making excuses, determinedly wearing a pair of shoes at a fashion show and standing to receive bouquets at a children's festival when she could have comfortably become seated The nuisance of mishaps in middle age had to be ignored, just as the ailments of age remained 'things largely of the mind.'

However, the fracture healed normally, and during the Queen's absence with Prince Philip on the 1963 tour of Australia, the Queen Mother again held the series of six New Year Investitures at the Palace as her daughter's deputy, and stepped pleasurably into her role as guardian grandmother to Princess Anne and little Prince Andrew. 'Tuck parcels' for Prince Charles were satisfyingly discussed, and at the

Gordonstoun mid-term, when flying conditions were difficult, she elected to travel by night train to Elgin and back rather than disappoint him. A friend recalls seeing her at Clarence House with the sixteen-month-old David Linley playing at her feet, possibly a grandmother solving a domestic difficulty on Nanny's day off. 'I'm beginning to believe that having babies around me is always important,' the Queen Mother said.

If not in so many words, 'keeping Mother busy' became a desired objective of the Royal Family, if only because she liked being occupied with every possible diversity of activity through the daily round. With Princess Alexandra's engagement to Angus Ogilvy, old Lady Airlie's grandson, Queen Elizabeth faced the rather disturbing fact that nearly forty years had passed since she had been endowed with royal status by marriage. If the possibility of public observance of this ruby milestone ever progressed beyond discreet inter-secretarial discussion, it was firmly declined.

'But you never travel *for yourself*,' a member of her staff reproached her, when official itineraries three or four years ahead were being planned. From some such remark there grew the thought of a private holiday abroad and, rarer than rubies, a vacation seldom experienced even in girlhood, a holiday in a hotel! On 'that lovely visit to Rome', four years earlier, friends had driven her to a quiet country trattoria one day where, like everyone else, she had lunched on the terrace, ordering from the menu, a pleasure unparalleled since Aunt Violet's excursions with her from the Villa Capponi. An unfulfilled dream of visiting the châteaux of the Loire presented itself and, with skilful encouragement from her daughters, the idea of playing truant with a few close friends took root.

As it happened, chilly draughts were blowing through the corridors of diplomacy after General de Gaulle's veto on Britain's desired entry into the Common Market. The Queen Mother's 'way round' this difficulty was to write personally to President de Gaulle of her plans and the President's reply was similarly a cordial letter in his own hand welcoming her on arrival at her hotel.

Lush and gilded, formerly the home of Françoise Coty of the perfume millions, the Château du Puits d'Artigny near Montbazon has all the Michelin stars of *situation très tranquille, isolée*, and the Queen Mother had taken the entire first floor for her fifteen friends, among them Lady Fermoy, her hip recovered, Lord and Lady Euston and Sir Pierson Dixon. But no secrecy had guarded the holiday and Queen

Elizabeth could not refuse the courtesy of receiving the deputation of local officials who wished to welcome her. On her sightseeing drives groups of people waited to wave to her in the villages, but these were salutations that, after all, heightened her pleasure. Lunching with the Marquis and Marquise de Vibraye at Cheverny, she thus saw the only sixteenth-century castle still in occupation by direct descendants of the original family, and it added to the fun that her hosts were unable to resist summoning the local hunt, pink-coated, to greet her with a fanfare of hunting horns.

In brief, the royal holidaymaker enjoyed herself immensely. She sampled some of the 365 rooms of Chambord and gazed at the unique reflection of the Château de Chenonceaux in its river moat. She ventured on foot through the streets of Chinon, though instantly recognized everywhere and presented with impromptu bouquets. She visited the twelfth-century Abbey of Fontevrault, the patterned gardens of Villandry, the Château of Ussé, and, as a sideline bonus, she trekked through Fontainebleau and lunched once again in a country restaurant. The ardent sightseer was moreover resolved to repeat such a holiday after visiting Australia the following year, but as the time approached she fell ill with appendicitis, the Australian tour was postponed and a placid cruise of the West Indies aboard *Britannia* occupied her convalescence. It was 1965, indeed, before Queen Elizabeth renewed her resolve and whisked her group of seven to Provence where the little eighteenth-century Château Legier, near Arles, was placed at her disposal at a token rental of a franc a week. As it chanced, the allure of Provence in April was marred by rain and days when the mistral blew unpleasantly. But the châteaux hereabouts bask in a privacy rare among their cousins of the Loire, and the Queen Mother's field of sightseeing extended from the tapestries of Aix-en-Provence to the Roman antiquities of Nîmes and for much of the time her complete freedom of choice and the pleasant illusion of anonymity prevailed.

No less pleasantly the New Year of 1964 found the Queen Mother looking forward to four happy events, for the Queen, Princess Margaret, the Duchess of Kent and Princess Alexandra were each anticipating a baby. Alexandra was the only novice of happy events, although her baby was expected first. At one time, indeed, Sandringham sheltered five pregnant ladies, Lady Rupert Nevill having arrived as an 'expectant' guest, a number probably unequalled in even Victorian times.

All the mothers-to-be wrily recognized the elements of comedy. Back at Royal Lodge, on Sunday 2 February, Queen Elizabeth may well have joked of sympathy pains when she retired early to bed complaining of discomfort. After a night of pain a doctor was telephoned and told, 'No, please do not come out all this way. Her Majesty will come into town to you.' The result was that by late evening their patient was in the King Edward VII Hospital for Officers and next morning had a successful operation for appendicitis.

On the far side of the world the situation appeared more dramatic than in London, for the Queen Mother was to have flown to Vancouver on the Friday as the first leg of her Antipodes tour. Indeed, there was some difficulty in convincing her that the journey could not be curtailed or deferred by a week or two instead of cancelled, but the doctors were adamant. Some symptoms of fatigue may also have justified their edict of two months' convalescence. And so she was at Royal Lodge to hear of the birth of Princess Alexandra's son on 29 February, and at Clarence House on 10 March when Prince Edward was born at Buckingham Palace . . . and she hastened to see her fifth grandchild. Calling at the same time to see the baby, Princess Margaret found her mother there with the five pound seven ounce charmer. The following day Queen Elizabeth left to fly to Jamaica – again by scheduled flight – where the *Britannia* was at her disposal for a three-week health cruise of the Caribbean. Thus it came about that a stallholder in Kingston straw market began to serve a tourist who seemed interested in straw hats and then realized that the chatty customer was the Queen Mother.

As a convalescent, Queen Elizabeth then sailed out of sight. Her companions were her secretary, Sir Martin Gilliat, her rota lady-in-waiting, Lady Jean Rankin (whose brother, the Earl of Stair, had married David Bowes Lyon's daughter) and the Countess of Leicester, ranking as an all but qualified guide by reason of her daughter Anne Tennant's joint interest in the isle of Mustique and other properties. If there were stowaways in the official party, perhaps sister Rose and the younger Elphinstone partisans so dear to her, the Queen Mother rarely resisted such sociable opportunities. Cruising for three weeks, between Antigua and Barbados, the odyssey was rightly of sunshine and silence until the Queen Mother returned to London by air on 2 April. Four weeks later, the Duchess of Kent's daughter, Helen, was born at Coppins, then the Kents' family home in Buckinghamshire; and on 1 May the Queen Mother's sixth grandchild, Lady Sarah Armstrong-Jones, made her appearance at Kensington Palace. Rarely bestowed as a royal name, Princess Margaret had only recently discovered that the ancient meaning of Sarah was Princess. It had 'really been a year of felicitous timing', in the royal grandmother's view.

The Queen Mother's physician, Dr Bodley Scott, had asked her to take things a little easier, as a lady nearing her middle sixties might be entitled to do, but the discovered ease of scheduled air travel and the full enjoyment of briefer visits overseas, Queen Elizabeth averred, made things easier than ever. In February 1965, she undertook another journey to Jamaica to receive a Doctorate of Letters at the University of the West Indies. A five-day jaunt to Canada, supposedly a private visit, became official by virtue of the engagements crammed into the few days. A presentation of new colours to the Toronto Scottish Regiment saw a regimental march-past the next day, with a sideline inspection of a Women's Army Corps unit; cathedral services, church ceremonies, a hospital visit floor upon floor, a visit to the new City Hall, and tours of art exhibitions and museums; with ceremonial books to be signed, presentation lines chatted up, dolls and children admired, and fainting choirboys, falling ladies and runaway horses to be noted and enquired about. Besides official banquets, E P Taylor's hospitality at Bayview Avenue was unflinching – and there was the fun that Martin Gilliat backed the winner in the Queen's Plate at the new Woodbine racecourse.

Nor was the traveller long home when she visited the British Army of the Rhine, matching in outline the visits of Prince Charles, Princess Anne, Princess Margaret and other royals, but emphasized more personally by her own style of readiness for 'whisky and broad banter' with other ranks. In 1966 the project of visiting Australia, Fiji and New Zealand, deferred two years earlier by appendicitis, provided a needed change to sunshine after a winter of recurring flu and laryngitis. But by coincidence Charles was spending his first term at the Timbertop outpost of Geelong Grammar School, with the notable and personal point here that a convenient exeat allowed him to fly from Melbourne to Canberra airport to welcome the Queen Mother when she flew in from Perth.

Grandson and granny laughed at the incongruity of meeting one another in the middle of miles of tarmac half the world away from home, intensely amused when the crowd seemed to applaud the enthusiastic kiss planted by Charles on his grandmother's cheek. The following week the Palace mail was enlivened by photographs of their car trip together through the Snowy Mountains and of the cottage they had shared at River Bend. The correspondence did not enlarge on the way grandson and grandmother had helped one another, as Charles said, to recover from 'shock and quite grim depression' on hearing that an Australian on the domestic staff had been killed in a road accident on his way to the cottage.

Incidentally, the temperature around Perth had been 102°F and from the *Britannia* the Queen Mother basked for three days in Fiji while, six days later, she landed in chill drizzle at Bluff, the southernmost port in New Zealand, where the nip in the air derives direct from Antarctica. Thence she made her way northward towards the sun, pausing for fishing lakes, mountain scenery, youth concerts, small friendly official luncheons – and at Wanaka the weather was so unexpectedly sunny that Jean Rankin and the Governor-General's wife made themselves paper-hats for shelter . . . and campers still tell of the little lady in windbreaker and floppy hat coming up the track to talk to them, who on drawing nearer turned out to be the Queen Mother.

Apart from her appendix operation and the seasonal affliction of colds or flu, the Queen Mother regarded herself through her sixties as 'fortunately mostly blest with good health', an attitude she maintained with bright determination. After returning from New Zealand she briefly entered the King Edward VII Hospital for Officers for a check-up, and when she again entered the hospital, taking an overnight bag, shortly before Christmas, 1966, her family regarded the routine with equanimity. On this occasion, however, the doctors discovered a condition necessitating surgery, and on 10 December it was announced that Queen Elizabeth the Queen Mother had undergone an operation 'to relieve a partial obstruction of the abdomen'.

The bulletin was signed by six doctors, among them two eminent in proctology, Sir Ralph Marnham, Surgeon to the Queen, a South African – and the New Zealander, Sir Arthur Porritt, Surgeon to King George VI, but the lack of precise information caused public disquiet. Concern was allayed when it was made known that tests for a malign element had proved negative. Subsequent bulletins mentioned a good night, a light diet and steady progress. But fuller reassurance, more comforting to the British public, came with the news that the Queen Mother was sitting up and watching the televised racing at Sandown Park. Holding court with the nurses, she was jubilantly enjoying, in fact, the victory of her horse, Irish Rover, which gallantly supplied the triumph of her 150th steeplechase win in her seventeen years as an owner.

The Queen Mother spent Christmas that year in hospital, but returned home to Clarence House in time to greet her entire family, her daughters and six grandchildren on their way down to Sandringham. By the New Year she was satisfyingly on the telephone to her racing trainers, Peter Cazalet and Jack O'Donoghue. 'And how are all my darling boys?' she would enquire, meaning her score of horses in training. For the public no other bulletins of her convalescence were needed and none was given. But for two months her Clarence House staff coped with probably the most extraordinary avalanche of well-wishing mail they had ever experienced, 300 such letters a day for several weeks on one estimate, with bouquets sufficient to cheer hospital wards throughout London and at Windsor and farther afield.

In January Peter Cazalet paraded several horses in the grounds of Clarence House for her inspection, and in February her first post-operative engagement was made known, her attendance at a regimental dinner in April, to be followed in May by a tour of the West Country and a private weekend in Normandy and then, most reassuring of all, a doughty thirteen-day tour of the Atlantic provinces of Canada in July. Thus the Queen Mother was indubitably back in business, and her friends knew of her quiet satisfaction, even a sense of triumph after suffering a phase of post-operative depression, not uncharacteristic after such an op. She had indeed coldly considered an enforced retirement. But instead she adapted readily to the need of a consistently regulated life, and the doctors for their part had reason for professional pleasure in an ideal patient.

A crisis of age in any event often clouds the seventies, and the adaptation needs must include a defensive philosophy against the losses seen among friends. Probably Queen Elizabeth drew courage from a maxim of her mother's, 'with much joy, one may also meet much sorrow'. The child of a large family, with many friends, learns earlier than most that the strongest links may inevitably be broken. The deaths of the Princess Royal, of Princess Marina and Sir Pierson Dixon, among others, were all separate griefs to the Queen Mother, although the world was unaware of the harsh and insistent repetition of sad news. In November 1967, word came that Queen Elizabeth's elder sister, Rose, Countess Granville, had died in a Forfar hospital at the age of seventy-seven, and now the Queen Mother was sadly the last survivor of all her girlhood family.

19.   'My Little Family'

There are times among comparatively new acquaintances, when the Queen Mother likes to chat away about 'my little castle', meaning the Castle of Mey. As a topic she will throw in 'my gingerbread cottage', her phrase for a small staff lodge embedded among the shrubs of the Royal Lodge drive. Or again she speaks affectionately of 'my little family', meaning neither the Royal Family nor her cluster of grandchildren but her Household and staff at Clarence House. The phrase is possessive, fond and reassuring, a point of anchorage against the gales of change.

In her accustomed London routine, unless Queen Elizabeth is lunching out – occasionally at the Ritz, but regularly at 'B.P.' or Kensington Palace – there occurs an interlude when the gentlemen of the Household gather from their offices along the passages and twisting stairs of the northward corridors, to await her in the morning-room on the ground floor: her Private Secretary, Sir Martin Gilliat; her treasurer, Sir Ralph Anstruther; her comptroller or staff chieftain, Captain Alastair Aird; Major Arthur Griffin, the press secretary, with the rota lady in waiting and one or two others. Extra guests are frequent. There are greetings, small talk, laughter, and the lady of the house steps from the small mirrored and gilded lift in the hall, pristine, smiling, relaxed and expectant.

If one is tempted to think for a moment of a woman chairman of the board joining her working colleagues in the directors' dining-room, the impression is lessened by the mere domestic informality. These are colleagues talking shop over a gin-and-tonic during the luncheon interlude from business pressures. One remembers the half-military urbane air of a Queen and her entourage. The room glistens with the sparkle of the crystal chandelier and the reflections in the gleaming display cabinets of Red Anchor porcelain; a gilt-framed looking-glass above the chimney-piece, caught and renewed every movement. The Queen Mother is poured a drink; the conversation flows with the easy, fluent pleasantries of a team.

When luncheon is announced Queen Elizabeth leads the way through the double doors into the library. The bookshelves form a cheerful background to the circular rosewood table in the middle of the room and here again the sparkling chandelier of Irish glass spread's an illusion of sunlight. One of the gentlemen will say a simple Grace, and the conversation and soft laughter flows again. Year by year this congenial hour is the nucleus of Queen Elizabeth's unobserved professional life.

The outside world knew little of the Strathmore family portraits – the blond young men in Highland costume, the dark and graceful Edwardian ladies – in the double drawing-room upstairs. Yet even in this favourite first-floor apartment with its Aubusson carpets and Nash ceilings, Queen Elizabeth occasionally surrendered privacy in her quest for good-doing. In Jubilee year, several hundred members of the National Art Collection Fund were shown around on different afternoons. They saw her Sisley study of the Seine, her Lowry of a Lancashire farm, some of her unrivalled Seago collection, the Piper drawings of Windsor Castle and a Monet invariably shown to French diplomats and formerly owned by Clemenceau. Here, too, was her unfinished Augustus John portrait of Queen Elizabeth, retrieved after his death from his cellar at Fordingbridge, that battleground of a portrait for which the then Queen gave thirty sittings until both protagonists were exhausted.

The camera can capture the Queen Mother effortlessly, time and again, but she is the despair of artists. John saw her clearly, 'one of those fine English skins and watery, translucent shadows and pearl highlights' yet the conception defeated him. His sitter provided brandy in the cupboard where he kept his paints, and supplied excuses in many a crisis. 'Mr John is quite cross with me today because I have been on holiday and changed colour'. It took the 1939 war, indeed, to end her patience and she at last wrote to John that it had been 'such an agreeable experience, posing in the spangled dress, but alas now it would have to be abandoned'. But she had not forgotten 'a hat of which he had said he would like to do a drawing, and one day she would come to his studio wearing the hat, as her own home (this was during the bombing) was dirty and dark . . .' It was a delightful letter which the old man never tired of showing to his friends.

Anthony Devas hungered to paint her in an apron, 'her milkmaid skin and her family qualities, the intimate woman inside the Queen' but his commissions were always for uniform or tiara, and he raged at the ribbon of the Garter, 'brutal and hideous'. Sir Gerald Kelly took five years to complete her State Portrait at Windsor, rubbing bits out and trying again, 'the many errors' – in his eyes – tormenting him. Graham Sutherland filled three sittings with 'preparatory and exploratory' drawings but then reluctantly abandoned the task. Annigoni felt that he missed 'the third image so vital in portraiture'. Preparing a fresco, Sara Leighton preferred to eschew formal sittings and was permitted to follow the Queen Mother with a sketchbook. The perfect moment, ultimately, was when her subject 'leaned down to speak to a crippled child in a wheelchair, the moment of warmth, compassion, dedication, her eyes like jewels . . .'

The portraits have lives of their own around the world today, but Queen Elizabeth's art collection at Clarence House embraces sixty years of discriminating royal patronage. In her sitting-room, the treasured Fra Angelico of *Madonna and Child Enthroned* outshines all others but also in that more intimate room, her preferences are more personal and revealing. There hangs the favourite study of her husband by Simon Elwes; the Sheraton bracket-clock bequeathed by Arthur Penn which lulls away her contented hours with friends; the delectable groups of miniature furniture that serve to charm her grandchildren; and, underfoot, the dark-blue Persian carpet, busy with tigers, deer and other animals, from the morning-room of 145 Piccadilly, a wedding gift showing remarkably little evidence of the decades of wear.

In the dining-room the Beechey and Hoppner portraits of George III and his family, inset white-framed into the plaster, are notable, and on great occasions Queen Elizabeth loves to embellish her sideboard and side-tables with some of her fine collection of plate: the four-centuries-old casket presented to her when she launched the liner *Queen Elizabeth*; the handsome silver tray by Paul Storr; the ancestral silver ewer and dish of 1718 with the arms of George Bowes of Streatlam, treasures according happily with the four modernist silver-gilt conch shells presented to her one year in Rhodesia. An array of her racing trophies might be brought out as background to the annual party she accords her racing associates, her trainers, jockeys and fellow owners. But this outgrew her available space and in her seventieth year became an ebullient party in the River Room at the Savoy, ostensibly to celebrate her 200th National Hunt win.

Her mere record achievement of winners was approaching 350 in 1980 when stable costs forced her to reduce her string. As an owner, Queen Elizabeth finances her steeplechasing entirely from her winnings and private funds, part deriving from Bowes Lyon interests, and jockey and similar charities have usually absorbed any small profit. Bargain shopping, implemented by feminine wiles, have kept down her initial outlay. Among first principles, where others may pay thousands, she shrewdly spends hundreds. She paid 250 guineas at the Dublin sales for Gay Record as a yearling and he handsomely had nine wins and twenty-three places, recouping £2,610 in prize money. Through the year, with secretarial help, she manages her own horses, usually buying yearlings inexpensively to have them broken in by a Sandringham neighbour. Some say that she judges by the expression and eyes of a horse. Stable lads talk of her 'gifts', however conjectural the second sight suspected by Glamis villagers. And one remembers that Helen Hardinge, among others, has written of her having 'a definite trace' of second sight, 'more than an insight'.

Her 'little family' follows her, of course, including Martin Gilliat, and great was the rejoicing in 1976 when Tammuz won the £10,000 Schweppes solid gold trophy at Newbury at odds of 18–1. That was the super-year, too, when her 300th win occurred at Ascot, thrilling her for a Royal Lodge gardener whom she knew had backed it. 'I'm so specially delighted it should happen at Ascot,' she said, beaming to everyone within earshot, with that comprehensive, smiling glance which seemed directed to each and every onlooker.

With the professional help of Bill Curling, formerly 'Hotspur', she keeps all her victories – and losers, too – chronicled in her racing albums, and occasionally browses through 'her boys' careers, bad or brilliant. The first horse raced in her (Strathmore) colours of 'blue, buff stripes, blue sleeves, black cap, gold tassel' was Manicou in 1950, who propitiously won the King George VI Chase for her during the King's lifetime. The second horse was M'as-Tu-Vu, who just before Elizabeth II's departure on her Coronation overseas tour in 1953, obligingly won at Sandown Park on the very afternoon when the Queen Mother was seeking enjoyment there with her two daughters.

It has become all but obligatory to write of Devon Loch, the horse who showed the invincible certainty of winning the 1956 Grand National by many lengths when less than fifty yards from the Aintree winning post, his legs suddenly splayed outward and he fell on his belly . . . to be passed the next instant by every horse remaining in the field. The tremendous ovation switched to an agonized hush. 'The Queen Mother never turned a hair,' wrote Harold Nicolson in a circumstantial letter to his wife. "I must go down," she said, "and comfort those poor people." So down she went, dried the jockey's tears, patted Peter Cazalet on the shoulder and insisted on seeing the stable-lads, who were also in tears. "I hope the Russians saw it," said the young Duke of Devonshire. "It was the most perfect display of dignity that I have ever witnessed." Malenkov and his party were in a box nearby.'

The tears were no metaphor. 'Please don't be upset,' the Queen Mother told the jockey, Dick Francis. 'That's racing. There'll be another time,' and so it proved. The lesser-known fact is that the Queen Mother had two horses in the National that year, but her M'as-Tu-Vu fell at the twentieth of the thirty jumps. Strangely, nothing was ever found wrong with Devon Loch. He remained in form and seven months later won his next race, to quote the Queen Mother's private racing albums, 'in such a run as could hardly be imagined. Though Northern King led over the last flight, and was still in front sixty yards from the post, Devon Loch passed him so fast that he won by two lengths.'

Then there was Manicou's son, The Rip, on whom the Queen Mother took an option after seeing him as a foal in a publican's field and later purchased against advice for £400. 'But make it guineas,' she said, conscience-stricken lest she had gained too much of a bargain. The Rip won thirteen races for his owner and became favourite for the Grand National, but he could be a vexatious horse and though he cleared every fence at Aintree he finished no better than seventh. As the intended star of a day at Ascot when the Queen Mother first took Prince Charles racing, the miscreant similarly trailed in last of seven. On the other hand, on a glorious day at Lingfield, he gave the Queen Mother her first treble, winning in succession to her runners Laffy and Double Star, a hat-trick repeated for her three years later with Arch Point, Gay Record and Super Fox.

These were the great days of Peter Cazalet, who once gave her twenty-seven National Hunt winners in a year and twice saw her in the first three of the winning owners' list. He was a notable friend and an eager collaborator whenever his royal patron wished to experiment. When she entered Laffy for the Ulster Harp National, for instance, the horse provided the first royal win seen on an Irish course for fifty years. Cazalet also supervized when her colours were carried over the jumps in France for the first time, putting in two runners in a bold attempt to make sure.

At Fairlawne, the Cazalets, Peter and his wife Zara, offered her the effect of a country home in Kent whenever she cared to stay for a weekend or more, a house replete with her enthusiasms even to

Augustus Johns in the drawing-room; and the study for confabbing was nearly an octagon room, curiously like her sitting-room at Royal Lodge. The Cazalets were in turn guests at Birkhall and Mey, and provided a racy contingent, of course, at the Queen Mother's seventieth birthday dinner party at Buckingham Palace, that superlative gathering of 120 friends and family when the Blue Drawing Room and adjoining State dining-room were turned into 'the happiest restaurant in town'.

A few days later the Queen Mother was to be found in the Orkneys, unveiling a memorial to the gallant lost crew of the local Longhope life-boat. Two years more and the contrast was directly displayed the very day after Trooping the Colour when the Duchess of Windsor came to London at St George's Chapel, Windsor, the distraught widow clutched the Queen's coat and was heard saying, 'Do I not go first? Should I not take precedence?' With gentle tact the Queen Mother took her arm and murmured 'May I not walk beside you?' But from that day forward compassion eased the rift of the years and Queen Elizabeth has never again visited France without sending the Duchess flowers and a kindly message.

Time in its flight indeed paused at the Queen Mother's desk. It happened back in 1952 that her departing secretary, Tom Harvey, commissioned from Laurence Whistler an engraved glass triptych to hold the typed sheet showing her engagements for each day, and through all the succeeding years that parting gift welcomes her every morning in London with her programme for the day. On the right hand of the crystal an engraved verse is remindful of 'DUTIES . . . the emblazoned document, the microphone . . . the moment when the ranks present . . . this tape to cut, that stone to lay . . .' On the left hand the inscription lists 'PLEASURES – a myriad to rehearse! The likely horse . . . the lucky hand . . . the leaping trout . . . the floodlit dome . . . the crowds, the lights, the welcome . . .' Etched in the crystal, drawings, too, express their ageless symbolism: the scrolls, regimental drums and insignia, a mortar-board cap (for academic occasions) the trowel for foundation stones, a key for opening buildings; only a helicopter absent. And for the pleasures the symbols of stirrups, a pack of cards, a fishing net and creel, a volume of poems, champagne, a cine-camera, a rose, a flourish of fireworks . . . Seated at her desk, Queen Elizabeth sees these reminders twinkling before her; and spaced on the white memo page are her appointments: the retiring officers to receive, the eastern prince to lunch, the conference to attend, the plaque to unveil . . . and perhaps next day new buildings to open, new Colours to present, nurses awaiting medals . . .

While in her seventies, when a Parliamentary select committee staged an enquiry into the Civil List as if checking the value for annuities received, they heard evidence that Queen Elizabeth had fulfilled 211 engagements second only to the totals for the Queen and Prince Philip. Audiences and luncheons bulked large, then came receptions and engagements concerned with her patronages, with commemorative church services and next the duties of universities and schools. Disentangling public from private tasks proved onerous: the Queen Mother then as now combined duty and pleasure beyond official analysis.

In 1955, for example she was installed as Chancellor of London University and her 'happy chores' varied annually: presenting degrees at the graduation ceremony one year, conferring honorary degrees the next; attending a reception at the Senate House or taking tea with students in the Provost's room, perhaps a visit to Paris with her Chancellor's Cap for an international ceremony. She conferred London University degrees in equatorial Africa, sweltering in her heavy Chancellor's robes. Regardless of her mid-seventies she enjoyed the University Ball, dancing with a youthful and unaccustomed President of the Union, clapping her crushed white gloves for more: 'How very clever of you, Mr President, to dance the Gay Gordons without knocking my tiara off!'

In 1975, she attended the Foundation Day dinner. 'I see they all retired at seventy-five,' she said, indicating a list of previous Chancellors. 'I've enjoyed it so much.' There was a pregnant pause. 'I've decided to carry on!' She retired when past eighty, the reins passing to Princess Anne.

Wet or fine, Queen Elizabeth still looks forward with zest to her annual outing with the London Gardens Society, each year into a different district of the metropolis, commending small back gardens, admiring the balcony bowers of council flats approving front gardens where good neighbours had created a floral street. There are greenhouses to be inspected, dogs patted, gardeners and their children to meet. Every year she has tea alone with one family, with an appreciative eye for the special best tea service, the amateur painting, the gifted child: one year a boy poet was asked to send a sample poem to Clarence House and was commended for his verse. The visitor was unhurried. Dorothy Laird tells of a seaman's wife who remarked over the teacups, 'I hope you have a happy time on 4 August.' 'How kind, but why do you mention it?' 'It is my birthday, too!' The conversation passed to other topics, but on 4 August a birthday telegram arrived from Queen Elizabeth.

There are also such hardy annuals as the candle-lit occasions of the Middle Temple when Queen Elizabeth was 'pleased to dine with her fellow Benchers in Hall', an event inaugurated one draughty evening during the war, when half the dining-chamber had been destroyed. There are unfailing commissions of work for the Royal School of Needlework, and occasional visits embracing one or other of the 300 and more societies, institutions, charities and kindred organizations, in which she actively and regularly interests herself. She reads their reports as they come to her desk and deals expeditiously with correspondence when needful. But papers are put aside when disinclined to decide an issue, and she once remarked of a 'Do It Now' slogan on her desk, 'I don't know why I leave it there: I never do, you know'. Yet overflowing 'pending' baskets are seldom in evidence.

Across the farther shores of good-doing enterprises, she visited a South Bank church crypt used as a haven for alcoholics and drug addicts. 'Well, she asked why I came and wished me good luck with my treatment, all credit to her for trying,' one of the junkies commented. For fuller understanding, she visited the drug squad office at New Scotland Yard and toured other departments to help spread the laurels. Her bouquets from the National Rose Society, and other floral offerings often serve other good purposes. At Smithfield meat market the smell of butchery is never entirely hosed away, but she visited the place unhurriedly for its centenary, and the meat porters serenaded her with an impromptu chorus of 'If You Were The Only Girl in the World'. Listening with broadening smiles to the end of the song, the Queen Mother had earned the 110 pound baron of beef ultimately taken home in the boot of her car. But probably this, too, was passed on, where it could be more useful.

She finds fun in meticulous draft schedules. 'Arrive 3.30 and proceed by roller-skate . . .' she pencilled marginally for a building notorious for endless corridors. Inspecting the Press Club (as its first woman member) she displayed unexpected skill with a billiards' cue, the natural dexterity of a Glamis girl. She held a reception at Clarence House one evening for members of the French Resistance and the Special Operations command. Bagehot's list of the three inalienable rights of a monarch – the right to be consulted, to encourage and to warn – was restyled in the Queen Mother's case as the right to give encouragement, to commend and to further all good purposes.

In different format, the exhibitions of the London Needlework Guild at St James's Palace, would not seem the same without the small stack of articles marked 'Made by the Queen Mother's guests at Birk-hall'. The knitters were not always regal. In a season of inexpert guests, the Queen Mother would be equal to inviting deserving nursing sisters to enjoy a holiday and perhaps help maintain the quota. Dress-making staff, milliners, a skilled old book-binder, her hairdresser Maurice and his wife are pleasantly invited to holiday at the Castle of Mey 'any time you like. Just ring the housekeeper', and she follows her offer up until the timid were gently urged into accepting. When her elderly chiropo-dist fell ill, Queen Elizabeth travelled across London to Wanstead to 'see how he was and cheer him up'. Driving through Lambeth one day, a young chauffeur apologized for slowing down, 'but I might see my wife on the corner to watch us drive past'. 'But of course we must stop!' the Queen Mother exclaimed. 'I would love to meet her.' And after a big City function, her presentation bouquet of red roses was sent straight to her milliner. 'Would you please give these to your work-girls? The won-derful hat gave me such confidence and pleasure.'

The presentation of shamrock to the Irish Guards on St Patrick's Day might involve a chopper trip to the Guards depot at Pirbright or a light-hearted ceremony at Clarence House: the event was once brought forward by a day to enable Queen Elizabeth to watch one of her horses as a Gold Cup favourite at Cheltenham. A young grocer once enquired if her car could pause near his shop on the way to the races 'which would give his customers much pleasure' and through ten years it became a semi-tradition for her car to stop and for the enterprising young man to present a bouquet and a box of mints. In her sixtieth and again her seventieth year the Queen Mother has deputized for the Queen in the distribution of the Royal Maundy money, a reminder of her satisfaction that throughout the havoc of the war years there was no break in the continuity of that ancient ceremony. In most years, the annual proces-sion of the Order of the Garter seems unchanging. Yet there had been only two Investitures of the Order this century until Elizabeth as Queen Consort, with her romantic ideas of chivalry, encouraged the King to retrieve the Garter from the dangerous ground of political honours and place it, with the Order of Merit, in the bestowal of the Sovereign alone.

The modernization of the British Crown, so often attributed to Prince Philip's enterprise and Elizabeth II's watchful heed of criticism, partly derives from the Queen Mother's readiness, especially in the earlier days of her daughter's reign, to examine, question and advocate the discard or remoulding of familiar ideas. Neither the Queen Mother when a girl nor any of the Bowes-Lyon family had attended the 1911

Investiture of the Prince of Wales – the later Duke of Windsor – but she remembered the nation-wide enthusiasm, the spectacular impact of the newsreel film, the special magazine and newspaper supplements of the then unprecedented ceremonial, and in 1958 she was in agreement with the Queen's broadcast promise to Wales on Prince Charles that 'when he is grown-up I will present him to you at Caernarvon'. Features of his tough education at Gordonstoun failed to appeal to his grandmother. 'Now he doesn't need to be toughened any more,' she once acridly told Cecil Beaton. At the point of no return the tentative 'presentation' became a full-scale Investiture, and she could see encouragingly that Charles was of very different fibre to his unwilling uncle. 'A good thing for the monarchy and a good thing for Wales,' summed up the Clarence House opinion.

The Queen Mother's dignified entrance into the Upper Ward of Caernarvon Castle, with Princess Margaret and Princess Anne, was ineffably moving and at once set the right atmosphere. The one moment amiss throughout the day was the thud of a distant explosion before the ceremony. Driving in the royal procession the Queen Mother could not be sure what was happening, and her substantial private subscription to the fund for the schoolboy injured by the bomb was one of the many gestures that mirrored her horror and compassion.

20. *Anniversaries*

The Queen's Silver Wedding in November 1972, and again her Silver Jubilee as Queen in 1977, were reminders to Queen Elizabeth the Queen Mother of family change and passing time. It could not have been other for her than an occasion of review and recollection as well as thankfulness. One of her most precious possessions is the Edmund Brock portrait of Princess Elizabeth at four years old, which had hung in the morning-room at 145 Piccadilly . . . and now 'Elizabeth' had made her a grandmother of four: Charles, Anne, Andrew and Edward, with Princess Margaret's two, of course. With Prince Philip, the Queen all but echoed her mother's thoughts when she said, 'It came as a bit of a surprise to realize that we have been married twenty-five years. Neither of us are much given to looking back and the years seem to have slipped by so quickly.'

The Queen Mother's closest friends and contemporaries found it similarly hard to believe how the years had flown since her own Silver Wedding, years equally of intense change and unfolding event. For the King and Queen's thanksgiving in 1948 they had driven to St Paul's with their two daughters past the bomb-damaged façades of Fleet Street, and the Cathedral itself stood amidst a wilderness of rubble, veiled by weeds and wild flowers. With consideration of her mother's memories of that occasion, the Queen with Prince Philip changed the venue of their own thanksgiving to Westminster Abbey, where they had been married, and then rode in procession with Prince Charles and Princess Anne into the civic square mile of the City of London to lunch at the Guildhall. In the second coach the Queen Mother rode with Princess Margaret and Lord Snowdon, 'Her Majesty wearing green which some consider an unlucky colour', one commentator noted, 'a bravura touch of springtime for this autumn day'.

To the Queen and Prince Philip at the Guildhall the Lord Mayor spoke felicitously of the game of Happy Families and the skilled player who had discerned the most valuable card in the pack, Mr Salt the Sailor. 'A marriage begins by joining man and wife together,' the Queen responded, 'but needs to develop and mature with the passing years. For that it must be held in the web of family relationships, between parents and children, between grandparents and grandchildren, between cousins, aunts and uncles. My Lord Mayor, we all know about the difficulties of achieving that Happy Family . . . but if it succeeds in real life there is nothing like it.'

The Queen Mother's thoughts dwelt on both her daughters and each of her grandchildren, without presentiment, on that day of happiness. Prince Charles made himself responsible for organizing the supper party and entertainment for his parents that evening, and consulted and indeed plotted with his grandmother on every detail from the comprehensive guest list of intimates to engaging the English Chamber Orchestra to open the evening concert with the Wedding March; and among the two hundred guests it may well have been Queen Elizabeth who suggested that Lieutenant Mark Phillips should be included.

Queen Elizabeth's relationship to Princess Anne is that of both godmother and grandmother. It will always be a moot point whether the Queen or the Queen Mother most influenced Anne in her phenomenal riding career. It was grandmama who gave the Princess the first saddle ever purchased for her, a birthday gift of Coronation year, and under her grandmother's watchful eye at Royal Lodge, the little girl liked nothing better than to clamber on to one of the aged rocking-horses that stood in the hall. Viewing her steeplechase films with her granddaughter beside her, the Queen Mother gave the child a slant on horsemanship extravagantly different from riding her docile pony with Mama. The founder and host of the Badminton Three-Day Event, the Duke of Beaufort, long known to Anne as 'Uncle Master', had of course married the Queen Mother's bridesmaid, Lady Mary Cambridge, and whether the Queen or Queen Mother presented the prizes, both furnished an example to the young Princess of the ultimate glories of riding adventurously.

Anne had no more eager partisan than the Queen Mother when, aged eleven, she won her first blue rosettes on her pony Bandit, first at Windsor and then at Allanbay Park; and at 14 justified her grandmother's enthusiasm with her first little-known competitive appearance at Badminton, when she rode a clear round over seven fences against nineteen other competitors. Lady Abergavenny had the laurels of first introducing the Princess to Mark Phillips at the competitors' party after the Eridge Horse Trials, but the Queen Mother brought them together again more insistently at Eridge the following year. Then, in 1968, the British three-day-event team won the gold medal at the Mexico Olympics, and the Queen Mother attended a party in their honour at the Whitbread cellars in the City of London, this time unexpectedly taking Anne along. Mark was the youngest ever reserve rider with the team, and there was no mistaking the Princess's admiring interest.

In 1971 Anne celebrated her twenty-first birthday at the Castle of Mey, coming ashore from the *Britannia* with the Royal Family for lunch, and before the fireworks that evening they all watched a re-run of the privately-edited movie of that year's Badminton. On the opening day Anne had headed the twenty-five entrants, and next day Mark led across the thirty-three fences of the rigorous cross-country course. On the third day, one show-jumping error reduced the Princess to fifth and Mark was the immaculate winner.

The victor later confessed that their romance 'deepened after Badminton', though which Badminton was never made clear. The Silver Wedding year intensified their rivalry in the saddle, but Anne's marvellous horse Doublet went lame and Mark on Great Ovation went on to win the leading trophy for the second year running. Anne had also won the 1971 European individual gold medal, the first member of the Royal Family ever to hold a European equestrian title; the phrenetic media variously elected her as Sportswoman and Sports Personality of the Year, and Queen Elizabeth followed her grand-daughter's remarkable career with all the more intense and attached interest, 'an unqualified fan', as she said.

In private life she championed the couple with an affectionate perception of their quickening mutual regard. When Mark was invited to Windsor Castle for lunch, Queen Elizabeth followed suit at Clarence House, and he was no sooner invited to Sandringham than she ensured that he came to lunch with Anne at Royal Lodge. Long a matchmaker at heart, the Queen Mother thoroughly enjoyed her sense of active involvement. With the equivalent rising barometer of public interest, some questioned young Mark's eligibility to wed the Queen's only daughter. At a remove, the Queen Mother riposted with the phrase she had used on discovering that a cocktail bar on the liner *Queen Elizabeth II* was to be called the Queen's Lounge. 'How snobby!'

Two months younger than Charles, two years older than Anne, Lieutenant Phillips was only twenty-four when he faced the need of asking the Queen and Prince Philip's permission to seek 'a deeper understanding' in his friendship, an ordeal for which the Queen Mother smoothed the way. Her preference in the affairs of young people showed readiness in setting the stage, but progress was then left to the actors in the hope that the sketched scenario will come right. Contrary to one branch of public opinion, the Queen Mother is no matriarch, whatever her certainty of feminine influence, but as a born matchmaker she finds a need at times of watching her step.

In the Silver Wedding year of 1972 the love-match of Prince Richard of Gloucester and Miss Birgitte van Deurs intervened as a sub-plot in the closer family interest of Anne and Mark. With some sympathy from his aunt, Queen Elizabeth, Richard had always been bent on going his own way, and was creating a promising career in architecture. While at Cambridge, he fell ardently in love with Danish-born Birgitte, whom he first met at a student party; and the passage of time heightened his determination to marry her in spite of family preference for an English bride. Ultimately the *Court Circular* announced that the Queen had 'gladly given her consent' but, rightly or wrongly, some read between the lines. The Queen Mother and Prince Charles went to Richard and Birgitte's quiet wedding in the Barnwell village church, while the Queen and Princess Anne remained in Scotland.

Not two months later, the tragic death during an air race of Richard's elder brother, Prince William of Gloucester, confronted the newly-weds with the heavier responsibilities of family life. Within two years more, on his father's death, Richard and his wife were Duke and Duchess of Gloucester, adapting in exemplary fashion to the tasks of royal rank, and they began to play an increasingly active part in occasions of State. With Richard's precedent of the wider freedom of choice in matrimony, extending indeed back to the Queen Mother's marriage, Anne and Mark at all events had no difficulties.

Easter in 1973 saw an exceptional house-party at Windsor Castle; and at Royal Lodge Queen Elizabeth's friends filled the house to the rafters. On the eve of the Queen's birthday – her forty-seventh – on 21 April, the Prime Minister of Australia and his wife, Mr and Mrs Gough Whitlam, arrived for an 'overnight' which Mrs Whitlam described hour-by-hour in her weekly published diary – 'In came the Queen Mother, Queen Elizabeth, in a lovely blue printed silk dress with an aqua cardigan . . .' In she came, too, later on, having changed for dinner 'in a most lovely white and gold dainty dress. She really is a pretty feminine person of enormous warmth.' The Whitlams presented the Queen with a handsome rug as a birthday gift, and Lord Snowdon climbed into its eight-foot travelling case to demonstrate its usefulness for smuggled guests. But Mrs Whitlam missed the main story after her departure. There began indeed a sustained four-day party.

Easter Day was on 22 April, and Easter Monday, the 23rd, felicitously St George's Day, was set aside for an intended early observance of a remarkable family milestone. On the Thursday, the 26th, it would actually and incredibly be the fiftieth anniversary of the Queen Mother's wedding-day, but Easter Monday was agreed as more convenient for the commemoration. At dinner that night the Queen proposed her mother's health with a speech said to have been 'charming, succinct, just right'. The Queen Mother responded in some jeopardy of emotion. Then, amid the happy babble of well-wishing, Prince Philip rapped for attention and so, 'among ourselves', the intimate news of his daughter's engagement to Lieutenant Mark Phillips was made known to the family.

Nothing could have given Queen Elizabeth more pleasure and delight than this wholly happy link of her half-century with the sentiment of Princess Anne's romance. The Queen so scrupulously included her mother in every detail of the wedding arrangements that one friend considered the Queen Mother in 'quite an elation of domestic happiness'. The forthcoming in-laws, Mr and Mrs Peter Phillips, were guests in London and at Birkhall during the summer, coming up from their country home in Wiltshire, and through their personal reticence one divines Queen Elizabeth's deft and sympathetic guidance through the practical and, on their part, totally unforeseen problems evoked by a royal wedding.

The Queen Mother gave Anne an exquisite aquamarine and diamond tiara, among other gifts, and nearly two years after the wedding, when the newly-weds had outgrown their Army home at Oak Grove Lodge, Sandhurst, she undertook several willing house-hunting excursions. Through her then assistant secretary, Alastair Aird, she gained news of Forest Lodge, a somewhat cumbersome mansion in Windsor Great Park, and the couple paid it several visits, primed on what Grandmother had once achieved at Royal Lodge with judicious demolition and just the right paintwork. At an early stage the Queen Mother also knew of the Queen's wish to find a suitable agricultural property for the young people: there were few personal secrets between mother and daughter. The ultimate purchase of Gatcombe Park came about, in fact, through a hot tip from Prince Charles that 'Rab Butler's place' was on the market. After thirty years Queen Elizabeth was heartened to see the persistent strength of the King's dictum, 'we are a family and a team: we must keep together'. And in an ever-remembered wedding letter he had widened this to include 'with additions of course at suitable moments'.

Altogether, when the years seemed to race as they usually do for the elderly, her elder grand-daughter's marriage lifted Queen Elizabeth's spirits at a point where her outgoing nature most needed the impetus. In glancing through the proofs of a biographic summary she noticed that she had not been abroad for five years. It was idle for friends to point out that the doctors had suggested she should lead a more restful life. 'But that was years ago!' she said, and future plans were to be more regardful of travel. Accordingly, in the summer of 1974, she again appeared in Toronto, first for the presentation of new Colours to 'her regiments', the Toronto Scottish and the Black Watch of Canada, and then to present a number of young people in Toronto and Montreal with the Duke of Edinburgh's gold awards, while also spending a day or two with E P Taylor in the world of horses which she always found stimulating. To Canadian friends, too, in one of her amusing moods, she mentioned that her son-in-law had once given her a gold medal, surely a recognition rare among mothers-in-law. Philip was in fact presenting her with the Royal Society of Arts' Albert Medal for 'personal service to Arts, Manufactures and Commerce', but the amusing point was scored. She spoke, too, with a sense of fun, of Prince Andrew's first year at Gordonstoun, a grandson already beyond being toughened. He had already suffered some slight concussion in a dormitory lark and at fourteen could hardly wait to start glider lessons. Then there were new prospects, for her other grandchildren, Princess Margaret's boy, David, who was thirteen, and his sister, Sarah, three years younger, with Canadian-style possibilities, as she emphasized in Toronto, that they might soon attend co-ed school together. The Taylor circle noticed her added affectionate interest in discussing 'her young people': Prince Edward's ingenuity in choosing a wedding-gift for Anne, 'he promised her something beautiful to look at, so he gave her a mirror!' And Sarah's ballet lessons, 'really ready for me to take her to Covent Garden!'

To awaken piquancy yet not appease their curiosity, the Queen Mother played guessing games with the youngsters. Her hints in 1975 of a romantic five-day package turned out to be a five-day visit to Persia as the guest of the Shah, a whirlwind of exotic places, blue-domed mosques and the fabled ruins of Persepolis in the days when the rule of the Shah and the uninterrupted flow of oil seemed eternal. In the same year, her expectations of going on a cruise 'only a brief one, perhaps five different islands' materialized as a busy voyage aboard HM Yacht *Britannia* to Guernsey, Jersey, Alderney and Sark with the Isle of Wight for good measure.

Of her own accord, Queen Elizabeth would have probably paid little attention to her seventy-fifth birthday but the Queen and Prince Philip decided that nothing would please her more than a surprise dinner-party followed by 'a small dance'. The occasion however ultimately called for 'seventy-five of us'. 'But how can she possibly be 75?' Lady Doris Vyner was heard saying. 'She never changes. She looks fifty. She stays looking young . . . because she's never bored.' The large world, too, remarked the anniversary. The Corps of Drums of the Coldstream Guards marched past playing 'Happy Birthday To You', the large London crowd joined in, and birthday cards and bouquets once again deluged Clarence House.

Unexpectedly every newspaper in Fleet Street greeted the birthday with lavish features, 'She has made the British monarchy much more easy and natural, much more good-natured and less severe,' said *The Times*. 'This great and unique lady,' said the *Telegraph*, as if reviewing a book. 'Impish, shy, tireless, humorous, irreverent . . . a gross libel that she is 75,' observed the *Express*. 'It is not in human nature to attack your nicest auntie, kindly, twinkling maternal,' added the *Standard*. And probably the 'nicest auntie' read with some indignation of 'being still actively engaged in public life, despite her age'. It was all a dress-rehearsal for the other landmark-birthdays ahead. In summer the Queen Mother often holds her lunch parties in her London garden, with a long table set on the lawns, while on the other side of the brick wall, passers-by have no suspicion of the pleasant al fresco scene so near at hand. The birthday gift from her Household was in fact two glass-topped cane garden tables to replace two older ones, and the Snowdons and their children came to the birthday lunch. At the Palace that evening the birthday cake was prestigiously three-tiered with one pink candle.

'Slowing down? Quite the reverse. We can't keep up with her,' her press secretary, Major Griffin, told the reporters. The energetic birthday lady, indeed, had choppered from Sandringham the previous day and was at the Castle of Mey two days later. During the winter, she fell ill with influenza almost as a matter of course, but with the Spring of '76 she was off with friends on another four-day jaunt into her beloved

France, this time the cathedrals and castles of Burgundy, Beaune and Macon, 'drinking it all in'. In September, she was in Paris; making a speech in French at the Sorbonne, opening a re-embellished mansion as a new British Institute, and above all enjoying another stay at the British Embassy, in the heart of the city, which had come to seem her Paris home. Next, 1977 brought a stay with the Rothschilds at Château Mouton, near Bordeaux, and 1978 found the royal tourist exploring the Dordogne, making her base at the Château d'Hautefort, while in 1979 she spent an unfettered week in Lorraine. Moreover, within the year, she was in Hanover to review her regiments, the Queen's Dragoon Guards and the Queen's Own Hussars — and fulfilling, on the sidelines, a long-cherished ambition to see the royal Hanoverian gardens of Herrenhausen.

A fondness for innovation so close to one's octogenarian phase is exceptional, but in 1979 before presiding in Canada over the first International Gathering of Scottish Clans, she could not resist the novelty of giving the *Toronto Star* a newspaper interview at Clarence House. 'We simply must keep up,' she told the writer, Val Sears. 'And how is the good old *Toronto Star* anyway?'

'Whatever you do, don't mention age to her,' Mr Sears was briefed beforehand. He was nervous and she set him at ease by mentioning a brave young sailor she had decorated at an investiture. 'He had crawled through scalding steam to save a ship. I said "It must have been terrible". And he said, "Not as bad as this, ma'am".' She laughed and seemed ready to chat unguardedly. The issue of Scottish and Welsh separatism came up, 'I'm dead set against it. Nobody really wants it. So much better if we stay together'. The Shah of Iran? 'Poor man, he really did try to help his people . . .' She obligingly went up and down stairs to change hats for the photographer, her 'props' as she called them. It was not so very different from the announcement of her engagement in 1923 when a London *Star* reporter had sent in his card from the Bowes-Lyon doorstep in Bruton Street . . .

In March, 1976, the deepest sadness of all her long widowhood befell Queen Elizabeth in the separation of Princess Margaret and Lord Snowdon. The shock came, not from an unclouded sky, but across a firmament long troubled by domestic storms; the tempest no less easier to bear in the violent ruin of hopes and the 'dismal and dreadful' aftermath in the divorce court. On any interpretation, any metaphor, the Queen Mother was stunned. In all her years, she rarely had cause to weep more, and it may be that she indeed shed tears: for her daughter, for her son-in-law, for the bewildered and frightened children.

There echoed in a memory of Royal Lodge, long ago, a child's scream of rage somewhere upstairs, the closing of a door, and presently the appearance of the same flushed endearing offender round the dining-room door, extending a plump little hand for crystallized sugar, good as gold. One meticulous commentator, at the time of the separation, likened the marriage crash to 'coming suddenly upon a jungle clearing — strewn with blood and bones and bits of flesh, all the evidence of a terrible lacerating battle': it mattered not who won. For the royal mother at the middle of the picture there could have been no relief from the numbing sense of devastation . . . until her natural optimism and good sense offered the forlorn hope that all might yet be well.

Two years earlier, in March 1974, the winds of discord were dismay-ingly evident when Margaret flew off to Mustique and her new-built Caribbean bungalow only four days before Tony's birthday, leaving him working in London, tied up with film conferences, his invalid chair commitments and his 'photo stills' contract for *Murder on the Orient Express*. But the quarrel, too, was murderous in its wounding unsen-timentality. Possibly the clash of travel arrangements and social and business interests was unavoidable, but Queen Elizabeth at the time recognized the stuff of which undesirable gossip is made. Tony was invited to dinner at Clarence House and the *Court Circular* next day hoovered the carpet, 'Her Majesty, accompanied by the Duke and Duchess of Kent and the Earl of Snowdon, was present at a gala perfor-mance of *Manon* at the Royal Opera House, Covent Garden'.

Ever since their honeymoon Tony had found viable reasons for not accompanying his wife to Mustique. Perhaps he genuinely disliked the place. Perhaps he felt indeed too busy to take two holidays a year, and he usually hated wasting time in sunbathing. But other dissensions and differences were becoming too evident. 'I sometimes feel I can do nothing right,' he once said of the running fire of curiously hostile press criticism that smouldered around him from the earliest years of his mar-riage. Entirely mythical breakdowns of the marriage were reported at least seven years before the real event. Latterly there may have been a masculine lack of sympathy in menopausal symptoms, and on Mar-garet's side a natural lack of understanding in the time-consuming drive, hazards and business hassles of a single-minded careerist. The Queen Mother, one may think, may have regarded these difficulties with judicious sympathy, and placidly made untroubled allowance for volatile flare-ups between two highly-strung, temperamental, and at times capricious people: one should not get too upset.

From the first the household at Kensington Palace was sharply divided into two financial sectors, each maintaining its separate loyalties, like Montagus and Capulets. Tony's bank account, which was not bottomless, paid for his business office suite, HQ of his photography and television films, and every normal husbandly responsibility, from private household bills and a share of the rates to the children's education. Princess Margaret's establishment was concerned with the business management of a Princess, her secretarial and wardrobe expenses and related upkeep allowed for by her Civil List annuity. But the necessary household division, so simple in origin, may finally have widened the rift, boulders rolling in a chasm.

Tony's commercial and artistic assignments in the United States and Australia created absences not always to be timed by Princess Margaret's physical need of wintering in the sun of Mustique or elsewhere. One writer of close insight, Ivan Rowan, could justly consider 'the state of the marriage still on the face of it perfectly manageable. Thousands of middle-aged couples in a similar impasse do in fact manage it . . .' At this point I must disclose a special interest, as the Parliamentarians say, having written separate biographies of both Lord Snowdon and Princess Margaret,* and in 1978 I shared what I believe to have been the Queen Mother's view, that behind any temporary unhappiness there was a firmer verity of mutual interest and family love.

The separation, when it came, was of incisive and wounding swiftness. One can only take into account, on one side, an ultimatum, and thus plans on ice for a separation, and perhaps, too, an ultimatum deliberately flouted, to call a bluff. 'I don't in truth know what is going to happen,' said Sir Martin Charteris, the Queen's private secretary, in this desert of assumptions. On his way to Australia, Lord Snowdon was caught by the television cameras in Tokyo, visibly shaken and overwrought, evidently taken by surprise by the Princess's separation announcement.

Either by a ghastly irony – or could it have been callous intention? – the BBC were playing the love-theme music of *West Side Story*, the Snowdons' favourite musical, immediately before the first announcement went out: 'HRH the Princess Margaret, Countess of

* *Lord Snowdon*, WH Allen, 1968.
  Princess Margaret, WH Allen, 1974.

Snowdon, and the Earl of Snowdon have mutually agreed to live apart. The Princess will carry out her public duties and functions unaccompanied by Lord Snowdon. There are no plans for divorce proceedings.' And that was all.

Later, Lord Snowdon 'slept on it' before making his one dignified statement. 'I am desperately sad in every way that this had to happen. I would just like to say three things. First to pray for the understanding of our two children. Secondly, to wish Princess Margaret every happiness in her future. And, thirdly, express with utmost humility my love, admiration and respect I will always have for her sister, her mother and indeed her entire family.'

The Queen Mother hoped for a reconciliation. Although she gave all her compassion to Princess Margaret and her sympathetic understanding to Lord Snowdon, she sorrowed for the children, and apparently did everything she could to urge the separated couple to remain good friends. From this she was to draw some shreds of comfort. The Queen's agreement to divorce proceedings after two years of separation evidently did not entirely quench a consideration that divorce itself is sometimes remedied. A decree nisi was made absolute in May 1978, with an agreement that Lord Snowdon should have access to the children. Kindred relationships are not so easily uncemented, and the Queen Mother maintained her unequivocal central status. Tony and the children indeed lunched with the Queen Mother at Clarence House on her seventy-eighth birthday with their own pleasant opportunities afterwards of conversation as of old. Four months later Lord Snowdon married a former television production assistant, Lucy Lindsay-Hogg, making her the second Countess of Snowdon.

With young David and Sarah at Windsor at Christmas, and the confirmation of Prince Andrew and Lord Linley in St George's Chapel, in the presence of their parents, the Queen Mother had retrieved the chains of affection. The children's holiday with their grandmother at Birkhall, and Tony's only partly professional presence at Gatcombe for Princess Anne's twenty-eighth birthday photographs, with other private occasions, continued to express Queen Elizabeth's desire of continued friendship.

'The only regret one has as one grows older,' she once told Dorothy Laird, 'is that things do not matter so strongly.' But regrets were soon to be partnered by joy elsewhere in her family. Eight months after the separation, the birth of a son to Princess Anne on 15 November 1977, made the Queen Mother a great-grandmother for the first time. 'It's one of the happiest days of my life,' she said. 'It's wonderful, wonderful. I'm absolutely delighted.' She was indeed nearly at a loss for words in the pleasure of greeting Master Peter Phillips. And presently there were again Snowdon photographs of a baby for her album and her desk, and again in 1981 when Anne and Mark's fair-haired daughter, Zara Anne Elizabeth was born. Both at Gatcombe and Clarence House Lord Snowdon's file of photographs has been sustained ever since.

21. *The Settled Scene*

After all, the stories are legion. David Shepherd, the artist, waits for his unpunctual sitter and is told, 'So sorry, Mr Shepherd. I've been up the road having coffee with my daughter.'

Noel Coward was invited to lunch for his seventieth birthday but the Queen Mother was laid up with flu and apologised sweetly, 'But my two daughters will understudy me,' which they did.

Then Cecil Beaton invited her to lunch and, from 'the huge limousine' out steps the 'smiling, delightful, familiar figure . . . dressed in brilliant puce and magenta . . . the delightful hesitancy, wistful eyes. 'How nice and warm your house is. I'm cold from sitting to Mr Ward. Sitting produces its own coldness, doesn't it?' Later, after long ignoring her waiting car, she stops to talk on the pavement, heedless of gawkers.

She enjoys the well-turned phrase in conversation and personal correspondence and the poetic touch in events. On her seventy-fifth birthday nothing gave her more pleasure than Benjamin Britten's gift of an album of seven poems by Burns, with the composer's manuscript of his musical setting for voice and harp. When Terence Rattigan in his last illness 'took the trouble' to send her the volume of his collected plays, her response was to take the Queen to see the play he had running at the time, *Cause Célèbre*. 'We have read it and heard it by radio, so we had to see it.' Among authors, her stock stands high for having, to take one quote, 'displayed the virtues of ordinary life in an extraordinary life'. She likes to wear Queen Victoria's favourite diamond jubilee brooch on occasions linked with that anniversary; top marks for remembrance, though one sometimes has to cudgel one's brains to discover the connecting sentiment.

Then there's the surprise effect. 'Turn down the sound,' she begged a house guest, when the National Anthem boomed from the radio. 'When you're not present, it's like hearing the Lord's Prayer while playing Canasta'. Max Bygraves mentioned that during a forthcoming visit of hers to the television studios he would probably be at the back of the crowd. 'Just pretend to faint,' she said. 'Then you'll be carried to the front. Lots of people do it. I've seen them.' She assured comedian Billy Dainty, 'I laughed so much I had to wring out my handkerchief.'

Show business was determined to please and compliment her at the last Royal Variety show during her eightieth year: Scottish singers, the Royal Scottish Ballet, the Royal Scots Guards Band, a backdrop of the Castle of Mey, celebrities as walk-ons, and an impersonation of Maurice Chevalier singing to her, as he once did, 'You must have been a beautiful baby'. Tireless, she joined in exuberantly with the choruses, seemed about to pitch out of the box at the personal jokes, and still had vivacity for the presentation-line of one hundred performers, close on midnight.

During the Queen's Jubilee year she scattered her commendation and congratulations around to those who had done well. A leading Chelsea restauranteur implemented the children's parties by inviting fifty neighbourhood pensioners to lunch. Getting to hear of it, the Queen Mother sent him her hand-written letter of thanks. Norman Hartnell received a knighthood and it fell to the Queen Mother that year to confer the accolade. But to surprise and please him she wore a peacock-blue version of a dress he had designed for her in mauve, having with her own touch of mischief taken pains to have it secretly copied in his workshop without his knowledge. From Sandringham she supported even her local football team, Norwich City, which received congratulatory telegrams as it climbed in the League Tables.

While in gaol, an admiring prisoner worked on a wool rug for her, basing his colours on the gold, blue and green of her coat-of-arms and, agreeing a purchase price, she found a place for it at the Castle of Mey. Long after the war, it made the Queen Mother's day when she received a letter from a woman who had been a bomb casualty unconscious in hospital when she passed by . . . and regretful ever since at missing her. So she invited the lady to Clarence House to come and have a chat.

'Is it genuine?' someone on her staff will ask, if her compassion is too readily touched by a please-help-me-letter. But mendacity is sorted out, sincerity readily proved. A soldier's bride complains of the unfairness of recalling her bridegroom to barracks while on honeymoon leave and the snag is sorted out. A simple Maori woman writes to thank her for coming to New Zealand, but the Queen Mother failed to realise that a copy also went to the Lord Mayor of London and would be read out, not sparing blushes, at a Guildhall banquet. Two ambitious schoolgirls wanted to invite two Canadian Mounties to tea, a dream denied, but five

Mounties presently visited their school. Supplicants no longer – or seldom – fling themselves at the feet of monarchs, but housing distresses, divorce tangles and old age troubles wait in the mail-basket to be referred to the right quarter. Every royal desk is a clearing-house of human problems, the Queen Mother vulnerable in sympathy and age-identity.

Then the unknown generosities, anonymous donations, sub-scriptions, gifts, an annual sizeable sum accounted to Queen Eliza-beth's charities. Her traditional oddities, too: crates of Christmas puddings distributed to her regiments, cartons of boxes of chocolates for hospitals and disablement homes on her visiting list. There are no echoes of Queen Mary's magpie concern with old lengths of ribbon or souvenirs and trifles that, after all, never came in useful. The Queen Mother has always been in the raffle and bazaar supply business for handbags, tea services, spare decanters, a great one for rummage in aid of the smallest church funds. In fact she has updated a whole field of goodwill. The sum total of consideration is another theme. It's a wet day, and the Queen Mother offers one of her office clerks a lift home to Staines in her car, 'I am going that way'.

The likely horse . . . the favourite waltz . . . the floodlit dome . . . *The crowds, the lights, the welcome . . . And (sweet as them all) the going home*! At the end of the week the Queen Mother likes to leave Clarence House early to avoid the business rush and, anonymous as thousands of Londoners, she goes home to Royal Lodge, in its secluded recess in Windsor Great Park, pleasantly little-known and never trespassed, her 'true and best home of all'. Twenty-two miles from Clarence House, just beyond the western orbit of the suburbs, it fortunately lies a little south of the flight paths of Heathrow that hurl an incessant air traffic across Windsor Castle.

As her car enters the park and the glade of scattered oaks, Queen Elizabeth invariably leans forward for her returning glimpse of her two trim cream-pink entrance cottages, and the smiling salute of her gate-keeper. 'I love the peace of this place,' her husband used to say, and the familiar rhododendron-banked drive, her welcoming housekeeper and then the enclosed domestic serenity all form a benison. Prince Charles has called Royal Lodge 'a unique haven of cosiness and charades'. She glances at once at the personal correspondence the last hour has brought to her desk, and all around are the tokens of friendship, her note pads, paperweights and pencil tray, books and blotter and paperclip box, the little mascot toys, photographs, books awaiting a spare minute and, of recent usage, a magnifying glass.

In the elusive perspectives of time, Queen Elizabeth can scarcely believe it is over fifty years since she first came to Royal Lodge. Yet through the French doors at her side, just beyond the paved garden path, stands the Little House, *Y Bwthyn Bach*, scaled down to child size, where her two daughters played when they were very young, the gift of the people of Wales, an essay in keeping house for her children, grandchildren and now her great-grandchildren and surely every child who has ever visited her. Everywhere, now, in every step, there are memories.

Trees that she helped the King to plant, happily at a safe distance from the house, are all now sturdy giants, some towering above the roof. Deeper across the garden is a miraculous glade of camellias, many scores that flower in their season, all the more cherished as her husband's gift to her of his last planting year.

Everywhere at the Lodge domestic history is suffused with tender sentiment. Protective secretaries are fond of saying that Queen Elizabeth does not live in the past, understandable in the ever-present events of Clarence House, yet everywhere there are sentinels to her private thoughts. In the Saloon the Lawrence portrait of the youthful George IV hangs over the fireplace in tribute to his former proprietorship. Yet one of the fireside sofas was banished from 145 Piccadilly; the fireside pole-screen, with the embroidered royal arms of King George VI, was a present from her husband after her first year as Queen. The rush log-basket has a Norfolk air; every item of hearth furniture tells of a birthday and in the background are modest water-colours of St Paul's Walden Bury that rival a classic ancestral landscape in oils depicting a racing scene on a northern moor. The blue eyes of the little girl who played at princesses surely sometimes peep from the gilded chair at the far end of the room, the Chair of State of the Queen Mother's Coronation; and a companionable nearby wing-chair was considerately upholstered to match its deep rose damask. The tapestry on the far wall came from Number 145. But the essence of the gothic Saloon is its changelessness, expressed in the much-trodden rose carpet, the old Persian rug at the fire, the unchanging three faded family photographs which have stood on their table as long as anyone – except Queen Elizabeth – can remember. Where so much has been swept away in the surf of time, here is security.

'This house has known only happiness,' the Queen Mother said not long ago, and curiously enough the phrase was soon to echo around another home she had thought relinquished and long vanished. The pace of change in her lifetime can be seen in the continuous challenge of the thriving new town of Stevenage to the rural calm of St Paul's Walden and the intrusion of peak summer tourist traffic that at times menaces Birkhall. And is it indeed fifty years since the demolition of 17, Bruton Street (the present Queen's birthplace) and its replacement by the brick heights of Berkeley Square House where, by strange coincidence, her dear brother David Bowes Lyon found himself working with the Ministry of Economic Warfare during the Second World War?

Even in the rural fastness of Richmond Park the ghosts have been evicted from White Lodge long since by the concentration and enthusiasm of the Royal Ballet School; and in more recent times the shell of 145, Piccadilly, bombed and in ruins, has made way for the traffic lanes from the park at Hyde Park Corner and its neighbouring towering cluster of hotels. Like many other pilgrim from when the twentieth century was new, Queen Elizabeth must surely feel like a desert traveller faced with a mirage as she considers the undreamed conjuring tricks of passing time.

Then, eleven years ago, not long before another 'wretched and delightful' birthday, as she termed it, she rediscovered a past she had considered even more inaccessible. In prosaic terms, after the first war, her father had surrendered the lease of 20, St James's Square and it had been sold to an insurance company and converted into offices. When she heard that an oil bomb had exploded there during the blitz she imagined that it had erased all but the stout façade of her girlhood home. To her astonishment, the Queen Mother learned instead that the Distillers' Company had not only repaired the building but had turned to the Robert Adams original sketches and faithfully restored the house in exact colour and detail to its former glory. What was more, the directors pleasantly invited her to lunch to see the painstaking and meticulous result.

It was like a shimmering dream. She found herself overjoyed to climb, if a little more arduously than of old, the same stone staircase. In the entrance hall she recognised the mahogany doors and brass door-handles, in fact precise copies of the original Adam design. In the strangely-named Eating Room there seemed to be the same white and green ceiling, and in the Music Room the paintings of playful nymphs, shepherds and musicians which she so well remembered. On either side of a niche at the top of the stairs, she recollected, there had been two romantic landscapes and here they were still, though brighter and more vivid than she could recall. Only the loss of the so-called Raphael (a copy) which had fallen to tatters in storage gave cause for regret.

It was then that the Queen Mother said, 'We only had happy times here,' warmed as she was by the chairman's finest dram. The following year she returned to show the splendours of Number 20 to a friend. Yet memory wavered in doubt, more in admiration of the semblance of the new perfected house that Robert Adam knew, its colours mint fresh, than in poignantly recapturing the dulled, used, familiar scenes of her girlhood so briefly 'long ago'.

Friends can fairly cherish the comforting illusion of Royal Lodge that time in its flight has faltered here: can it truly be so long ago since Bertie and Elizabeth first saw a gloomy conservatory and a shabby villa, materials with which to begin their struggle of building a garden and founding a home? Gradually wing by wing, they raised a *petit palais*, washed pink as it should be for rose-coloured spectacles. And is it really nearly forty years since young Philip came to plead for Elizabeth, and presently Charles and Anne were playing coaches with a garden chair, grandchildren without a grandfather?

Fate cast the darker events at Sandringham, even at Birkhall, while in summer, cheerful voices echoed around the pool at Royal Lodge. Alexandra and Angus came to tell Aunt Elizabeth of their betrothal, and soon Andrew and Edward and their young cousins are whirring their toy cars down the lawn. Then Charles and Diana are there, holding hands, talking of marriage plans and nothing seems to have changed at all. The Ascot festivities fill the house with guests, with music and laughter. Autumn sees the dancing flames of the log-fire in the octagon room, the cosy tea-cups and conversation. And still one of the days of Christmas brings the children's party, grandchildren, grand-nephews, grand-nieces, cousins, the hubbub of the youngest generation. Presently there will be duties to consider, 'the emblazoned document, this tape to cut, that stone to lay . . .', but there's time enough.

Within the settled scene, the years are sweetened by fulfilment; and when, writing at her husband's desk, Queen Elizabeth the Queen Mother knows a delectable contentment.

To an elderly dutiful royal the regal yet continuously scheduled way of life could become a thief of time, if habitual willingness to serve should fade. Daunting as the stealthy approach of her eighties may have been, Queen Elizabeth the Queen Mother had to consider many aspects of her eightieth birthday more than a year ahead of time. Her first inclination for a thanksgiving service at St George's Chapel, Windsor, flowered into a thanksgiving and commemoration at St Paul's Cathedral in which Anglican and Catholic Archbishops and the Moderator of the Church of Scotland should all take part. As a prelude in July the proposal of a Guildhall reception was heightened by her wish that all the remaining RAF flyers of the Battle of Britain should be invited. Asked what else the celebrations might include, the birthday girl made mocking wide eyes: 'There will be a gun salute, I expect.'

But first came her 'delightful appointment' – so she styled it – as Lord Warden of the Cinque Ports, in fact an embellishment in the gift of her daughter, the Queen. It was a whiff of Liliput and Gilbert and Sullivan infused with the British sentiment for tradition, and Queen Elizabeth played it with a sense of lightest comedy. She regarded it as a delicate compliment, she avowed, to be placed in the illustrious line of Sir Robert Menzies, Winston Churchill, William Pitt and the Duke of Wellington who were among her predecessors in the wardenship. As 166th Lord Warden, she was the first woman ever to promise to protect the five former ports at the white chalk toe of England, and instead of a bleak town hall installation she prompted a ceremonial of charm and pageantry.

It was her imaginative touch to embark at Greenwich in the royal yacht Britannia the previous evening with three of her teenage grandchildren – Prince Edward, Lord Linley and his sister Sarah – and sail down the Thames in the sunset. Next morning at Dover a band of the Queen's Regiment welcomed them and headed their procession. A Captain's escort of the Household Cavalry in shining breastplates accompanied the State carriage, and her three youngsters added their beaming smiles to the cavalcade. The Queen Mother vigorously climbed the steep stone stairway of Dover Castle as if twenty years younger. That evening aboard the royal yacht she was an alert and vivacious hostess to her Cinque Port notables, Dover's first woman mayor among them, and the day ended with the pop, crackle and splendour of fireworks.

Privately, besides, she revelled in the peculiarly personal satisfaction that the little coastal fort of Walmer Castle went with the job as official residence of the Lord Warden, and she could surprise her guests by telling them that it had once been in her sister's family. Elizabeth had been a bridesmaid at Rose's wedding to a young naval lieutenant, grandson and ultimately heir of the first Earl Granville, a notable Lord Warden of Victorian days who had laid out the Walmer garden and added the pleasant residential range that now formed Queen Elizabeth's private apartments.

It spiced the Queen Mother's sense of fitness to picture her own first great-grandchild, Princess Anne's baby, Peter Phillips, soon playing with toy bucket and spade on the beaches below. The old castle remains open to the public. A sheltered rampart is often the scene of picnics for one or other of her handicapped children's charities: 1986 prompting redecoration for family visits with young Prince William and Prince Harry coming to exercise their small boys' prerogative to build sandcastles.

But to return to the pleasures of installation, the Britannia, like Cinderella, sailed at midnight on a second mission with her passengers, setting them ashore after breakfast to rendezvous on the Norfolk coast with a car from Sandringham. This was Bertie's courtship country and, now that Edward and his cousins were such good company, a compulsion had beset the Queen Mother to show them the scenes of their grandfather's romance, to travel the same narrow lanes, as she had so often with the King, and share a lunch hamper in the car. Year by year these were the sources of her resilience and strength, and the young people were sympathetic and responsive, praising the adventure to their darling Granny as one of the best of their lovely secret days.

And so on 3 August they all voyaged back to Portsmouth, ready for her birthday at Clarence House next day . . . the people crowding the opposite pavement, the bands swinging by with *Happy Birthday to You*, the children running across to her with posies, the Queen and Princess Margaret, the cousins, the house police and footmen, all enjoying the bright fun when the Queen Mother appeared at the gate. Such was her 79th birthday, the stepping stone to her eightieth year.

That summer she had already visited France to stay at a chateau in Lorraine with a couple whom she had known in London, in the De Gaulle and Eisenhower days, to see something of the Vosges and pay wistful respects at the birthplace of Joan of Arc. Jaunting across the Atlantic in a Canadian military Boeing she inaugurated an international Gathering of the Clans in Halifax, Nova Scotia, and stayed with the turf-minded E. P. Taylor family in Toronto for the weekend, with racing pleasures mixed with regimental reviews, and time, too, for a sightseeing drive to see the year's changes along the highways.

Then there were housefuls of guests both at Birkhall and the Castle of Mey, where an early topic was of the proliferating portrait exhibitions of the Queen Mother's eighty years. The National Portrait Gallery was drawing on its own collections and the resources of Clarence House; while the Royal Photographic Society turned eagerly to the family photo albums at St Paul's Walden Bury for exhibitions in Bath, at Woburn Abbey and even in Westminster Abbey. 'The best they need do for me at present', flashed the impending octogenarian.

In contrast, Queen Mary at eighty had complained, 'It's so tiresome getting old . . . a great bore'. But on every testimony Queen Elizabeth is never bored. She genuinely delights in her annual birthday fiesta with the public at the gates of Clarence House. Queen Alexandra, on the other hand, privately wrote bitterly of 'that tiresome horrible Alexandra Day drive, *which I dread*', and 'that horrible Rose Day drive'. It was made known that at film premieres the Queen Mother disliked over-close close-ups, but the rule was quietly relaxed. 'I suppose after all, people want to see me as I really am'. On 'tiara nights' her hairdresser comes to ensure that her tiara is secure, her coiffure as it should be, and she frets and worries until he is at the door. Then composure takes over.

Visiting an ex-Services convalescent home, she went out of her way to walk smilingly under a ladder, knowing that it would make a nicely unusual camera shot for the newsmen. Here again when 'just looking around' her resistance to fatigue seems that of a woman many years younger. To quote Mrs Vera Drew, who accompanied her round a big crafts exhibition in London, 'She was on her feet walking round for two hours, really seeing each of 800 items on display, asking questions. She was intrigued by a hand-painted goose-egg and told me, "I shall have a go myself!" She wouldn't sit down or take a break with a cup of tea. I suggested, "Well, Ma'am, I hope you can take it easy tomorrow for a time". She just laughingly echoed me and said "Don't you realise it's half-term tomorrow? I have the boys on my hands and shan't have a minute to myself. I'll be playing cricket with them most of the day!"'

In the winter of 1979–80 she resigned her 25-year Chancellorship of London University. 'I must leave before this very midnight in case my car is turned into a pumpkin,' she joked. But the following summer a so-called strike-bound Day of Action and the stoppage of public transport meant that her final presentation of degrees had to be cancelled. Instead, she signed a letter of apology to each graduate, a self-imposed chore taking three or four weeks to complete.

She still rarely agrees to curtail working time. The first of her eightieth birthday garden parties was given at Knole by the National Trust and the Sackville family but the weather was atrocious. As Trust president she nobly squelched around in the mud for a time, but the programme ended early, whereupon she paid an entirely unexpected visit to a local school. At Buckingham Palace the Queen gave an extra garden party for her mother, especially including as many personal friends and key personnel of her 300 charitable foundations as possible. On 4 August the little-known side of the celebration saw the birthday lady as hostess of the most crowded family lunch Clarence House had ever witnessed. The evening saw a gala ballet performance at Covent Garden, a light buffet supper stage-managed by Prince Charles behind the scenes and a cake to be cut on stage. And unnoticed among the familiar mass of Brabournes and Knatchbulls, Kents and Ogilvys, was an extremely pretty blonde whom Queen Elizabeth had also known from babyhood, none other, of course, than Lady Diana Spencer.

The Spencers had closely known and served the Royal Family for years, so long that they had even acquired a rented house on the Sandringham estate, and on her 1961 birthday visit the Queen Mother had walked over to Park House to see their latest baby in her cradle. So linked were the families that one of her Bowes-Lyon nieces became the new baby's godmother in Sandringham church; and the present Queen was also to sponsor Diana's younger brother, another Charles.

The younger set among the Queen Mother's grandchildren used to play around in the Park House swimming pool innocent of future prospects, although Prince Charles rarely put in an appearance among the small fry. At some time the Queen and her husband are thought to have considered a cousinly alliance with Prince Philip's niece, his sister Princess Sophie of Hanover's daughter, the revival of a dynastic link closely akin to Earl Mountbatten's mysterious foreign conjectures. In 1980 the Sandringham New Year house party included several 'continentals', and the Queen Mother must have watched the turn of events with anxiety. The young lady however had found an alternative sphere of her own at university in British Columbia, and with happy optimism the Queen Mother suddenly found herself whirled into a familiar matchmaking course of luncheon and dinner invitations, now with Prince Charles, now with Lady Diana, and then triumphantly both together at Clarence House and Royal Lodge.

The press first noticed the couple aboard the Britannia in Cowes Week and then at Birkhall with the Queen Mother. Out came the old sheet music for piano duets with Ruthie Fermoy and it was like the old distant days when Ruth was launching a concert career in Aberdeen admiringly encouraged by Lady Elizabeth Bowes Lyon at Glamis. But now there was the agreeable youthful counterpoint of Charles and Diana's laughter and fun. With the official engagement of the happy pair the Queen Mother offered both Diana and her Fermoy grandmother a refuge at Clarence House and, as everyone remembers, within forty-eight hours the chaperonage was exchanged for a guest-suite in Buckingham Palace.

On the wedding day, riding to St Paul's in the landau with Prince Edward, her millinery a triumphant turquoise halo, the tumult of Queen Elizabeth's ovation echoed far back through the procession of carriages. In the great cathedral she found a small added detail of her own. Eight probationary choristers had attended all the rehearsals but had not quite served the two terms necessary to become full choristers and had to be sadly told they could not be seated there on the day. An indignant parent wrote to the Queen Mother of their disappointment and Clarence House wrote to the Dean of her hope that they could 'be squeezed in somewhere.' And there they were, squeezed but happy. Thus with her own small candle Queen Elizabeth was buoyed forward to her eighty-first birthday a week later.

The Queen and her mother exchange one another's itineraries for months ahead as an essential check in the family firm's routine. On Investiture days the Queen Mother still maintains her duty rota, usually one such day in every six, to be ready to take over should her daughter be taken ill. The emergency, though remote, has occurred at least twice in the present reign. Prince William's 4 August christening appeared to be timed to coincide with his great-grandmother's eighty-second birthday, but this was partly because not all the godparents and other principals could be brought together any other day.

The Queen's engagements follow a rarely changing pattern. The Queen Mother through her eighties allows herself more latitude to repeat favourite adventures, and initiates untried experiences as if asking, 'What haven't I done yet?'

She went down to the notorious Railton Road in Brixton to open a new day centre but also danced a calypso to the massed steel bands. She visited a training barge in London's dockland climbing up and down ladders – and tearing her coat – as if it were something she did every day. She had been patron of that inestimable institution, the London Library, for years, but had never paid it a visit, it seems, except for an unauthorised exploration of the book aisles in her teens with her young brother David. The omission was made good by attending a reception one evening, animated in conversation for two hours, yet deftly evading any ageing hint that she had once lived (at Number 21) five doors down.

Then there is her partiality for Smithfield Market, a rightful interest for an honorary member of the Worshipful Company of Butchers. Children prepare to press flowers shyly into her hands, brawny meat porters kiss her fingers, some still in blood-stained aprons because 'she wants to see us working'. In 1982 they sang *Maybe it's because she's a Londoner* and she promised to push a barrow 'next time'. In 1986 she indeed accepted a barrow 'useful for my garden at home', and agreed to join the Transport Workers Union as an Honorary Bummaree, a senior freelance porter. She then passed on the day's gifts from barons of beef to quails' eggs to hostels and hospitals both inside and beyond her patronage orbit. At another level she visited the headquarters of the Intelligence Corps in Kent and the SAS regiment, never mind where. She once called herself a veteran of the Special Forces club, that haunt of James Bond characters in Knightsbridge, and agreed – a veteran in her eighties – to grant six sittings for a portrait for them. The artist, Brian Stonehouse, was suitably a former wireless operator in occupied France, though happily less tight-lipped than of yore. 'We talked of everything. She loves to talk, about her life and her travels, world affairs, anything. We used to talk about the Resistance. If topics ran dry, we began practising French.'

One July weekend she flew off to Oslo for her cousin-in-law King Olav of Norway's eightieth birthday 'to help him get used to it – but we shan't talk about salmon.' Six months earlier she had been due to lunch with Olav when, a night or two earlier at Royal Lodge, she had swallowed a salmon bone which lodged in her throat. It was one of those dire moments when she could have choked to death. 'We had to persuade her to stop trying to make conversation,' her table companion, Hugh Cavendish, recalled. In the small hours of the morning the police had to clear the western road into London in a dramatic dash with her two doctors to the Edward VII hospital. 'It was the salmon's revenge,' she gasped, on coming round from the anaesthetic and surgery.

There were other hazards she royally ignored: to fly to Northern Ireland to take an anniversary salute of the Territorials at Ballymena menaced though it was by IRA threats, and to dine and sleep at Hillsborough Castle, meeting old local friends many of whom could remember her sister Rose as Governor's lady.

Twice a year she takes a medical check-up, the birthdays flying, she once intimated, faster than anyone could check. In 1984 she was reminded that, astonishingly, she had never been to Venice. Before the Kaiser's war she had visited Florence three or four times with David to stay with their grandmother, Mrs Scott, at her old Medici villa in the hills. The morning devotions in the little private chapel with its guardian stone angels and red damask walls appeared 'rather too high church' to some Cavendish-Bentinck cousins, and an aunt had skilfully guided the happy youngsters through the Pitti and Uffizi galleries down in the town. But Venice had remained an unfulfilled dream.

She could have seen the city in luxurious comfort from the barge of Britannia. Instead she chose to walk over cobbled bridges, clamber up and down church steps, change from sunlight into chill interiors, try out her girlhood Italian on the mayoral officials and observe only a comfort adage of changing her shoes every hour. She took marble stairways with careful calm, seeming not to notice the helpful arms offered. She sipped tea in Florian's: had not her sisters Rose and May been there long ago? On her third day, having set at rest all the fears lest she should stumble on wet steps, she gratified every cameraman by cruising the canals in a gondola – and came home bubbling as everyone does of the operatic scenes on the quaysides, the crumbling palaces, the wonderful fun.

The prospect of undertaking another overseas tour also possessed her. Invitations had been coming in and were due to be harvested. 'Just a few days, it won't be tiring at all,' she vanquished anxious protests. Like Winston Churchill, she was increasingly able to snatch strategic naps. Her 1985 'week in Canada' was in quick statistics her ninth official tour in the Dominion, programmed for nineteen official appearances, supposedly with only one evening function although the 'days' usually extended to 8 pm. A sunny Saturday arrival in Toronto saw a Sunday walkabout in pouring rain and the gift of the deep see-through umbrellas she has used ever since. There ensued three separate flights to three provincial capitals, smiles and speeches for ten different groups of local dignitaries, and between stops she was bounced about in turbulent electric storms until her plane had to be diverted 100 miles from Edmonton to an RCAF air-base; 'lovely unexpected tea and sandwiches in the officers' mess' was her dismissal of a touchdown which ultimately saw her arriving in Edmonton four hours late. Back again in Toronto concerned officials felt that the 58 seconds' elevator ride to the 1822 feet top of the Post Office tower might prove upsetting. But she wanted to see the view and found everything 'fascinating', expansively promising another visit in 1986. It made main page news when she dropped a glove and gracefully retrieved it before anyone could pick it up for her.

Three weeks later Sandringham saw another birthday, her eighty-fifth. This was observed with an evening ride into King's Lynn to hear Rostropovich, the Russian cellist. But lest her London well-wishers should be disappointed she went up to town next day for her street party, her little figure all but lost in an unhurried walk-around of about two thousand children and parents.

Her week had also included a leisurely trudge around the Sandringham flower show, a helicopter flight to open a new Norfolk village hall, two other King's Lynn concerts and the Festival exhibition of seventeenth and eighteenth century drawings, kernel of the Queen's 1986–87 Queen's Gallery exhibition. On 6 August the chairman of British Airways, Lord King, having heard that she had long cherished a wish to fly Concorde, accordingly laid on a private supersonic flight round Britain as an extra celebration. She had first tried for a trip, she confessed, when the plane was still undergoing its Atlantic test-flights without its certificate of air-worthiness. Now, past her mid-eighties, she began lunch with her daughter, Princess Margaret, and her two children, David Linley and Sarah, somewhere over Glamis at 66,000 feet, and she flew through the sound barrier. And how it took her back, back to 1952 and her trip with Margaret and the Salisburys in the first jet airliner, the Comet, flying over the Alps for lunch.

In those days she had felt 'banged about by sorrow . . . nearly senseless', as she had written, and yet had landed with a new sense of exhilaration and within a month she had found the Castle of Mey. Circling Britain and the North Sea by Concorde she spent much of her time on the flight deck, 'excited and asking many questions' said Captain Brian Walpole – and was still there behind the pilot's seat, seat-belt fastened, thrilled in sharing the excitement of the landing. The flight deck would have been awash with air sickness if Walpole had permitted the giddying spectacle to many oldsters. And, again, millions of television viewers could see for themselves the lady's intrepid endurance involved in visiting the Scillies, the barge of Britannia almost standing on its stern in the heavy seas in transporting her to shore, the steep and narrow stone steps of the quay not by no means clear of perilous sea slime as she clambered up, with low-heeled shoes her sole concession in the effort.

'She's younger than any of us, extraordinary, delightful but exhausting, wearing everyone out,' Sir Martin Gilliat reiterates with genial realism. The word 'octogenarian' is anathema, which led a household wag – or was it Prince Charles? – to coin the word 'octogen' – a powerful elixir, a draught of life, used by youthful great-grandmothers to inspire, encourage and fortify all those around them.

Some years ago, when Queen Elizabeth was away, a Clarence House housemaid allowed a cleaner to peep into the Queen Mother's bedroom, and the intruder had a fright. Standing on either side of the handsome brass bedstead were two tall figures in white, stone angels each with staff and halo, not quite 'clad in white samite, mystic, wonderful', but robed in starched cotton needing to be laundered every few weeks. Perhaps they were exiles from Grandmama Scott's chapel at the Villa Capponi or certainly descended from them in sentiment. 'May angels guard me while I sleep, till morning light appear'. The Queen Mother recently had her bedroom redecorated in blue silk, as prudent house-wifery, friends said, should she ever need to spend more time there, and one does not know whether her angels still keep their vigil.

When Martin Gilliat joined her staff thirty years ago, after serving as Mountbatten's military secretary, he noticed that never a day went by without her mentioning the late King, and never the February anniver-sary of his death without a private family service of Holy Communion, linked with prayers of dedication and remembrance, in the little chapel of All Saints at Royal Lodge, a consecration totally unknown to the public. Bound up with this commemoration is Queen Elizabeth's whole existence. 'At one and the same time, we can be truly contemporary and yet have our thoughts and lives rooted in truths that do not change,' she once wrote to a bereaved friend, Lady Elizabeth Basset. 'It is difficult to convey at all clearly the faith and hope that is in us, what in our hearts we believe but find so hard to say'.

No one ever ventures to talk with harsh realism of the Queen Mother as a little old lady. Whether in her energy or her rare days of hidden fatigue, the truth is cushioned in a tacit agreement to regard the passing years as an illusion. 'Every day with her is a new adventure', says Gill-iat. One day after lunch at the Royal Air Force Club in Piccadilly her car broke down, a non-starter. 'It's a lovely day,' she said, 'Let's walk!' She led the way along the pavement, a true adventure, the first time she had walked along Piccadilly for fifty years. More recently she has derived pleasure from becoming an Old Etonian, enhanced by Martin in his year as President of the Old Etonian's Association in welcoming her to their number, his speech quickly a skilful exchange with her as a comedy duo. One or two Eton boys often appear at Sunday luncheon at Royal Lodge, sons or grandsons of old friends. In some ways there's an extra dimension of flashback to teenage days, when her younger brother David was at Eton. In her Coronation year David had been the anony-mous donor of the 'born and worshipped here' plaque in St Paul's Walden Church. How they had all laughed at the Bury after the unveiling when sister Mary telephoned on hearing that David had been completely mistaken. He simply hadn't known that Elizabeth was born in London, either at St George's Hospital or St Mary's: even Mary couldn't remember after all that time.

'Indeed all there'. Mrs Reagan briskly summed up the Queen Mother's IQ when she gave a dinner for the Reagans and other economic summit leaders in London. President Reagan had begun quoting from *The Shooting of Dan McGrew*, and the Queen Mother promptly capped his lines with 'the bunch of the boys who were whooping it up' and the 'lady that's known as Lou', ensuring hilarity throughout the rest of the evening.

Like all veterans, the lady of Clarence House sees her old acquaintances thinning out and gradually disappearing. Talking of bygone friends she will sometimes explain they have 'gone upstairs', as if climbing to a heavenly attic. In the run-up to the New Year at Sandringham in 1986 she had caught cold going down to inspect her brood mares and had to spend the New Year in bed. It was all the more a shock to hear of the death on New Year's Day of her old friend Lord David Cecil at the age of eighty-three. He was the invalid boy, another David, three weeks older than her brother, whom she had gone to see with her governess as he lay listlessly on his couch, amusing him with a pretended playlet of patient and visitor while a gale whipped the windows. He alone had early divined the dramatic skills she demonstrated in playing at princesses. 'They are part of a unique performance . . .She thinks she *ought* to wave and give pleasure, and she is able to perform these feelings to the public. Hers is an honourable and simple view of life, and she has been able to put it across to the millions because of this gift of performance.' And now sadly – though she had once written of sorrow as 'small and selfish' – he too had gone upstairs. In April the Duchess of Windsor had also slipped away, Princess Anne being her grandmother's close support during the bleak ritual of the funeral.

Between these two extremes, the poles of affection and dislike, the Queen Mother had more happily enjoyed a characteristic light interlude of personal pleasure. The atrocious weather had barred racing for a month when she went to Sandown one Saturday to watch three of her horses on the card. Her veteran, Special Cargo, opened the day by winning the Grand Military Gold Cup, his third successive year of victory in that event. The Queen Mother's Insular then gallantly became her next winner, the hat-trick being completed by The Argo-

naut. Moreover, it was her second treble as a National Hunt owner –
and to her delight one of her Clarence House staff won £1,340 for £10
invested on the 134–1 treble . . . her ninth win, too, of the season, a
cornucopian racing chance. Does this presage a new run of health,
happiness and good fortune?

For the older generation there are more fortifying facts. The Queen
Mother's father lived to be eighty-nine. His nearest brother, her Uncle
Frank, survived to within a week of ninety-two, when he died in 1948,
and since then the march of medical science has added ten or twelve
years to the human life span.

Throughout this twentieth century the British sovereign has followed the felicitous custom of sending a telegram of congratulations to
every newly-qualified centenarian, a former happy average of thirty
such messages a year. In 1985 the figure was 1,819 within the British
Isles and an additional 1,200 to British-born centenarians overseas.

'I am hoping that perhaps one day my elder daughter will send me a
telegram,' says Queen Elizabeth the Queen Mother.

Author's Note: On 19 March 1986 Buckingham Palace announced, 'It is
with great pleasure that the Queen and the Duke of Edinburgh
announce the betrothal of their beloved son, Prince Andrew, to Miss
Sarah Ferguson . . .'

Without further ado the Queen also conferred with her mother on her
wish to create Andrew Duke of York on the eve of his marriage, and
Queen Elizabeth responded with an instant sense of benison and
completion. Nothing could be better than to see Bertie's and her own
former married titles as Duke and Duchess of York bestowed afresh on
her second grandson and his bride.

Among the Queen Mother's younger friends, the Duke and Duchess
of Grafton invited her to join them in celebrating the engagement with a
few days in Tuscany. Prince Andrew is the Duchess's godson, and their
guest learned that the tour was to include her dearly-held dream of
revisiting her grandmother's home, the Villa Capponi. The present-day
owner, Paula Piaggio, widow of the motor-cycle magnate, invited the
party to lunch . . . and so the Queen Mother revelled once more in the
spectacular view of the domes and towers of Florence, the villa's
ramparts of pencil cypresses and roses, the coolness of the lemon
garden, and shared for a few minutes with Ruth Fermoy the ineffable
peace of the private chapel.

On the return home, the prospects of a winter jubilee appeared to be fading. 'No discussions have taken place concerning any celebration to mark the fiftieth anniversary of Queen Elizabeth the Queen Mother becoming Queen Consort,' Sir Martin Gilliat wrote to this author on 17 June. No preparation was necessary for a private observation and, God willing, a celebration of the fiftieth anniversary of the Queen Mother's Coronation as Queen Consort offered a brilliant and felicitous Jubilee alternative for May 1987.